The
Pocket Guide To
Victorian Writers And Poets

by
Russell James

REMEMBER WHEN

First published in Great Britain in 2010 by
REMEMBER WHEN
an imprint of
Pen & Sword Books Ltd
47 Church Street
Barnsley
South Yorkshire
S70 2AS

Copyright © Russell James, 2010

ISBN 978 1 84468 083 2

A CIP catalogue record for this book is
available from the British Library.

Printed and bound in Great Britain by
CPI Antony Rowe, Chippenham, Wiltshire

Pen & Sword Books Ltd incorporates the imprints of
Pen & Sword Aviation, Pen & Sword Maritime, Pen & Sword Military,
Wharncliffe Local History, Pen & Sword Select, Pen & Sword Military Classics,
Leo Cooper, Remember When, Seaforth Publishing and Frontline Publishing

For a complete list of Pen & Sword titles please contact
PEN & SWORD BOOKS LIMITED
47 Church Street, Barnsley, South Yorkshire, S70 2AS, England
E-mail: enquiries@pen-and-sword.co.uk
Website: www.pen-and-sword.co.uk

CONTENTS

1. Introduction 7
2. The Victorian Myth Exploded 11
3. Settle Down to a Victorian Book 19
4. A to Z Guide to Victorian Writers and Poets 23
5. Index 199

At the very least my books kept me aloof from the ring, the dog-pit, the tavern, and the saloons, with their degrading orgies.

From a letter to the *Manchester Athenaeum*, July 1843,
sent in by Thomas Hood.

INTRODUCTION

IF THE novel was born in the 18th century it grew to adulthood in the 19th. Everything we associate with the novel today was developed then: the unreliable narrator, the use of several storytellers, the false ending, the fictional biography, the psychological study, the author who interrupts; the use of photos, diagrams and 'handwritten' letters; time sequences which reverse or shift unexpectedly; stories told by animals, pieces of furniture, babies, ghosts ... all of these were familiar tools to the Victorian author. The novel was new, yet was continually subverted – even if no novel has ever been so playfully subversive as the 18th century's *Tristram Shandy*.

Poetry, though, was a long-established form. The world's earliest literature – from *The Iliad to Beowulf* – is told in verse. It is extraordinary, in fact, how long it took for prose to replace verse as the natural medium for storytelling, almost as if prose was harder, as if any fledging author would find it easier to write in verse – just as when a child tells its first stories it often does so in simple rhyme. But in the 19th century, verse – that primordial form – blossomed into its final glorious flower and was loved by millions. In the 20th century poetry found itself analysed to death and its popularity declined. It's a minority art now; most poetry books sell in tiny numbers and lose money for their publishers. But in the 19th century, poets sold in enormous numbers. Their verses were learnt by heart, not because poems were crammed in by rote at school, but because readers loved them and wanted to make the words part of their soul.

All that has gone. Yet in any poll of the nation's favourite poems today a good many will come from the Victorian age. And in any listing of classic novels the sturdy Victorians still burst to the fore. This book includes some 250 writers, giving each a brief biography, a critical outline, and a note of important works to look out for. Their biographies can be surprising.

Glance, for example, at the extraordinary lives of Amelia Barr, the Countess of Blessington, Wilfred Scawen Blunt, Edward Bulwer-Lytton, Sir Richard Burton, Baron Corvo, George Egerton, George Gissing, A J Munby, Ouida, Laurence Oliphant, H M Stanley, and the campaigning W T Stead. Remind yourself of Victorian scandals, such as those involving William Aytoun (and the 'Spasmodic' school of poetry), the feuding Bulwer Lyttons, the scandalous divorcees Ménie Muriel Dowie and Caroline Norton, the pugnacious Charles Reade, and the self-destructive Oscar Wilde.

But to many Victorians the greatest scandal, already raging before Charles Darwin's belief-battering book, was 'The God Debate' (see below) and, while this guide will not burden itself with the interminable details of that fight, it does give space to some of its leading combatants: Robert Chambers, Charles Darwin, T H Huxley, Benjamin Jowett, John Keble, Charles Kingsley, John Henry Newman and the peaceable Mark Rutherford. Less expected might be the inclusion of several sexual revolutionaries, such as Edward Carpenter, George Egerton, Havelock Ellis and the poet, John Addington Symmonds. And I found it impossible to ignore those notorious literary marriages, some unconsummated (Thomas Carlyle, Anna Jameson and John Ruskin), some never legitimised (the most famous being that of George Eliot).

Not all of the 250 writers in this book led unconventional lives. Some were merely unfortunate. Consider Valentine Durrant, W E Henley, Lionel Johnson, Amy Levy, Philip Bourke Marston, Hugh Miller, and the two unrelated poets, Francis Thompson and James Thomson. Others were – or were considered to be – great thinkers, though I'm sure you can spot the odd man out among Walter Bagehot, Thomas Carlyle, William Lecky, John Stuart Mill, Walter Pater, John Ruskin, Samuel Smiles, Herbert Spencer, and the conjoined Beatrice & Sidney Webb. Others simply wrote. Potboilers flowed from the pens of many, including Harrison Ainsworth, Mrs Mary Braddon, Thomas Prest, J M Rymer and Mrs Henry Wood. Children's stories came from many hands; famous ones here include Helen Bannerman, J M Barrie, Lewis Carroll, Mrs Ewing, George MacDonald, Mrs Molesworth and the unfortunate Anna Sewell.

Best-sellers were produced by real-life travellers such as Sir Richard Burton, David Livingstone, J H Speke, H M Stanley – and, in his different style, Robert Louis Stevenson. Those seeking the contemplative life might turn to poets – and although you may already have your favourites, may I suggest you spend a moment looking at the lives of these: William Allingham, Malcolm Arnold, Alfred Austin, W E Aytoun, William Barnes, The Brownings, Ernest Dowson, William Morris, Coventry Patmore, Christina Rossetti, Swinburne, Tennyson – even the excruciating William McGonagall and Martin Farquhar Tupper.

So many names. Yet there are many in this book that I have not listed in this short introduction. Some may complain that there are names which don't appear at all, and which ought to have been included. I can only reply that, first, I have left out writers who, although they were alive during Victoria's reign, published the bulk of their work either before or after her time. Second, that in sixty years of writing (Victoria reigned for more than sixty years) there were literally thousands of working writers, and I have had to miss some out. I don't think any major names have been omitted and I do think that among the minor names are some genuinely interesting ones. In the following pages I hope you will find some old friends – and one or two new ones whose works you will hunt down and enjoy for yourself.

Take from me things gone by – oh! change the past –
Renew the lost – restore me the decay'd;
Bring back the days whose tide has ebb'd so fast –
Give form again to the fantastic shade!

From *Heart's Ease* by Caroline Archer Clive

1

THE VICTORIAN MYTH
EXPLODED

H AS ANY age had as much twaddle written about it as the Victorian?
The rot started with their sneering, vengeful offspring, those children
of the early 20th century upon whose testimony we have relied too long.
Because they knew the Victorians, because their lives overlapped, we
assumed those children knew the Victorians better than we ever could.
They did know them. But they couldn't judge them.

No generation is as dated as one's parents, no one's values more
condemned, and for the bright young things of the early 20th century the
Victorians *were* their parents. Most of us, when young, scorn our parents,
scorn everything they stand for, though, perversely, we may form a bond
with *their* parents, our grandparents, who carry about them traces of a
world we never saw, a world of memory and anecdote – a golden age. But
our parents' age was not a golden age. How could it be? How could our
parents get anything right?

For us today, a century later, the Victorians are emphatically not our
parents. There is not a single Victorian, not even a person born in the dying
seconds of Victoria's reign, still alive today. They are all dead, all history,
and much of what we know of them – their history – was written by their
disenchanted children. The most damning – and lasting – of those

indictments was Lytton Strachey's *Eminent Victorians*, written while other men were fighting a war, in 1918, and achieving its success not for its historical insight, certainly not for original research (Strachey admitted that he hated research and simply read up on other people's works) but for its impudence. The book was mildly amusing and, in the jazzy Twenties, seemed rather shocking. Strachey, a supremely supine, sneering sybarite, exerted himself enough to toss together a slim volume in which he claimed to sum up the age by skimming the lives of just four Victorians (eminent as they were, four sketches don't describe an age) and showing those four to be hypocritical, uptight, afraid of sex, stuck in their ways, God-fearing, timorous, didactic and conservative. He painted the picture and the public bought it. (They were encouraged to do so by Strachey's friends, the Bloomsbury set, who by then – better men fighting a war et cetera – had seized the citadels of criticism and had become the self-styled arbiters of taste.) Strachey, they whinnied, had shown us the Victorians, warts and all. Mainly warts.

But had he? Every smear of his thin paintwork was awry. No portrait has ever been more false. The Bloomsbury belles delighted to loll on sofas and mock their parents (who had, of course, provided the money to support their cosy lifestyle) but we should not join them in their scorn. Unlike their parents, the Bloomsbury set were narrow in outlook and closed to argument. Consider their claims:

Hypocritical? Yes, one can find evidence of hypocrisy – but one can find that in any age. Dickens may have been hypocritical when he stoutly proclaimed family harmony while maintaining at least one long-time mistress and discarding his worn-out wife, but in his novels he exposed the hardships of factory life, the abuse of children, the plight of women, the bought elections, the hidden horrors of the workhouse and board schools, the cruel distortions of utilitarianism, and the uncaring, self-serving machinations of bureaucracy and the legal system. Not only did he expose these and other faults, but he caused them to be talked about and met head-on. Which Bloomsbury type did a tenth of that?

Uptight is the second charge. To counter, let's move from Dickens – though before we do, how can anyone claim believe *his* prose was uptight and Virginia Woolf's was not? – and let us look at just a few of his contemporaries. Uptight, are they? The Victorians delighted in uninhibited and often shocking tales. Their 'Penny Dreadfuls' relied on stories which simultaneously appalled and delighted readers – and, as with tabloid newspapers today, there were enough delighted readers to generate huge sales. Think of Thomas Prest (creator of Sweeney Todd), J M Rymer (*Varney the Vampire*), Mrs Braddon (that naughty *Lady Audley*), Marie Correlli (whose romances swept from the supernatural to swirling love), Harrison Ainsworth's historical sagas, Ballantyne and Reid and Stevenson writing for boys. Even the Reverend Barham's *Ingoldsby Legends*, while thoroughly decent, cannot be thought inhibited. And as for Wilde and Aubrey Beardsley ... No, the Victorians were certainly not uptight.

Afraid of sex, said Strachey. (Well, he could talk.) In the supposedly frigid Victorian age – for much of which the age of consent was a mere thirteen – rates of illegitimacy were higher and the proportion of legitimate marriages was lower than today. For many, sex was easy and uncomplicated (Gissing and Collins will show you that). But sex was easier for some than for others. The marriages of Carlyle and Ruskin were never consummated, and Lewis Carroll was by no means the only Victorian male who (as far as we know) died a virgin. But be honest: are sexual hang-ups unknown today? Against these unlucky Victorian virgins we soon find contrasts. George Gissing stole money to help a prostitute, he married her and was let down – then he made much the same mistake again. Wilkie Collins never married, but kept two households, with a mistress in each one. George Eliot wrote of religion while she lived openly 'in sin'. Swinburne, Pater and Edward Carpenter made no secret of their homosexuality. Beatrice Harraden, Violet Hunt and Rhoda Broughton were only three of the overtly feminist writers of the time. Each of these writers wrote of sex and sexual relationships. (As did many other Victorian writers whose own sex lives were more conventional.)

Stuck in their ways, maintained the Stracheyites. There has never been a generation *less* stuck in its ways. Victoria's reign began with the industrial revolution, and by the end of it the lives of every citizen had been transformed. Railways, schools and hospitals, books and newspapers: all flourished and became cheap for all. Health and sanitation – above all, perhaps, antiseptics, anaesthetics and immunisation – improved out of all recognition and increased the common lifespan. In Britain the 19th century ended with near universal literacy and education. Were Victorian *books* stuck in old-fashioned ways? No. All the great literary tricks and modernisms of the 20th and 21st century were alive and well in Victoria's reign: unreliable narrator; multiple viewpoint; switches of sequence, time and tense; fantasy; magic realism; authorial overview – all these arrows flew from the author's quiver and struck their targets in Victorian writing. Each can be seen in Dickens's quiver alone. The Victorians were not stuck in their ways.

But surely they were God-fearing? God, certainly, was an obsession, one of the great themes of an age divided between believers and atheists, in which a good number of honest agnostics held the central ground. While the Oxford Movement (originating around 1833, just before Victoria came to the throne) sought to bring back into the church much of the old ritual and ornament that had been stripped away in the Reformation, the very existence of God was challenged by the scientists. Darwin is the most often quoted and was the most strongly attacked, but his theories – while they are, perhaps, the most important of the 19th century – were but part of a continuous onslaught from scientists such as Wallace, Lyell, Chambers, Huxley and many more. Their rationalist view was countered not merely by the many pounding tracts of faith (generally unreadable today) but also by some of the finest and most beautiful Victorian writing. Poets, perhaps, expressed it best – faith being more easily expressed in verse than prose – and where faith mingled with doubt the resultant writing is still capable of thrilling, or at least intriguing us today. Malcolm Arnold, to express his thoughts more clearly, turned in later life from the inspirational vagueness of verse to the clean hard bullets of prose. One can argue which works best: his *Dover Beach* (one of the nation's favourite poems) or his *Culture and Anarchy* (Arnold's most influential prose work, among whose lesser achievements was that it made the word 'philistine' the cliché it is today).

Timorous, some people say – about a breed which, like it or not, sucked half the world into its self-styled Empire and made itself the 'greatest country in the world'. Timorous is not a word that could be applied to Thomas Carlyle, Sir Richard Burton, Sabine Baring-Gould or to R B Cunninghame Graham. How about the claim that they were didactic and conservative? Didactic, yes, in that many Victorian writers – by no means only men – stated their views strongly, even imperiously; but conservative: no. In parliament, the Whigs held office longer than did the Conservatives,

MATTHEW ARNOLD

LONDON & GLASGOW
COLLINS' CLEAR-TYPE PRESS

15

and in print the Victorians were progressive, sometimes outrageous, ever seeking something new.

So let us forget forever those out-of-date views of Victorian culture. This book brings you some 250 Victorian writers. It demonstrates their freshness and variety, and shows what *mattered* to them. Like today's writers, many Victorian writers set out principally to entertain – few could afford to write to please themselves; they wrote to *sell* – but, to a greater extent than today's writers, they wrote of society and its ills. From their books we discover how it was to live in the Victorian age. We find the same financial scandals and disasters (think of Merdle in *Little Dorrit*, or the 19th century Veneering yuppies in *Our Mutual Friend*; think of Melmotte in Trollope's *The Way We Live Now*). We see the 'condition of England' – from a future Prime Minister! (Disraeli's novels.) We see scandalous public services, run for private gain and worse: the workhouses (Dickens again), the abusive schools (add the Brontës), the private asylums (Wilkie Collins), the snobbish upper classes (Thackeray pins them tightest in *Vanity Fair*, while Ouida, in trying to defend them, didn't realise how awful she made them seem). And in every decade we find books that keep on campaigning: for a wider franchise, for women's rights, for children, for religious or racial tolerance.

We also find unashamed Victorian pride and bigotry. If Britain was greatest, then everyone else must be a lesser breed; thus do the foreigners described in many adventure books make us cringe. The voice of feminism was smothered, in apparently reasonable terms, by (among others) Ruskin ('Each book that a young girl touches should be bound in white vellum') and Coventry Patmore ('Within her face / Humility and dignity / Were met in a most sweet embrace'). Politics, religion and social justice were the themes of countless Victorian books – as was education: from the presses of publishers great and small poured an enormous number of worthy tomes you will never read. But in their day they were a vital food to the many thousands who saw education as a ladder to self-improvement. (In those days, as today, self-improvement books were a solid line: Samuel Smiles is perhaps the most famous example.)

Above all, Victorian writers wrote to sell. To entertain. In an age before radio, cinema or television, print was the universal home entertainment medium. Writers used print to give their audience comedy and tragedy, science fiction, romance bitter and sweet, intellectual nourishment and downmarket thrills. I admit that, partly in order to help fill the long hours of evenings before television, Victorian books tended to be over-written and padded – no more than a TV soap opera is today – but that's because they were fulfilling the same role: whiling away the hours. Like a soap opera, the better books – those you find still in print today – were designed to hold the attention of the audience. One can put down a book as easily as one can switch a channel, and the aim of the writer, then as now, was to keep the reader glued to the page.

Writers' private lives were different from those of their heroes; some were less exemplary while the lives of others were more extraordinary than their creations. (See their entries later.) Many Victorian books have disappeared – although, prompted perhaps by this 21st century guide – you may stumble across one or two at knockdown prices in our disappearing second-hand bookshops. (You can, of course, leap two centuries and track them down on the internet.) But a lot of first-class Victorian books, despite all the jeremiads about our dwindling reading culture – which are the same gloomy forecasts you might have read in Victorian magazines – are still available in popular paperback editions. That's a triumph that many of their authors would never have expected – that as many as half the titles mentioned in this guide can be bought, brand new, from a decent bookshop. They are out of copyright, so they should be cheap (small editions, though, can be costly) and the fact that not only do they exist but they are easily accessible is living proof that Lytton Strachey was wrong (and who reads *him* now?). Contrary to what he wrote, the Victorians were vibrant, forward-looking and – I will use the word again – entertaining.

So seek them out. Enjoy them. Share their world.

2

SETTLE DOWN TO A VICTORIAN BOOK

W E'VE ALL seen those stupendous Victorian menus: course after course of rich, sometimes indigestible food, every scrap of which, presumably, is to be consumed at a single sitting – a long sitting, admittedly, since part of the purpose was to give satisfaction throughout a long, long evening. To the uninitiated, Victorian literature seems like a Victorian meal, comprising course after course of indigestible prose. How could a Victorian consume it all? Evenings, of course, were long – *every* evening was long. There was no television, no radio, and little other entertainment to fill the hours. In such a world there was little merit in a book that could be consumed in a single evening, but there was great merit in a book that not only required several evenings – supplying entertainment perhaps for weeks – but was one in which the reader met and became familiar with characters who lived throughout those evenings, who lived beyond them, in the reader's own memory and in conversations with friends. Some books, indeed, filled the space occupied by television soap operas today; many books, especially in the middle years of the century, were issued first in instalments (weekly or monthly 'parts') before being bound up in omnibus editions to be read again and kept where we would today keep our DVDs, on the bookshelf.

But only some books were like modern soap operas. Others were what we might disparagingly call 'improving works' (modern TV's documentaries), high-class fiction (TV's up-market dramas), books of poetry (the 'arts programmes'), and a considerable amount of hard-hitting campaigning works (the *Panoramas* of their day). As TV viewers confine themselves to certain channels but switch between them,

Victorian readers selected and, at times, stoutly defended their own channels of reading preference. Some wanted entertainment; others wanted richer fare.

Entertainment came from famous names (Dickens, Thackeray, Wilkie Collins, Mrs Braddon), the infamous (J M Rymer, Thomas Prest) and many barely known or perhaps anonymous writers. Richer fare could be very rich indeed. Books, as with television sets half a century ago, began as the prerogative of a privileged minority and, by the end of Victoria's reign, found their way into every household. Print was the main source of information: in print were cookery books and guides to household economy, how-to manuals for every trade, school books, science manuals, theological discourses. These books were quietly revolutionary, because in 1838 when Victoria was crowned, there were no public libraries. In an average bookshop one found few essential guides. It is hard for us today to conceive of a time when there was almost nowhere to look something up; not only was there no internet but there might not be *any* book on the subject. Literally, not one book. You want an overview to the poets of the 17th century? Compile your own. It was the Victorians who, for the first time, produced vast numbers of textbooks, guides and encyclopaedias and made painstakingly garnered information available to ordinary people.

'How to Live' could be gleaned from the works of writers as diverse as Samuel Smiles, Ruskin and Henry Newman. Print was the great new medium through which information could be shared, facts disseminated, opinions argued, and debates could rage. What debates! At times, what rage! Noble causes were argued – the abolition of slavery, an end to child labour, the reform of prisons, a better health system, the need to widen our limited franchise, and emancipation – if not of women, then at least of under-represented working men. And then there was God. Or was there? The God Debate raged through the 19th century; in the face of rising agnosticism and blatant disregard of the Church (more people ignored church than ever went to it) religious thinkers and professionals turned inward on themselves, quarrelling and condemning each other and indulging in ruinous theological splits. The Protestant Church tore itself apart, there was violent anti-Catholicism, and against the challenges of revitalised science the Church defended itself with fierce and fearful fundamentalism.

The Church's approach was disastrous in an age that saw itself, rightly, as an age of Change, an age of Progress and Achievement. Anyone over fifty today thinks the world has transformed in their lifetime, but those changes are nothing to those experienced by Victorians. Space travel affects far less people today than did the railway. Medical advances today have less impact than had the 19th century's discovery of anaesthetics and antiseptics. No public works today compare with the 19th century's drainage and sewerage system below ground, and its illumination of cities, first by gas light, then by electricity, above. We tinker with our education system where the Victorians created schools for all. We struggle to retain our position as a world-class power, where they dominated the world through their British Empire. Knowledge is expanded less by our internet than it was in their day by books and inexpensive newspapers. It was a truly exciting age and people knew it; they were excited by their times.

And what Victorians talked about, they wrote about.

I have suggested that, to the uninitiated, Victorian literature can seem like an indigestible Victorian meal. There is certainly a lot of food in it, not all of it well cooked. Some which was well-cooked is no longer to our taste. Victorian writing can seem ponderous – a good deal of it *is* ponderous – but let's face it, more recent writing, from the mid and early 20th century (a mere fifty years ago, say), can seem ponderous to the speed-reader of today. To the Victorians, when they compared their books to those written a century before, their own seemed full of movement, content and thought. And they are; their books are packed with movement. There is far more *thought* in a Victorian novel than in almost any today. There is more argument, more propaganda, if you will. Today you will struggle to find writers like Carlyle, Mill and Ruskin whose secular sermons were proclaimed throughout their books; writers like Eliot, Arnold and Meredith who used their books to explore religion and ethics; writers like Dickens, Charles Reade and Bulwer Lytton whose characters *and* whose arguments were familiar and fiercely debated in ordinary people's homes. This was an age when, as has not happened since until Barack Obama, a leading politician and Prime Minister, Benjamin Disraeli, could write best-selling 'state of the nation' novels arguing for change. *All* of these writers, in fact, along with the Brontës,

Mrs Gaskell, Charles Kingsley, Wilkie Collins and more, took important and topical issues and made them headline news. Their books mattered, they were part of an unceasing flood of change. They changed government policy, they changed the way people thought, and the legacy they left helped to create *you*.

As Tennyson wrote in *Locksley Hall:*

> *Forward, forward let us range,*
> *Let the great world spin for ever down the ringing grooves of change.*

An A to Z Guide
To Victorian Writers And Poets

Gilbert À BECKETT (1811-56)

Though he claimed descent from St Thomas à Beckett he is remembered – and was known at the time – as a comic writer for *Punch*. Collectors of John Leech illustrations still look out for Beckett's *Comic History of England* (1847) and *Comic History of Rome* (1852). Beckett also wrote plays, and his son once collaborated with W S **Gilbert**.

William ACTON (1813-75)

Doctor and writer specialising in 'indelicate' topics whose first book (1841) was on the 'generative organs' and whose most famous (1857) was on their 'functions and disorders'. His 1858 treatise on prostitution led to the Contagious Diseases Act of 1866 and his 1870 revised edition criticised and helped improve the Act. He was one of the few writers brave enough to view the 'social disease' and its purveyors with sympathy, though the guidance in his texts was impaired by his impracticable morality.

W Harrison AINSWORTH (1805-82)

Journalist and author of thrilling historical stories, the *Newgate Novels*. He had enormous success with *Rockwood* (1834) which glamorised Dick Turpin as much as *Jack Sheppard* (1839) did for its own criminal hero,

though he wrote a touch more soberly in *Old St Paul's* (1841) and *The Lancashire Witches* (1849) et cetera. (He wrote almost 40 novels.) His serial, *The Tower of London* (1840), sumptuously produced by publisher Bentley and lavishly illustrated by Cruikshank, was so successful that Bentley made Ainsworth editor of

Bentley's Miscellany. Ainsworth went on to produce his own *Ainsworth's Magazine*, in which a few more of his novels were illustrated by Cruikshank, till the two fell out in 1844. (Cruikshank later claimed not only to have collaborated but to have invented these novels – but he laid a similar charge against Charles **Dickens**. The claim was as nonsensical as his drawings.) A huge seller in his day, both in book and magazine serial form, Ainsworth is wisely ignored today.

Grant **ALLEN** (1848-99)

Best remembered for his light fiction, Allen was, in fact, a much-travelled and well educated man. Of Irish descent, he was born in Kingston, Ontario; was educated in America, France and England; became an Oxford graduate, a teacher and, for a while, a scientist, whose early works were of a scientific nature. (*Physiological Aesthetics*, 1877, is little read today, though *The Colour Sense* of 1879 was well thought of.) He contributed scientific articles to magazines such as *Cornhill*, and sold short stories to an increasing number of magazines, beginning with *Belgravia*, the fiction magazine founded by Mrs **Braddon**. The success of these tempted him to write full-length novels, beginning with *Philista* (1884) and climaxing with *The Woman Who Did*, an 1895 shocker he wrote in support of feminine freedom but which only outraged contemporary feminists and prudes. In that same year appeared his *The British Barbarians* in which a 25th century anthropologist looked back scathingly at Victorian society. With that novel, Allen managed to upset nearly everybody.

BY GRANT ALLEN.

I.—THE EPISODE OF THE MEXICAN SEER.

Science fiction and fantasy fuelled many of his stories. He wrote nearly 30 novels, and among his fictional creations are Lois Cayley, the bicycling, sporty, ex-Girton amateur detective whose exploits in short stories were amalgamated into two anthologies (1899 and 99); and Colonel Clay, the gentleman crook who could disguise and reshape his face as if it were made of modeller's clay. (Clay's 1896 *Strand* serial was reissued as *An African Millionaire* in 1899.) Allen's final, uncompleted novel, *Hilda Wade*, was finished for him by his good friend Sir Arthur Conan **Doyle**.

William **ALLINGHAM** (1824-89)

A poet of some standing in his day but now remembered best through his associations. His poetry of the 1850s, when collated, was illustrated by major Pre-Raphaelite artists such as **Rossetti**, Hughes and Millais – and for that reason the books are collectable today. (His *The Music Master* of 1855 is especially desirable, and Rossetti's *The Maids of Elfen-Mere*, shown

here, is from it.) Between 1874 and 79 he edited the influential *Fraser's Magazine*– though it is for the contributors, rather than his own work, that the magazine is still collected. His posthumous *Diary* (published 1907) is a mine of gossip and information on Victorian life and notables – including the *fin de siècle* aesthetic movement – and contains many snippets on friends such as **Dickens, Leigh Hunt, Carlyle** and **Tennyson**. He even managed to marry sensibly: in 1874 he married the watercolourist and illustrator Helen Paterson. (She edited his

diary for publication.) His famous poem, *The Fairies*, begins:

Up the airy mountain,
Down the rushy glen,
We daren't go a-hunting
For fear of little men;
Wee folk, good folk,
Trooping all together;
Green jacket, red cap,
And white owl's feather!
Down along the rocky shore
Some make their home, -
They live on crispy pancakes
Of yellow tide-foam;
Some in the reeds
Of the black mountain-lake,
With frogs for their watch-dogs,
All night awake.

Matthew ARNOLD (1822-88)

Son of a famous father, Thomas Arnold, historian and headmaster of Rugby School (fictionalised by Thomas **Hughes** in *Tom Brown's Schooldays*), Matthew grew to outshine his father. He won the Newdigate Prize at Balliol, was a fellow of Oriel, and became Private Secretary to Lord Lansdowne. In his travels he met and fell for a Swiss miss, Mary Claude, and although in his poetry he immortalised her as 'Marguerite', he later married Miss Frances Wightman. It was a happy but afflicted marriage: three of their four sons died before reaching adulthood. Between 1849 and 1867 he published poems to growing success and acclaim, producing work that will be found in any proper anthology of 19th century or major English verse. *Dover Beach, The Scholar Gipsy, The Forsaken Merman* (sweetly illustrated overleaf) are the most memorable. Arnold could turn even Kensington Gardens into an arcadian dreamworld:

In this lone open glade I lie,
Screen'd by deep boughs on either hand;
And at its head, to stay the eye,
Those black-crowned, red-boled pine-trees stand.

Arnold had always been engaged in the God Debate or, in his case, the challenge to faith which roared through the century, and it was in his last anthology entitled, with no hint that it was to be his last work, *New Poems* (1867), that he encaptured the Victorian fear that faith might ebb away:

The sea of faith
Was once, too, at the full, and round earth's shore
Lay like the folds of a bright girdle furl'd;
But now I only hear
Its melancholy, long, withdrawing roar,
Retreating to the breath
Of the night-wind down the vast edges drear
And naked shingles of the world.

Though he had been professor of poetry at Oxford since 1858 his focus gradually shifted to prose. His 1865 *Essays in Criticism* (two years before his last poetry anthology) was persuasive in its conviction that criticism should be applied beyond art and literature, and the collection led almost inevitably to his even more famous *Culture and Anarchy* of 1869:

> *The whole scope of the essay is to recommend culture as the great help out of our present difficulties; culture being a pursuit of our total perfection by means of getting to know, on all the matters which most concern us, the best which has been thought and said in the world....*
>
> *I propose to try and enquire, in the simple and unsystematic way which best suits both my taste and my powers, what culture really is, what good it can do, what is our own special need of it.*

A short book by Victorian standards, with a Preface, Introduction and seven chapters, it includes his essays on *Sweetness and Light, Doing As One Likes* and *Barbarians, Philistines, Populace*. Arnold's message is timeless:

> *The people who believe most that our greatness and welfare are proved by our being very rich, and who most give their lives and thoughts to becoming rich, are just the very people whom we call Philistines.*

His later books were in defence of the church. His death came unexpectedly, as he hurried for a tram to take him to the docks where he hoped to meet his newly-married daughter.

Henry Spencer ASHBEE (1834-1900)
Under the pseudonym 'Pisanus Fraxi' he compiled a massive *Index Librorum Prohibitorum* (1877), the first serious bibliography of erotica and pornography. *Centuria Librorum Absconditorum* expanded it in 1879 and *Catena Librorum Tacendorum* completed the work in 1885. Biographer Ian Gibson claims that Ashbee also wrote as **'Walter'**.

Alfred AUSTIN (1835-1913)
A much-mocked Poet Laureate, awarded the post after the popular success of his *prose* work *The Garden That I Love* (1894). Before that he was, nevertheless, a poet (though his work is now considered to be of little merit) and, as joint founder of the *National Review*, was its editor for eight years. Shortly after his appointment as Poet Laureate he made the mistake of publishing an ode celebrating the abortive Jameson Raid (unaware that Britain had just lost the battle) and that pre-emptive slip, together with his tendency to criticise his peers, assured his ode of a derisory reception. His poetry, while not great, is not as bad as his reputation suggests.

William Edmonstoune AYTOUN (1813-65)

A Scottish poet and critic remembered now – and perhaps best known at the time – for having coined the word 'spasmodic' as part of his sneer against the Romantic poetry of the early century. A parodist also, he collaborated with Theodore Martin on *The Bon Gaultier Ballads* (1855), while at the same time he exposed himself to possible ridicule with his own precious and high-minded *Lays of the Scottish Cavaliers* (1849) and *Ballads of Scotland* (1858). Dealing with Scottish historical subjects and heroes, the poems in these books aped those of Sir Walter Scott and Thomas Babington. But the reading public didn't laugh at them: despite his reputation as a humorist they thought the poems rather good – authentic even. Then he produced his parodic masterstroke. It began in May 1854 when for *Blackwood's Magazine* he contributed what appeared to be a review of the unpublished poetry of a young 'Spasmodic', T Percy Jones. His review was so glowing that readers called for the young poet's work to be published. In July 1854 Aytoun duly obliged with *Firmilian, or, The Student of Badajoz: a Spasmodic Tragedy*. The parody – taken seriously – sold out, though not everyone was fooled. The *Times* praised *Firmilian* as 'the most perfect, as it is the most elaborate and the most legitimate, parody that has ever been written.' It was enough to kill off the modish Spasmodic school, which Aytoun had always detested.

All this made critics wary when judging his more serious work, including the two-volume *Ballads of Scotland* (1858) and his semi-autobiographical novel *Norman Sinclair* (1861), but these were good enough to be generally well received. By now the fun had slipped away from him: his wife had died in 1859, his health deteriorated and, although he remarried at the end of 1863, he died in August 1865. His one-time writing partner Theodore Martin published a biography in 1867.

Walter BAGEHOT (1826-77)

Public opinion is a permeating influence, and it exacts obedience to itself; it requires us to think other men's thoughts, to speak other men's words, to follow other men's habits. Of course, if we do not, no formal ban ensues; no corporeal pain, no coarse penalty of a barbarous society is inflicted on the offender: but we are called 'eccentric'; there is a gentle murmur of 'most unfortunate ideas', 'singular young man', 'well-

intentioned, I dare say; but unsafe, sir, quite unsafe'.
From his essay on *The Character of Sir Robert Peel*

He is one of the Victorian historians you can still read with a degree of pleasure. Bagehot's *The English Constitution* (1867) remains a classic work, and was reissued in 1963. At the time he wrote it he was editor of *The Economist* (he had married the founder's daughter) and had previously been editor of *The National Review*. 'The best reason why Monarchy is a strong government,' he said in that book, 'is that it is an intelligible government. The mass of mankind understand it, and they hardly anywhere in the world understand any other.' He was both a political and literary critic, and most of his works still stand up well, even if *Physics or Politics* (1872) is at times an awkward marriage of state politics and theories of natural selection. Among his works on literature, *Literary Studies* (1879) stands out.

He was sound on financial analyses, as in his *Lombard Street* (1873) and *Economic Studies* (1880) – though it is said that he spelt badly and could barely add up. His words of 1880 seem especially pertinent to the economic maelstrom whipped up in 2008 and 2009:

The result is that we have placed the exclusive custody of our entire banking reserve in the hands of a single board of directors not particularly trained for the duty – who might be called 'amateurs' – who have no particular interest above other people in keeping it undiminished – who acknowledge no obligation to keep it undiminished – who have never been told by any great statesman or public authority that they are so to keep it or that they have anything to do with it – who are named by and are agents for a proprietary which would have a greater income if it was diminished – who do not fear, and who need not fear, ruin, even if it were all gone and wasted.
From *Lombard Street*

It is to Bagehot that we owe the comforting belief that the role of the Bank of England is to underpin confidence and to be the 'lender of last resort'.

Philip James **BAILEY** (1816-1902)
Father of the 'Spasmodic School of Poetry' and thus mocked by **Aytoun**

and others, Bailey published his epic blank verse *Festus* in 1839 – or he began it then, because over the years he added to it until it became a grossly extended 40,000 line drama in 52 scenes, into which he had incorporated chunks of his other works such as *The Angel World* (1850), *The Mystic* (1855) and *The Universal Hymn* (1867). *Festus*, in case you don't get round to reading it, is a romantic blend of Goethe's *Faust* and Milton's *Paradise Lost*.

R M BALLANTYNE, (1825-94)

A once-popular children's author, Robert Michael Ballantyne achieved his greatest success with *The Coral Island* (1858), a merry tale of three boys shipwrecked on an island, whose adventures are far more pleasant than those inflicted upon the characters in Golding's 20th century *Lord of the Flies*. The book's sequel, *The Gorilla Hunters* (1861), is by today's standards unacceptable, given its cheerful theme of killing animals, and many of his works (written, we should remember, by one who had been an Elder of the Free Kirk) would be deemed too pious and instructive to meet the tastes of modern youth – though they were Adventure stories: that was the reason for their success. He had lived an active life himself, having traded with 'Red Indians' for the Hudson Bay Company and having worked as a London fireman. His biographer, Eric Quayle, says that Ballantyne was less interested in writing than in acting out the lives of his "boys' heroes". (As 'research' for his tales he played at being a train driver, a diver, a detective and an Arab in Algiers.) Ballantyne was a big seller in his day and for decades afterwards. In his 40 year career he wrote some 80 books, the first of which, should you seek it out, was *The Young Fur Traders* (1856) – a book he originally called *Snowflakes and Sunbeams*. Just as well he had second thoughts.

Helen BANNERMAN (1862-1946)

Could she have guessed, with her first book, how long its fame would live? It was *The Story of Little Black Sambo* (1890), a tiny, Beatrice Potter sized book decorated, like Potter's, with brightly coloured pictures – done by Bannerman herself. She had written it while travelling with her doctor husband in India and she sold the copyright to the publisher Grant Richards for five pounds. Seen at the time as delightful and entirely unobjectionable, *Sambo* was followed (just outside the Victorian age) by more books about *Little Black* people: *Mingo, Quibba, Quasha* and finally *Little Black Bobtail* in 1910. She was understandably impervious to the charges of racism – since, by and large, they were made long after her death – and indeed she wrote *Sambo and the Twin* in 1938. Her unpublished *Little White Squibba* was published posthumously in 1966.

The Reverend R H **BARHAM** (1788-1845)

Although much of his writing came before the Victorian age, Barham's most successful work began in the year Victoria came to the throne, 1837, when his *Ingoldsby Legends* began in *Bentley's Miscellany* and *The New Monthly Magazine*. These supposedly medieval ballads, copiously illustrated by Cruikshank, Leech and Tenniel (seen here), were a riot of puns, slang and non sequiturs, keeping Victorians amused for decades. None of his other work (a novel, *Baldwin: or a Miser's Heir* and sundry journalism) came to much, but the Legends are still funny today.

Sabine **BARING-GOULD** (1834-1924)

Some men might be content to have composed *Onward Christian Soldiers* but Baring-Gould was as prolific as a man who reached his tenth decade could be. His prose works covered an enormously wide field, from antiquaries to zoology. His first novel, *Through Fire and Flame* (1868) described his own marriage to a mill girl (they had 14 children); he wrote travel books, devotional literature, works of natural history, *The Lives of the Saints* (1872-7), biography, a great deal of journalism and a number of important works on folklore and folk song. He was a prodigious walker – indeed, he was prodigious in nearly everything. *Mehalah* (1880) is generally considered his finest novel, and was reissued half a century after his death with an appreciation by John Fowles.

William **BARNES** (1801-86)

A dialect poet and philologist, and thus obscure to most of us, Barnes resisted the dilution of English by foreign words and called for a return to the Anglo-Saxon. Perhaps because of his three collections of *Poems in the Dorset Dialect* (1844, 59 and 62) his funeral was marked by a poem from fellow Dorset man Thomas **Hardy** who later (1908) edited a compilation of his poems. But can any reader today continue with a poem that begins (all too typically):

> *Ov all the birds upon the wing*
> *Between the zunny show'rs o' spring, –*
> *Vor all the lark, a-swingèn high,*
> *Mid zing sweet ditties to the sky,* et cetera

Amelia **BARR** (1831-1919)

Amelia Barr personifies the Victorian struggle of triumph over adversity. Her father, a Methodist minister, lost what little fortune he had when a friend defrauded him. Her mother was left rentable property by a relative but, under the Married Woman's Property Act, saw her property revert to her husband. Amelia married, her own husband's business failed, and in 1853 the couple sailed for America. In Chicago she opened a school for girls – but her husband upset the locals and they had to leave. They lived in Tennessee and Texas, and she had eight children, five of whom survived – until, when they moved again in 1866, her husband and two more children died of yellow fever, leaving Amelia with five dollars and three children to support. While teaching in New York, she began submitting short stories to magazines. Encouraged by their success she wrote a novel, *Jan Vedder's Wife* (1885), which was well enough received to start her writing more novels in that vein (historical romances set in England and the United States, the most famous of which was *Remember the Alamo* in 1888). Amelia Barr was resolutely professional, sticking to the genre her public preferred and producing more than sixty novels which, if predictable, were what her readers wanted. She earned enough from writing to live comfortably in a country house at Cornwall-on-Hudson, New York, and she was buried in Tarrytown, New York, in Sleepy Hollow cemetery.

J M **BARRIE** (1860-1937)

Though immortal as the author of *Peter Pan*, he was a prolific novelist and dramatist. Much of his early fiction was sentimentally Scots, and irritated his countrymen who dismissed it as being of the 'Kailyard school'. These late 1880s stories were set in 'Thrums' (based on his native Kirriemuir) and were followed by unashamedly sentimental novels such as *Sentimental Tommy* (1896) and *Tommy and Grizel* (1900). This latter anticipates his most famous creation, yet to come. (Barrie described the unhappily married Tommy as a 'boy who could not grow up.')

Only in the 1990s did he begin writing for the stage (*Richard Savage* came first in 1891, though his first real success was with a dramatisation of *The Little Ministerin* 1897) and just after Queen Victoria died he had true smash hits with *Quality Street* and *The Admirable Crichton*. Then in 1904 came the play *Peter Pan* – subsequent development and beatification of whom belongs to the 20th century.

Barrie was a small man, five foot two, and, especially after the death of his older brother in a skating accident, was a lifelong mother's boy. (The Thrum stories were based on ones she'd told him, and he wrote a hagiographic biography, *Margaret Ogilvy*, in 1896.) Barrie's troubled marriage to the actress Mary Ansell has been well documented (imaginatively at times) and seems not untypical of the Victorian age.

Aubrey **BEARDSLEY** (1872-98)

Known principally as an artist and illustrator and for his involvement with the *Yellow Book* and fin de siècle decadence, Beardsley did publish a few snippets of provocative prose and poetry. *The Story of Venus and Tannhauser* was an erotic take on Wagner's German legend and was sufficiently explicit to be shortened for publication in the *Savoy* as *Under The Hill*. Whether that version was expurgated or was edited down by Beardsley for artistic reasons is a matter of slight debate (though an unexpurgated version appeared in 1907, and the original *Yellow Book* text together with other scraps and letters was published as a separate book, called *Under The Hill* again, in 1904). Beardsley had never been healthy, and he died early and not unexpectedly of tuberculosis.

Thomas Lovell **BEDDOES** (1803-49)

Beddoes wrote what little there was of his work before Victoria came to the throne but, since 1825, continued to fiddle with the text of his *Death's Jest-Book*, a revenge tragedy in verse which was not published until 1850, after he'd committed suicide. This macabre work was taken up nearly half a century later by the poets of the *fin de siècle* who relished its morbid tonality, and it is from his 1850 and 1851 collections that a few poems are still anthologised. His *A Voice From The Waters* prophetically begins:

> *The swallow leaves her nest,*
> *The soul my weary breast;*
> *But therefore let the rain*
> *On my grave*
> *Fall pure; for why complain?*
> *Since both will come again*
> *O'er the wave.*

Mrs **BEETON** (1836-65)

Isabella Mary Beeton died before her thirtieth birthday, wrote (some say co-wrote) one book, and became a national household legend. Like many Victorian works, hers was serialised in a magazine, in this case one published by her husband, *The Englishwoman's Domestic Magazine*, between 1859 and 61, and was then issued by him in volume form as *Household Management* in 1861. As the original title suggests, the book was far more than a cookery book; in 1172 pages of exhaustive detail it covered all the duties of the Victorian housewife, including management of staff, the intricacies of cleaning, the care of pets and other domestic animals, health, hygiene and financial management. Isabella knew whereof she spoke: her mother had had seventeen children, to which her stepfather brought in four more. She herself died of puerperal fever after delivering her own fourth child. Her husband, a successful publisher, also died young, of consumption.

Hilaire **BELLOC** (1870-1953)

Most of Belloc's output came after the Victorian period – indeed, he himself didn't become a British citizen until 1902 – but his *Bad Child's Book of Beasts* and his *Verses and Sonnets* were both published in 1896. He also squeezed in a biography of Danton in 1899. The much-loved *Cautionary Tales* did not appear till 1907 and, although he wrote till the middle of the 20th century, he was in essence an Edwardian. For this reason, perhaps, much of his other writing seems removed from us and is held in less regard than once it was. Fiercely political, he was against the Boer War, against Imperialism and against party politics, although this did not stop him becoming Liberal MP for Salford. He was half French and staunchly Roman Catholic.

Arnold **BENNETT** (1867-1931)

A late Victorian, more a 20th century figure, but his output was so voluminous that, although his first stories appeared as late as 1890, more than a million of his words had been printed by the time Victoria died. He came from resolutely middle class stock; his father was a solicitor and young Arnold was expected to follow that profession, but at the age of twenty-one he left home to make his way in London, starting as a clerk while trying to establish himself as a writer. The first stories appeared in *Tit-Bits* (1890) and the *Yellow Book* (1895), and his semi-autobiographical *The Man From The*

North came out in 1898. Earlier, in 1893, he had become editor of *Woman* magazine and, for much of his life, journalism was to play a large part in his career, although it is for his 20th century fiction, brilliantly describing middle class and usually provincial life, that he is most remembered. *The Clayhanger* series and, best of all, the many stories, short and long, set in his 'Five Towns' (broadly based on the pottery towns around Stoke on Trent) have been his most successful, although *The Old Wives' Tale* (1908) is perhaps his greatest. It is also worth seeking out his lively and revealing diaries, begun in 1896 and continuing till 1929.

February 13th, 1897
Yesterday afternoon, a sandwich-man in Coventry Street, stooping with difficulty owing to his encumbrances, picked up a cigar-end out of the gutter.
'My first today,' he exclaimed to his mate who was in front of him.

Tuesday, June 29th, 1897
I wonder if women realize the acute pleasure which men derive from the sight of them in their fresh, cool, clean, summer toilettes – openwork stockings, diaphanous sleeves, and general impression of musliness.

Sunday, December 31st, 1899
This year I have written 335,340 words, grand total. 228 articles and stories (including 4 instalments of a serial of 30,000 – 7,500 words each) have actually been published. Also my book of plays – 'Polite Farces'.... My total earnings were £592 3s 1d, of which sum I have yet to receive £72 10s.

Walter **BESANT** (1836-1901)
His life almost exactly coincided with Victoria's reign and was almost as crowded. Educated at King's College, London and Christ's College, Cambridge, he became secretary to the Palestine Exploration Fund, a post he held from 1868 to 1886, during which time he wrote several best-selling novels, including *Ready-Money Mortiboy* (serialised in *Once A Week* in 1872) and *The Golden Butterfly* (1876) while at the same time becoming active in campaigns to publicise and ameliorate the dreadful social conditions of industrial workers. In 1897 he helped found the enormous and hugely beneficial educational establishment, the *People's Palace* in Mile

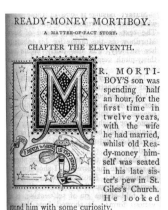

ADY-MONEY MORTIBOY.
A MATTER-OF-FACT STORY.
CHAPTER THE FIFTH.

N THE THURSDAY morning, Dick Mortiboy went up to town to see the "partner" of whom he had told his father. "Meet me," he wrote to him, "at Euston, in time for the two o'clock train." At ten minutes before two there arrived on the platform of the
us a thin, slightly built man, who pacing up and down, and irritably ng every moment at his watch.

READY-MONEY MORTIBOY.
A MATTER-OF-FACT STORY.
CHAPTER THE ELEVENTH.

R. MORTI-BOY'S son was spending half an hour, for the first time in twelve years, with the wife he had married, whilst old Rea-dy-money him-self was seated in his late sis-ter's pew in St. Giles's Church. He looked
round him with some curiosity.

READY-MONEY MORTIBOY.
A MATTER-OF-FACT STORY.
CHAPTER THE TWENTY-NINTH.

FTER walking through a num-ber of narrow and dark pas-sages, Frank found himself at last in the North London Palace of Amusement and Aristocra-tic Lounge.
Dingy and dirty by day, light it ap-peared.

End. He also worked to improve the lot of fellow writers, founding the Society of Authors in 1884 and laying the foundations for a standard contract between them and their publishers, a contract which still broadly pertains today.

Augustine **BIRRELL** (1850-1933)
Literary essayist who in 1889 descended into politics (becoming MP for West Fife and ultimately President of the Board of Education and, in 1907, Chief Secretary for Ireland). His approachable literary essays of the 1880s, anthologised under the title *Obiter Dicta* and issued in 3 volumes in 1884, 87 and belatedly 1924, became almost essential reading for the educated reader. He also wrote some literary biographies.

William **BLACK** (1841-98)
Prolific but now-forgotten Scottish author of Scottish tales – lumped like the early J M **Barrie**, into the sentimental 'Kailyard school' of writing – produced his first novel, *James Merle, an Autobiography*, in 1864 and achieved his first commercial success with *A Daughter of Heth* in 1871. When, in 1880, he broke from the mould to bring out his sea story, *Sunrise*, the critic of the *Athenaeum*, could not conceal his relief: 'No yachting, no highland lochs.'

PART I. APRIL. ONE SHILLING.

SUNRISE
A Story of These Times
by
WILLIAM BLACK
author of "A Daughter of Heth"
&c. &c.

LONDON
SAMPSON LOW-MARSTON-SEARLE-&-RIVINGTON
1880

R D **BLACKMORE** (1825-1900)

The author of *Lorna Doone* (1869) must have written something else, and indeed he did, though none achieved anything like the same success. Having preceded his best-seller with *Clara Vaughan* (1864) and *Cradock Nowell* (1866) he followed it with titles such as *Alice Lorraine* (1875) and, breaking away from girls' names, with *Cripps the Carrier* (1877) and *Springhaven: A Tale of the Great War* (1887). Richard Doddridge Blackmore was the occasionally epileptic son of an Exmoor clergyman and, although he trained for the law, he divided his life between authorship and market gardening. Exmoor, nature and the country life permeate many of his stories, most of which are far more peaceful than *Lorna Doone* Perhaps that's why they never sold as many copies.

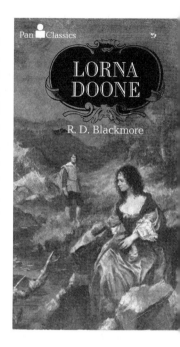

Marguerite, Countess of **BLESSINGTON** (1789-1849)

Her story is that of a spirited heroine in a 19th century romance – one cannot think of her as Victorian. Born in near poverty in County Tipperary, she was a mere fourteen when her dissolute farmer father sold her off to marry an equally dissolute English army captain (splendidly named Maurice St Leger Farmer) who she quit after just three months. She did not go home. Instead she rose colourfully in London and abroad until, in 1817, she married the First Earl of Blessington and made his home in St James's Square a focus for literary and artistic society. She began writing, and courting literary men.

The most notable was Byron, with whom her friendship may have been no more than extremely cordial, but the most intimate was with the young and dashing (though probably homosexual) Count d'Orsay. Blessington himself remained remarkably tolerant. (He died in 1829 of apoplexy and left her only moderately well off.) Her Kensington salon, now run jointly with Count d'Orsay on a financial knife-edge, remained a social Mecca, and she busied herself with a deal of writing. Much of it was pretty journalism but she also became editor of two much-treasured annuals, *The Book of Beauty* and *The Keepsake*. She wrote a number of novels (little read today) and two decent travel books, *The Idler in Italy* (1839) and *The Idler in France* (1841). But her income never matched her splendid lifestyle and in 1849 she was forced to flee to France to escape her creditors. In less than two months she was dead. *The Keepsake* is sought out today mainly for its deadeningly respectable illustrations, but her *Journal of Conversations with Lord Byron* (1832) is still a useful work.

Wilfred Scawen **BLUNT** (1840-1922)

The last person to tell your secrets to – or, if you were a respectable woman – the last person to go to bed with, Blunt seems to have believed it was a writer's job to tell. Well-born, handsome, devil-may-care, he began adult life in the diplomatic service – not that diplomacy was ever his personal forte. After a decade of youthful passion (during which he bedded the famous courtesan 'Skittles' among others) he married Byron's granddaughter. Inevitably, perhaps, his first volume of poetry, *Sonnets and Songs by Proteus* published six years later in 1875, sung the praises of several other women. His next volumes blended amorous songs to women with odes to nature and paeans to his new love, Arabia – to whom he would, for once, remain faithful. He wrote in support of Egyptian, Indian and Irish independence – eventually landing in an Irish prison where he wrote *In Vinculis* in 1899. His scapegrace, sometimes scandalous lifestyle did not limit his large number of friends in literary and artistic high society – though those who survived to read his *Diaries* (1919 & 20) may have wished he had been more circumspect. He had, in 1887, founded a male-only literary salon, the Crabbet Club (meeting at his fine ancestral home, Crabbet Park) to which were invited famous names as disparate as Oscar Wilde and Lord Curzon, and the first clause of its constitution read: "*The Crabbet Club is a convivial association which has for its object to discourage serious views of life by holding up a constant standard of its amusements.*" Among Blunt's romantic amusements, apart from the famous 'Skittles', were Jane Morris (wife of William), Mary Elcho (his longest-lasting lover), Dorothy Carleton (the cousin of Mary Elcho), Gay Windsor (Lady Paget's daughter and considerably younger than him), Lady Gregory, Minnie

Singleton (Lady Currie, a.k.a. the author Violet **Fane**), and Madeline Wyndham (his cousin's wife). The full list is much longer.

Charles **BOOTH** (1840-1916)

A Unitarian shipping magnate remembered as a social campaigner and reformist and as the author of a monumental study, *Life and Labour of the People in London* which, although published in its final form in 1902 and 3, is a portrait of Victorian times. The 17-volume work was released in stages (as it was written), the first part as early as 1889, when it was called *Labour and Life of the People.* Subsequent volumes came out from 1891 onwards. His wife's cousin Beatrice **Webb** (or Beatrice Potter, as she was misleadingly named before her marriage) described this tall, gaunt man as having 'the complexion of a consumptive girl, a prominent aquiline nose, with moustache and pointed beard barely hiding a noticeable Adam's apple.' He should not be confused with William Booth, leader of the Salvation Army.

George Henry **BORROW** (1803-81)

Borrow was an inveterate traveller through much of Europe and a deal of Russia, and he did more to document Gypsy life and lore than anyone, yet he began adult life respectably articled to a solicitor, during which time he edited *Celebrated Trials, and Remarkable Cases of Criminal Jurisprudence*(1825). In the same year, by contrast, he translated *Faustus: His Life, Death, and Descent into Hell* and produced his own *Life and Adventures of the Famous Colonel Blood*. He continued hackwork until 1832, when he secured a peripatetic post with The British and Foreign Bible Society, for whom he worked for seven years, travelling extensively. From his experiences he then produced two commercially successful books, *The Zincali, or An Account of the Gypsies in Spain* (1841) and *The Bible in Spain* (1843). This latter, despite its sober title, was an adventure story, recounting his clashes with Gypsies, bandits, fellow travellers and officialdom. Borrow was not the only travel writer to lace his stories with large dashes of colourful fiction, but his accounts of Gypsy customs have always been regarded as broadly authentic. Other notable books are *Lavengro* (1851) and *The Romany Rye* (1857), although his *Wild Wales* (1862) remains a travel classic also.

Dion **BOUCICAULT** (1820-90)

A colossus of the Victorian stage, his first success came in 1841 when *London Assurance* was put on at the Theatre Royal, Covent Garden. (The RSC revived this comedy with some success at the Aldwych in 1970.) Boucicault had a succession of crowd-pleasers, including in 1852 two big hits, *The Corsican Brothers* and *The Vampire*. The following year he emigrated to America, and he continued to dominate the theatre both there and in Britain, satisfying American, British and Irish audiences. (He was Irish himself.) His biggest hits were probably *The Octoroon* (1859, a melodrama about a glamorous freed female slave), *The Colleen Bawn* (1860, an outrageously Irish

romantic melodrama), and *The Shaughraun* (1874, roping in all three audiences with a swirling tale of an escaped Irish convict betrayed by a fellow Irishman, reluctantly arrested by a noble Englishman, and a final emigration of the hero and his sweetheart to America). Apart from being a successful dramatist, Boucicault strove to improve the rewards for his fellow writers, earning for them the right to royalties from their plays (rather than a niggardly once-off payment) and copyright protection in America.

Mrs **BRADDON** (1835-1915)

When your first novel is a sensation – indeed, when it is disparagingly called a 'sensation novel' – it can be hard for you to get your later work looked at seriously. So it was for Mrs Braddon. She (or rather, her husband, the publisher John Maxwell) published her first novel, *Lady Audley's Secret*, in 1862. This vigorous saga of a bigamous blonde femme fatale who murders her first husband, shoves him down a well, then has a good crack at both her second husband and his interfering nephew, was an enormous smash hit. What should Mary Braddon do next? She tried some more in the same vein (she would have been foolish not to) with rapidly-produced titles such as *Aurora Floyd* (1863), *John Marchmont's Legacy* (1863), *The Doctor's Wife* (1864), *Sir Jasper's Tenant* (1865) et cetera, but the bulk of her later titles were placed a rung or two up the intellectual ladder. She did her own take on *Madame Bovary* with *The Doctor's Wife* (1864), wrote satires, society novels, historical romances, tragedies and ghost stories – some 80 novels in all – and found time for a good deal of journalism. She also edited *Belgravia* and *Temple Bar*.

Her early life could have provided source material for her novels. An actress, fatherless, who took to the stage in part to support her mother, she lived with John Maxwell and looked after his children for a decade and a half before his insane wife died and Miss Braddon (as she then was) could marry him. He and she added six more children to his original brood of five. She had written several serious books before *Lady Audley's Secret*, including *Garibaldi and Other Poems*, a quite different work. These early pieces are difficult to find. In her day she was extremely well-known.

Robert **BRIDGES** (1844-1930)

Educated at Eton and Corpus Christi, he became a doctor and wrote poetry on the side, publishing *Poems* in 1873 and *The Growth of Love* in 1876. The success of these and later works allowed him to give up medicine in 1881, whereafter he concentrated on poetry, drama and criticism. (In 1913 he would become Poet Laureate, a post he held till his death.)

Anne **BRONTË** (1820-49)

Youngest and least effective of the three sisters, she lives on (almost literally, since her two novels have autobiographical elements) in *Agnes Grey* (1847) which draws on her own experiences as a governess to spoilt children, and *The Tenant of Wildfell Hall* (1848) in which the villain, Arthur Huntingdon, is generally thought to be a portrait of her dissolute brother Branwell. The Brontë sisters shared the Haworth rectory with their hard-working widowed father and brother Branwell, and their stern aunt Elizabeth as governess. In this grim household (less grim than legend has it, since the rectory was quite comfortable and was conveniently situated at the edge of a large village) the three sisters – and to an extent, their brother Branwell – began to write. Anne's first work was a volume of poems she published with her sisters in 1846. *Agnes Grey* (originally pseudonymous, by 'Acton Bell') is a bittersweet romance, only for the dedicated today, but *The Tenant* is an ambitious and more turbulent romance. Its unflinching portrayal of Huntingdon's alcoholism aroused censure at the time, but in a preface to its second edition Brontë defended her decision to tell the truth: 'To represent a bad thing in its least offensive light is doubtless the most agreeable course for a writer of fiction to pursue; but is it the most honest?'

Charlotte **BRONTË** (1816-55)

Eldest of the three sisters and the last to die. Following her mother's death, Charlotte and three of her sisters were sent to Cowan Bridge school, an appalling place which Charlotte blamed for the death of two sisters and for her own impaired health. She would reinvent Cowan as 'Lowood School' in *Jane Eyre* – but that came later. First, as a young adult from a Yorkshire curate's family, Charlotte had to earn a living. Options were limited. She taught, became a governess, then scraped together the means to study languages in Brussels. Here she had a clandestine,

almost certainly unrequited, romance with an older teacher, Monsieur Heger. On her return to Haworth she initiated the publication of *Poems by Currer, Ellis and Acton Bell*, but it didn't sell and, like her sisters, she switched to her first work of fiction: *The Professor* (based, inevitably, on Heger), which also failed to find a publisher. To add to her dejection, both her sisters' novels were accepted. She plunged into a second story, *Jane Eyre*, and wrote it quickly enough for all three Brontë sisters to have their novels appear within the same year. *Jane Eyre* (1847) was an immediate success – leaving her readers agog: who was Currer Bell?

Charlotte Brontë
1816-1855

'Who the author can be I can't guess,' wrote **Thackeray** to her publisher, George Smith. 'I wish you had not sent me *Jane Eyre*. It interested me so much that I have lost (or won if you like) a whole day in reading it.' Charlotte was so pleased with his praise that she graced her second edition with a fulsome dedication to the famous author – unaware that, like a milder version of Rochester, he had his own unstable wife locked away. Rumours quickly started that 'Currer Bell' was Thackeray's governess and hence, by implication, his mistress. 'I am very, very sorry that my inadvertent blunder should have made his name and affairs subject for common gossip,' she wrote – but in vain: even Thackeray's mother thought the rumour might be true. 'I never spoke 3 words to the lady and had no more love for my Governess than for my grandmother,' he grumbled. Reviews praised and lambasted her. The author was, wrote Lady Eastlake, 'one who had forfeited the society of her sex.' Other reviewers felt differently. It was the cleverest novel, wrote Lockhart, 'since Austen and Edgeworth were in their prime.'

PENGUIN CLASSICS

CHARLOTTE BRONTË

Jane Eyre

Charlotte could not enjoy her triumph: tragedy struck at home. Both her brother and her sister Emily died the following year, and Anne would die the year after that. During this painful time she wrote *Shirley* (published in 1849). London, meanwhile, yearned to fete her. She visited, but was never comfortable. 'Extremely unimpressive to look at,' sniffed Jane Carlyle. She was, said Thackeray's daughter Annie, who met her at a publisher's party: 'a tiny, delicate, serious little lady, pale, with fair straight hair, and steady eyes. She may be a little over thirty; she is dressed in a little barège dress with a pattern of faint green moss. She enters in mittens, in silence, in seriousness; our hearts are beating with wild excitement...' But: 'Everyone waited for the brilliant conversation which never began at all ... brilliance was not to be the order of the evening. "Do you like London, Miss Brontë?" she said; another silence, another pause, then Miss Brontë answers, "Yes and No" very gravely.' It was, declared another guest, one of the dullest evenings she had ever spent in her life.

Charlotte returned to Haworth, where she issued memorial editions of her sisters' works and produced a further selection of Brontë poems. In 1853 she published *Villette*, a novel some maintain to be her greatest, finer even than *Jane Eyre*. In *Villette* she returned again to her time in Brussels and, although her identity was now well known, she published again as Currer Bell. The following year, to her father's disappointment, she married his curate Arthur Bell Nicholls, but that too led to tragedy: she died the following year from complications during pregnancy. *The Professor* was published posthumously, in 1857. There have been several biographies but the best may still be that written by Elizabeth **Gaskell** in 1857.

Emily **BRONTË** (1818-48)

I am the only being whose doom
No tongue would ask, no eye would mourn:
I never caused a thought of gloom,
A smile of joy since I was born.
A verse from her poem written in 1839

EMILY BRONTË
Poems of Solitude
Foreword by Helen Dunmore

Emily was the second youngest of the Brontë sisters and the first to die (of the tuberculosis that took Anne also). She died so soon she had no chance to enjoy the praises that would be given her. *Wuthering Heights* had been published the year before she died but had been met with caution by reviewers, for its dark, brooding, complex psychology was too advanced for the 1840s. Emily seems to have taken their reaction stoically: her first book, after all, the *Poems* written by all three sisters, had achieved an initial sale of just two copies. Yet her poems were the finest of the Brontës, and many would claim her novel to be the finest that a Brontë wrote. She was reclusive and, although she spent short periods away from Haworth as a governess and was with Charlotte for nine months in Brussels, she was never happier than in the Yorkshire moorlands.

The story of Heathcliff and Cathy Earnshaw sails out beyond melodrama into the churning storms of psychological and even psychopathic agony and distress. Heathcliff, the embittered, perpetually angry orphan, sheltered by Mr Earnshaw but later bullied by Earnshaw's son, wrongly believes himself disdained by Catherine, whom he loves. He quits the house and, on his return three years later, finds her married to someone else. From here an already troubled story darkens into madness and despair; Heathcliff's bitter fury becomes more irrational and his behaviour more self-destructively violent than any previously seen in Gothic fiction. There was no easy ending and little comfort in the tale, so it is hardly surprising the novel took some decades to establish itself with readers. Now, perversely, it is seen as one of the greatest romances ever told.

(Charles William) Shirley **BROOKS** (1816-74)

Brooks was a *Punch* stalwart and, after being right-hand man to the editor, Mark Lemon, he succeeded him as editor in 1870. ('The most promising journalist of the day,' said Douglas Jerrold.) Brooks had trained originally in law but soon switched to authorship and journalism. He was reputed to be fast enough to turn out an article an hour, although Lemon insisted that 'Shirley's pen is the gracefullest in London.' He had strong views on social matters (and occasionally exercised them

in *Punch*). 'Castrate your ruffians after the second offence,' he suggested to Mark Lemon. 'Logic says exterminate the nuisance.' Unlike many contemporaries, he was strongly in favour of birth control: 'Poor people have two pleasures – to get children and to get drunk. Since they are denied the luxuries of the rich, one cannot wonder at their having large families, though they have nothing to live on and know that half their sons must either steal or starve.' An author of workaday serials also, his worst was his first: *The Gordian Knot* which began in *Bentley's Magazine* in January 1858, vanished for almost a year, then came back to limp sadly along till the knife fell in December '59. He died still working, with his latest work papers on his bed.

Rhoda **BROUGHTON** (1840-1920)

Women who offend Victorian propriety often turn out to be daughters of the church. So it was with Rhoda Broughton, born in Wales to a country parson. At the time her lively and witty novels seemed both audacious and feminist, and through several decades she was regarded as a champion of the 'new woman'. But in the later part of her life changing fashions and, in particular, society's greater freedoms, made her seem quite harmless. She found this amusing, and once remarked to Herbert Henry Asquith: 'I began by being the Zola and I have now become the Charlotte Yonge of English fiction.'

She began with novels in the conventional three- and two-decker format: *Not Wisely, But Too Well* and *Cometh Up As A Flower* (both 1867) and *Nancy* (1873), but as her novels shortened so they sharpened. *Mrs Bligh* (1892) and *Dear Faustina* (1897) both stand out. Nevertheless, in another tale told against herself, she said she'd once seen a railway bookstall with a bundle of second-hand novels tied with string and labelled: 'Rhoda Broughton – soiled and cheap.'

Doctor John **BROWN** (1810-82)

Whimsical Scottish essayist, known mainly (then and since) for his sentimental stories about a dog, first seen in his three-volume collection, *Horae Subsecivae* (which, as any decently educated Victorian would have known, meant Hours Of Leisure) published in stages between 1858 to 1862. The dog anecdotes were then issued separately as *Rab and his Friends.*

Elizabeth Barrett **BROWNING** (1806-61)
When one thinks of her one pictures a delicately frail young woman with long dark tresses, permanently reclined on a chaise longue, tucked beneath a tartan blanket, and perhaps feeding titbits to her red cocker spaniel, Flush (born 1842). A precocious student when a child, Elizabeth Barrett suffered a spinal injury at fifteen which left her semi-invalid for the rest of her life (hence the chaise longue).

Her first book of poetry, *The Battle of Marathon* (juvenile but not without interest) was privately printed in 1820. A second work appeared in 1826 but must have seemed of little consequence against the sudden death of her mother in 1828. The family moved to Wimpole Street in 1835, and it wasn't until 1838 that she produced her first notable book, *The Seraphim and Other Poems*. That same year she was sent to Torquay to recover from a haemorrhage. (It was there that her beloved brother Edward would be drowned in a sailing accident two years later. She lost another brother, Samuel, who died in Jamaica around that time.) She returned to London in 1841, but it was not until 1845 that an exchange of letters began with the younger, less popular poet, Robert Browning. Her renownedly tyrannical and widowed father had forbidden any of his (originally) twelve children to marry without his consent but, in September 1846, she and Robert married secretly and fled to Italy. Their only child (Robert Wiedermann) was born there in 1849. After 15 years of happy marriage she is said to have died in her husband's arms.

Her book, *Poems* (1844), had been enthusiastically received (one of its poems, *The Cry of the Children*, being widely quoted and discussed) but it was not until 1850, after the birth of her son, that she published a second *Poems*, a book which included her famous *Sonnets from the Portuguese* (verses she had actually composed during her courtship). *Casa Guidi*

Windows followed in 1851 (*Casa Guidi* was their Florence home) and perhaps her greatest work, Aurora Leigh, appeared in 1857. The theme of Italian liberation had been visible in *Casa Guidi Windows* but it came to the fore in her late work, *Poems before Congress* (1860), where it alienated many of her readers. After her death, her husband prepared a final *Last Poems* and had it published in 1862. Volumes of letters and memorabilia swiftly followed from several pens.

Robert **BROWNING** (1812-89)

Perhaps it helped that his father, a clerk in the Bank of England, had a library of 6,000 books. Attracted to political romantics like Keats and Shelley, the young Robert had a youthful infatuation with atheism and vegetarianism, before he dropped out of university and set off on travels to Russia and Italy. After an unsuccessful attempt at poetry (*Pauline: A Fragment of a Confession*, 1833) his long monologue *Paracelsus* (1835) attracted notice in literary circles and encouraged him to continue in dramatic vein. An 1837 play, *Strafford*, was staged to muted response at Covent Garden, but in 1840 he blew his small reputation with *Sordello*, a complex (nigh

incomprehensible) narrative poem. Though he continued writing, few readers were interested, and it was during this interregnum that he courted the more successful Miss Elizabeth Barrett. Perhaps she helped redirect him, as it was only after their marriage that his works began to be accepted again for publication. *Christmas-Eve and Easter Day* (1850) was followed by the better *Men and Women* in 1855, leading to real success with *The Ring and the Book* (1868-9).

After Elizabeth's death he returned to England. Here he was forgiven his unimpressive time at university and was given an honorary Oxford degree and an honorary fellowship at Baliol. A Browning Society formed in 1881. Few of his later works are held in much regard today, nor were they much read by the Victorian public. He tends toward the cranky, wordy and obscure, and it is hard to reconcile his writings with the popular, often fictionalised image of Elizabeth Barrett's romantic young lover and besotted husband in sunny Italy.

Robert Williams **BUCHANAN** (1841-1901)
Though a poet, essayist, novelist and playwright, he is remembered for his attacks on **Rossetti** and **Swinburne**. After a comfortable start – born well-off, finding it easy to get published, being praised for his poetry – he began spitting venom as a critic. He hit Swinburne first, striking him twice, first with an anonymous article in *The Athenaeum* where he accused Swinburne of being morbid and 'unclean for the sake of uncleanness', then with *The Session of the Poets*, a satirical poem in the *Spectator* in 1866. Swinburne hit back, a literary storm erupted, and Buchanan, again anonymously, turned his scorn on Rossetti with a critical article entitled *The Fleshly School of Poetry*. (It was printed in the *Contemporary Review* in 1871 and issued as a pamphlet in 1872. Rossetti responded with *The Stealthy School of Criticism*.) Swinburne took his grievance to court, but lost: Buchanan was awarded £150 damages – and the wholesale scorn of the literary world. He later recanted, and in 1892 made an unsuccessful pitch for the post of Poet Laureate. He lost out to Alfred **Austin**. Buchanan's own volumes include his first, *Undertones* (1863), then *London Poems* (1866), *White Rose and Red* (1873), and *Balder the Beautiful* (1877).

Henry Thomas **BUCKLE** (1821-62)
Typhoid robbed Buckle of his life and may have lost us a potentially great historian. His mammoth *History of Civilisation in England* started outside England and was meant to work in. But he died too soon, at a point where he had managed a comprehensive if unfriendly history of Spain and Scotland but little of England itself. Today, Buckle's 'scientific' approach seems startlingly modern and almost Marxist: change happens according to natural laws rather than from the acts of heroes; civilisations grow as a result of their climate, food and soil, their agriculture, manufacture and size of population, rather than – again – from the acts of leaders. Men are the by-product of change, and not its cause. Only two books of his projected work were published: the first in 1857, the second in 1861.

Edward **BULWER-LYTTON** (1803-73)

When, at the age of 40, he added a second 'Lytton' to his already impressive name of Edward George Earle Lytton Bulwer, it was a move irresistible to satirists such as Thackeray who, in *Yellowplush Correspondence* jumbled his name to become 'Sawedwadgeorgeeearll-ittnbulwig' (a drawled version of Sir Edward George etc.) and in his later *Novels By Eminent Hands* Thackeray signed his pastiche 'E.L.B.L.B.B.L.L.B.B.B.L.L.L.'

Bulwer Lytton was an easy man to parody. Well-born and dandified, he claimed ancestry back to William the Conqueror. At Cambridge he was President of the Union and, after he left, he began an affair with the notorious Lady Caroline Lamb – he the young romantic, she the ex-mistress of Lord Byron. She, at 39, was eighteen years older than him, and their affair lasted several months until she dropped him for another man. Bulwer then met the woman who would become his wife, the wild and beautiful Rosina Anne Doyle Wheeler – an Irish adventuress, declared his mother who refused to sanction the marriage. When the pair married she cut off Bulwer's generous allowance, and he decided to earn his living by writing books.

That must have seemed an unwise decision, but in the next decade the young aristocrat turned out an astonishing total of a dozen novels, two dozen short stories, five plays, two volumes of poetry, a history of Athens, a sociological survey of English life, and over a hundred essays and reviews. He ended that decade as 'without doubt, the most popular writer now living,' according to the *American Quarterly Review*. Although his first novel, *Falkland* (1827) had been of little consequence, the next, *Pelham, or, The Adventures of a Gentleman* (1828) was a great success, and began a trend for the 'silver fork' novel, set in a romanticised high society.

In 1830, he shocked his readers with an anti capital punishment crime novel, *Paul Clifford* (1830), beginning with the famous lines 'It was a dark and stormy night.' He followed this with another crime novel having a murderer as its hero: *Eugene Aram* (1832) – a prime example of 'the Newgate School of Fiction' (stories based on tales reported in the *Newgate Calendar*). It raised a storm of reproof because of its supposed immorality – sending it, almost inevitably, into several editions. He published his next novel, *Godolphin* (1833), anonymously, but it was not a success, his health was affected, and he set off with his wife to Italy. What he saw there inspired his most successful book, *The Last Days of Pompeii* (1834). The following year brought another popular success: *Rienzi, Last of the Tribunes*, set in 14th century Rome, and in a clutch of further books he continued to plunder Europe: *The Pilgrims of the Rhine* (1834); *Athens: its Rise and Fall* (1837); *Leila, or, The Siege of Granada* (1838); and plays such as *The Duchess de la Vallière* (1836) and *The Lady of Lyons* (1838). A verse satire, *The Siamese Twins* (1831), formed the basis for a famous caricature of the author by the artist Daniel Maclise. Another of Bulwer's stage pieces, the verse drama *Richelieu* (1839), contains the famous words: 'The pen is mightier than the sword'.

He became MP for St Ives in Huntingdonshire in 1831, then for Lincoln the following year, and during his parliamentary career he led campaigns to establish dramatic copyright (1833), to curb the monopoly of performance in Covent Garden and Drury Lane (1843), to abolish the royal patent (1843 also), and to reduce stamp duty on newspapers (1855). He was a handsome, well-connected and increasingly famous man, and in April 1836 he and

Rosina separated, giving as their reason 'incompatibility of temper'. Nine years of stormy marriage were followed by forty years of acrimony. Rosina claimed he had kicked her in the side when she was eight months pregnant, and that he had caused his daughter's death from typhus fever. She had posters printed in an attempt to baulk his parliamentary career. After a while he turned to a remedy all too familiar from Victorian fiction: he had her committed to an asylum. She was out within a month, whereupon he had to pay off her debts and increase her allowance. She died, an angry woman, in 1882.

Bulwer was a close friend of Dickens, and is renowned for having advised the great man to alter the ending to *Great Expectations*. (In his lifetime Bulwer Lytton outsold every author except Dickens.) He understood the market. For £20,000 (a vast sum then) he sold a ten-year lease on the copyrights to his nineteen existing novels. They were then reprinted in cheap editions, and by 1857 he had become the most requested author at station bookstalls. Unfortunately, the high Victorian prose and sentiment makes his books indigestible today.

Rosina **BULWER-LYTTON** (1802-82)

Perhaps her stormy marriage, part covered above, can be explained by her stormy upbringing: her mother was an active feminist, her father an alcoholic (not, presumably, *because* his wife was an active feminist) and, after her parents separated, the ten year old Rosina was brought up by relatives. As a young woman she was a friend of the notorious Lady Caroline Lamb, and she was perhaps too spirited a woman for her noble husband. Certainly she was angry when they parted. Her *Cheveley, or The Man of Honour* (1839) was a barely disguised attack on Bulwer – part of her long-running attack – and she was still bitter in 1880 (seven years after his death) when she published her memoir, *A Blighted Life*.

Sir Richard **BURTON** (1821-90)

A man of many parts – explorer, swordsman, anthropologist, linguist, historian, expert on exotic sexual techniques – he left Oxford in the time-honoured way for heroes, by being rusticated and not taking a degree. From 1842 to 49 he served with the Indian Army, then off he went in disguise (with a long beard, shaven head, and face stained with walnut juice: incredibly it worked) to Mecca in 1853; then on through Africa (looking for slave-traders and, hopefully, the source of the Nile); on again to the Crimea, Salt Lake City (to study the Mormons); to Brazil (as Consul), to Paraguay, Iceland, Damascus and Trieste. In 1858, along with John Speke, he discovered Lake Tanganyika. From these peregrinations he produced some 40 travel books, alongside books of poetry and folklore, and his famous translations of the *Kama Sutra* (1883) and *The Perfumed Garden* (1886), as well as *Arabian Nights* between 1885 to 8. Given the frankness of his translations and his undisguised interest in sexual behaviour it is not surprising that he was prosecuted several times under the Obscene Publications Act. Within his personal library were works more shocking than those he published, books which he could enjoy in the company of like-minded friends such as Richard Monkton-Milnes and Algernon Swinburne. (Some of these were destroyed by his wife Isabel upon his death.)

Samuel **BUTLER** (1835-1902)

He was the son of a clergyman but had religious doubts; he denied the Resurrection; he told the Canadians they were philistines; he disputed Darwin's theory of natural selection; he championed Lamarck when everyone else decried him; he theorised on 'unconscious memory' and the 'Life Force'; he declared that Homer must have been a woman; he developed his own theory over Shakespeare's sonnets – he was, in short, the great contrarian. He also painted and composed music. From 1859 he spent several years as a sheep farmer in New Zealand (to see how far he could go?), out of which came his book, *A First Year in Canterbury Settlement* (1863), a book he would plunder later when writing *Erewhon* (1872). That book, *Erewhon* (an anagram of Nowhere), is a satire about an imaginary country in which all things are contrary, including names: Yram for Mary, Nosnibor for Robinson, etc. Crime is an illness there, and morality is health and beauty; the Unborn select their parents; the development of machinery is forbidden. Contrary is as the contrarian writes.

The Fair Haven (1873) was his satirical attack on miracles and the Resurrection; *Evolution, Old and New* (1879), *Unconscious Memory* (1880) and *Luck or Cunning* (1886) were his espousal of Lamarck over Darwin; *The Authoress of the Odyssey* (1897) was his declaration on Homer's gender; *Shakespeare's Sonnets Reconsidered* (1899) 'proved' that the bard's lover was of humble birth. Posthumously, in 1903, Butler surprised many with a minor masterpiece, an in-part autobiographical novel that lambasted the Victorian family: *The Way of All Flesh*. It shocked but satisfied, and remains in print.

Thomas **CARLYLE** (1795-1881)

The son of a stonemason from Ecclefechan, Carlyle was to become one of the most admired thinkers of the Victorian age – an assessment which has been re-evaluated since. While a teacher (1822-4) he privately tutored the attractive and intelligent Jane Baillie Welsh, six years his younger, whom he courted and practically insisted should become his wife. Having won his prize he never – according to most biographers – managed to consummate the marriage. He plunged instead into study and polemic.

Before marrying Jane in 1826 he had written on German literature and philosophy, and while in the early years of their marriage they lived, for financial reasons, on her lonely farm at Craigenputtock, he wrote *Sartor Resartus* (serialised in *Fraser's* Magazine in 1833 and 1834), a bizarre philosophical potpourri and early example of what was to become his characteristic style, splattered with redundant capital letters, exclamation marks, made-up words, rambling digressions and biblical sounding

protestations. While the pages ranted off the press the Carlyles moved to Cheyne Row in Chelsea – Jane now being relegated to the role of put-upon housewife as her obsessive and cranky husband tried to build himself a soundproof room while sampling the plaudits of literary London outside the home, and writing his *History of the French Revolution* (published in 1837) – an extraordinary and idiosyncratic production, brilliant in patches, almost comically bad elsewhere, and unlike anything seen before. Yet for many present-day readers, Jane's letters on their time in cramped Cheyne Row are far more entertaining than her husband's *Revolution*, though his book remains a gem of literary anecdote because the entire and only manuscript of Book One was accidentally used by John Stuart Mill's maid to light a fire.

The book was a success, and Carlyle began a series of lectures on a subject for which he has since become notorious: *On Heroes, Hero-Worship and the Heroic in History* (published in 1841). Here he developed his anti-democratic paean to the 'Great Man', a work seen today – though not then – as an early text in fascism. Carlyle, like Donne, believed no man was an island, that we are all connected, and that we are never happier than when allied together in the same cause. But a great end cannot be achieved without direction, and for direction the masses need a leader, a good leader, a hero. How can an ideal leader be defined? Carlyle was on much the same ground here as Plato, though he derided him for his logic-chopping and obscuration. Pots and kettles, Thomas, surely? He had now become a political pundit extraordinaire, writing *Chartism* (1839), *Past and Present* (1843), and various extremist pamphlets. *(Latter-day Pamphlets*, published in 1850, make his points more strongly.) Throughout the 1840s he wrote biographies and a treatise on Cromwell and he shut himself away in his never sufficiently soundproof room to labour over a biography of *Frederick the Great of Prussia* (finally completed after 14 years and then issued in six interminable volumes from 1858 to 1865).

The following year, 1866, Jane Carlyle died. He mourned spectacularly. Though he lived another fifteen years, he wrote only one more book, an unremarkable *The Early Kings of Norway* (1875) which, surely, even he couldn't have expected would find a market. He fired off occasional political squibs, earned a Prussian Order of Merit from Bismark, and gave up writing when, he said, he lost the use of his right hand. Back in 1871 he had given Jane's papers and letters to his friend J A **Froude**, asking him to publish them when he was dead. Froude duly did, together with Carlyle's own *Reminiscences* and a 4-volume biography, in the year of Carlyle's death. They created a sensation – revealing far more than Carlyle would have liked about their marriage and his inadequacies as a husband (clearly he'd never read his wife's own papers). It is quite possible to read these posthumous accounts as evidence that she was not only cleverer than him, certainly more rational, but also that she had contributed in no small way to his writings and had received in return no thanks but, instead, a good deal of selfish, self-centred, intemperate domination. Though she is now remembered more fondly than her husband, he had the consolation of knowing that in his day he was regarded as a great man, a leader – but a hero? No, not even then.

Edward **CARPENTER** (1844-1929)

His was a difficult time in which to be both an open homosexual and a curate, so he gave up the cloth in 1874. Vigorously involved in politics and issues of the day, he lectured on astronomy at Leeds (where he lived), campaigned against conditions in manufacturing towns, and began a lifelong dedication to experimental farming (organic and vegetarian). Now influenced by the works of Whitman, Thoreau, Ruskin and Morris, he took to living in a wooden hut and writing poems: *Towards Democracy* was published in 1883 and sold 400 copies. With the help of a small legacy he set himself up as a market gardener, living in a cottage with his lover, Albert Fearnehough, a former scythe maker, and in his spare time he made sandals. He wrote the earnest *Modern Money-Lending and the Meaning of Dividends* in 1883, and became more involved in new socialist organisations, for whom he wrote such stirring tomes as *England Arise: a Socialist Marching Song* (1886). His second enlarged edition of *Towards Democracy* came out in four parts between 1883 and 1902. *England's Ideal* appeared in 1887, *Civilisation: Its Cause and Cure* in 1889.

He is more remembered today for his writings defending male love. In 1894–5 Manchester's Labour Press published four of his pamphlets: *Sex-Love, and its Place in a Free Society; Woman, and her Place in a Free Society; Marriage in Free Society; Homogenic Love, and its Place in a Free Society* (which was reissued as *Love's Coming of Age* in 1896 and enlarged in 1906). He initiated the use of the word 'urning' for homosexual men and women (he derived it from Uranos, meaning 'heaven'). Among those who were influenced by his works were Siegfried Sassoon, Robert Graves, E M Forster, and D H Lawrence. He remained committed to socialism and produced a fine autobiography, *My Days and Dreams*, in 1916.

Lewis **CARROLL** (1832-98)

Charles Lutwidge Dodgson excelled at Mathematics at Christ Church, Oxford, went into the church but, as he was afflicted with shyness and a bad stammer, preached only occasionally. He produced some mathematics textbooks before, under his famous pen-name, he wrote in 1865 the book originally called *Alice's Adventures under Ground* which, as has often been retold, was developed from tales he told the three young Liddell daughters while sharing boat trips with them in 1862. From his diary:

> *August 6 (Wednesday): In the afternoon Harcourt and I took the three Liddells up to Godstow, where we had tea; we tried the game of 'the Ural Mountains' on the way, but it did not prove very successful, and I had to go on with my interminable fairy-tale of Alice's Adventures*

The 1865 publication date (three years after the boat trips) is explained in part by the author's endless fussing with the text, in part from his wanting to illustrate it himself, and in part from the chosen illustrator, John Tenniel, taking an uncharacteristically long time to complete his drawings. (He was already behind schedule, then his mother died ...) Tenniel objected (on slight grounds) to the first printing, the edition was scrapped, and an approved edition was finally issued in November 1865 (though dated 1866). The rejected sheets from the true first edition were sold to Appleton in New York who used them to make the first American edition. From the original British first edition Dodgson had inscribed around 20 presentation copies – so, one way or another, there has always been some dispute over what constitutes a 'true first' of this extremely important and therefore valuable work. Reviews were mixed; sales healthy but not tremendous; but it gradually became the greatest children's book ever written. It has frequently been reissued; many illustrators have relished the challenge but all have laboured behind the Tenniel heritage.

Through the Looking-Glass and What Alice Found There appeared in 1871 (dated 1872), *The Hunting of the Snark* followed in 1876, *Sylvie and Bruno* in 1889. There are a number of other works, all of interest to collectors.

Dodgson himself is remembered almost entirely as 'Lewis Carroll', although he was an inventive mathematician, puzzle-maker and putative inventor. His interest in photography has become undeservedly notorious. He never married, and he died early in 1898 of bronchitis caught the previous Christmas.

Robert **CHAMBERS** (1802-71)

Co-founder of the publishing firm W and R Chambers (*Chamber's Journal*, founded 1832 and *Chamber's Encyclopaedia* begun 1859) he was the initially anonymous author of the important pre-Darwin classic *Vestiges of the Natural History of Creation* (1844). This book showed through geological evidence that Earth was not created in seven days some six thousand years ago, but was in fact millions of years old and had evolved gradually through time. The book was an essential reference in the 'God Debate'. His theory of biological evolution was roundly applauded and attacked.

Charlotte **CHANTER**

Younger daughter of Charles **Kingsley**, sister of 'Lucas **Malet**' and, in her own right, author of one best-seller, *Over The Cliffs*, in 1860.

Caroline **CLIVE** (Mrs Archer Clive, 1801-73)

Though she had written *IX Poems* in 1840 (using the pseudonym 'V') and had followed it with several other volumes, she is remembered for her 'sensation novel', *Paul Ferroll* (1855), in which the hero murders his wife, then spends 18 happy years married to his true love (before confessing all; Mrs Clive was, after all, Victorian and, as Oscar **Wilde**'s Miss Prism observed: 'The good ended happily, and the bad unhappily. That is what fiction means.'). The book was successful enough to justify a sequel: *Why Paul Ferroll Killed His Wife* (1860). Lame from birth, Mrs Archer Clive was accidentally burned to death while writing.

Arthur Hugh **CLOUGH** (1819-61)

Friend of Matthew **Arnold**, with more religious doubts than his friend, he was memorialised by Arnold in the poem *Thyrsis*. Though he wrote a great deal of lyrical poetry, only two volumes were published in his lifetime: *The Bothie of Tober-na-Vuolich* (1848) and *Ambarvalia* (1849) to which he co-contributed with Thomas Burbridge. His admired long poem *Amours de Voyage* was written in 1849, appeared in *The Atlantic Monthly* in 1858, and is still anthologised. A cousin by marriage of Florence Nightingale, he suffered constantly from ill-health. In the hope that continental air would help, he went to Florence, where he caught malaria and died. His verse became far more popular after his early death.

> *Say not, the struggle naught availeth,*
> *The labour and the wounds are vain,*
> *The enemy faints not, nor faileth,*
> *And as things have been they remain.*
>
> from his *Say Not, The Struggle Naught Availeth*

Wilkie **COLLINS** (1824-89)

Close friend and colleague of Charles **Dickens**, with whom he sometimes co-wrote and in whose house he was often found, Collins made little attempt to maintain the marital facade and respectable image that Dickens felt essential. Dickens wrote of domestic fidelity while his marriage collapsed and he looked elsewhere for his pleasure; Collins maintained two households – but married neither of his long-term mistresses (though he treated each as decently as most Victorian men did their spouses). Dickens spiced his stories with fictional descents into opium dens; Collins lived with his own very real addiction to opium for many years. Collins's life was packed with more incident than was Charles Dickens's, yet while there any number of Dickens biographies, there are hardly any for Wilkie Collins. In their novels they each tackled burning social issues of the day. Collins was the better plotter; Dickens had the more richly imagined characters. But then, no one created more memorable characters than Charles Dickens.

Collins was the son of the artist William Collins and was named after his father's friend, Sir David Wilkie. His brother Charles would be on the fringe of the Pre-Raphaelite circle. When he first met Dickens, Wilkie Collins already had three books beneath his belt, but Dickens drew him in as a contributor to *Household Words* and they began collaborating on short pieces, melodramas and serial stories. Collins moved from his more serious early books into popular fiction: *Basil: A Story of Modern Life* (1852), *Hide and Seek* (1854), and *The Dead Secret* (1857). These dramatic stories were a training ground for his set pieces of the 1860s: *The Woman in White* (amateur sleuths, multiple narrators, and a hot issue of the day – the incarcerated wife, 1860); *No Name* (illegitimacy costs a young actress her inheritance, 1862); *Armadale* (a melodramatic tale of murder and a wicked woman, 1866); and *The Moonstone*, generally considered the first full-length novel to feature a detective (1868), though Collins had written of detectives before *The Moonstone* – in several short stories and, particularly, in *Armadale* within which is 'the necessary detective', a

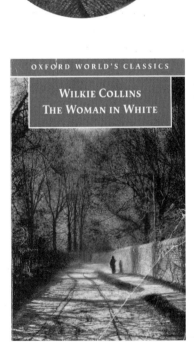

man 'professionally ready on the merest suspicion (if the merest suspicion paid him) to get under our beds, and to look through gimlet-holes in our doors.' Collins understood the medium; his famous dictum was "Make 'em laugh, make 'em cry, make 'em wait." Sometimes, it has to be admitted, he "made 'em wait" too long.

Dickens died in 1870 and, though this can hardly be the reason, so did Collins's facility. He was, by now, badly addicted to laudanum, often unwell, and his relationship with the two women in his life was far from trouble-free. As ever in his life, he was willing to 'speak out', and in his stories he began to put tub-thumping before plot. Perhaps twelve long novels in the next two decades were too many for a man in his declining state of health. Perhaps, like many writers, he had used himself up too soon. Whatever the reason, it is the 1860 novels which remain a testament to a writer who, at his best and in his own way, was as good as Dickens.

Joseph **CONRAD** (1857-1924)

He lived his life in the 19th century, and wrote about it in the 20th. Born of Polish parents in Russian Ukraine as Teodor Józef Korzeniowski, he lost his parents while a child and spent his youth and young adulthood as a sailor, gunrunner and all-round adventurer (becoming a naturalised Briton in 1886) and not leaving the British merchant navy till 1894 – by which time he had become fluent in English (though his spoken English would never be as fluent as his written) and had begun working on his first novel. *Almayer's Folly* appeared in 1895 but was barely noticed. *Outcast of the Islands* (1896) fared little better, as did *The Nigger of the Narcissus* (1897) – a title for which, unlike Agatha Christie's *Ten Little Niggers*, there has never been pressure to have changed. (He had sailed on the Narcissus in 1884.) Conrad sailed on through the doldrums. Despite producing fine novels such as *Lord Jim* (1900), *Heart of Darkness*

(1902), *Nostromo* (1904), *Under Western Skies* (1911) and the land-based, quite different, *The Secret Agent* (1907) it was his lesser story *Chance* (1913) which broke through and established him with a 20th century public.

Eliza **COOK** (1818-89)

A verse-maker rather than a poet, she was prolific and popular, though many of her verses show Victorian mawkishness at its worse (sometimes at its comical worst). Amidst all the doggerel are a few accidental gems, such as her most successful poem, *The Old Arm Chair*. ('I love it, I love it; and who shall dare / To chide me for loving that old Arm-chair?') Her first collection, *Lays of a Wild Harp*, came out just before Victoria's reign (1835), and throughout her reign Miss Cook's rhymes cropped up in numerous periodicals and magazines (and, later, on greetings cards). She edited *Eliza Cook's Journal* from 1849-54, giving it up on grounds of failing health, although she lived another 35 years. Her complete works were published in 1870. Poems within it include: *Old Dobbi; To A Favourite Pony; The Gipsy Child; The Acorn; The Loved One Was Not There*. One that perhaps only she could have got away with was *Song of the Dying Old Man to his Young Wife* whose final verse declaims:

> *Bury me in the churchyard where the dark yew-branches wave,*
> *And promise thou wilt come sometimes to weed the old man's grave!*
> *'Tis all I ask! I'm blind – I'm faint – take, take my parting breath –*
> *I die within thy arms, my Kate, and feel no sting of death.*

Marie **CORELLI** (1855-1924)

The extreme romantic, her novels, whatever their apparent subject, were extremely romantic too. She could write on love, morality, religion, music, vegetarianism, animals, radioactivity – whatever the topic, it would be wrapped in an exotic miasma of romance. However whacky the subject, it seems, not only did she write about it, but she believed in it as well. Many of her readers were swept along with her; during her life it is said that the Queen and Gladstone – even Oscar Wilde! – admired her (but on what grounds?). Her first book was *A Romance of Two Worlds* (1886) and from an extensive list the curious today might sample those that sold the best: *Barabbas* (1893) or *The Sorrows of Satan* (1895). Perhaps *The Soul of Lilith* (1892) or *The Mighty Atom* (1896) are to your taste? It is easy to scoff – and many have – but Corelli knew her audience. Consider *The Sorrows of Satan*, which she begins like a skilful angler, knowing precisely in which pools her readers swim, and casting her first line skilfully to reel them in:

> *Do you know what it is to be poor? Not poor with the arrogant poverty complained of by certain people who have five or six thousand a year to live upon, and who yet swear they can hardly manage to make both ends meet, but really poor, – downright, cruelly, hideously poor, with a poverty that is graceless, sordid and miserable? Poverty that compels you to dress in your one suit of clothes till it is worn threadbare, – that denies you clean linen on account of the ruinous charges of washerwomen, – that robs you of your own self-respect, and causes you to slink along the streets vaguely abashed, instead of walking erect among your fellow-men in independent ease, – this is the sort of poverty I mean.*

Oh yes, the reader thinks: I know exactly what she means. Which is why she sold.

She was born Mary Mackay to Charles Mackay, a Scottish poet and newspaper editor who penned *A Good Time Coming*. She learnt early the value of publicity, dashing off letters to papers and magazines and speaking wherever an audience was guaranteed. In her later years she ensconced herself at Stratford (with her moustachioed companion, Bertha Vyner) where she would parade the streets or sail along the Avon in her version of Cleopatra's barge (a gondola imported from Venice). Many tourists went to see Miss Corelli rather than the Shakespearian sights.

Baron **CORVO** (1860–1913)

About himself he was a fantasist. Born in Cheapside, rejected by Oxford, he converted to Roman Catholicism, was a putative priest, and assumed the name Baron Corvo while in Rome. His real name was Frederick Rolfe (he sometimes called himself Father Rolfe) and it was towards the end of the decadent *fin de siècle* that he set out to be a writer, leaping straight into the *Yellow Book* in 1898 with his *Stories Toto Told Me*. A larger collection of stories, *In His Own Image* and a study of Renaissance Italy, *Chronicles of the House of Borgia*, both appeared in 1901. Other works dribbled out in the 20th century, including his most famous, *Hadrian the Seventh* (1904) in which he portrayed a thinly veiled version of himself as a failed priest and writer who became Pope. An acerbic scrounger, much of his real-life fame came from his unfailing ability to repel ex-friends, either by maligning them behind their backs or by repeatedly pleading for money and assistance. He was the basis for the eponymous rogue and conman in Pamela Hansford Johnson's *The Unspeakable Skipton* (1959). His own autobiography, *The Desire and Pursuit of the Whole* (1934) is, as one would expect, hopelessly unreliable.

Mrs **CRAIK** (1826–87)

Her real name was Dinah Maria Mulock but she wrote either as Mrs Craik or, even more discreetly, as 'The author of *John Halifax, Gentleman*', her most famous book. She had no need for modesty: she was a prolific and competent writer of fairy stories, children's books, essays and novels for grown-ups. Her first novel, *The Ogilvies*, appeared in 1849, and she maintained a steady flow thereafter. *John Halifax, Gentleman* (1856) told of an orphan from

Tewkesbury who, by steady industry and endeavour, pulled himself up in the world to become 'a gentleman'. A very Victorian theme.

It has been suggested that her 1859 novel, *A Life for a Life*, gave Wilkie Collins the idea for how to present *The Woman in White*, a novel told by several narrators. Her forerunner was written in the form of two diaries telling the same tale, of a doomed love affair, from different viewpoints. Her 1863 collection of traditional tales, *The Fairy Book* was one of the best of its time (and continued to be reprinted in the 20th century). Her 1875 fantasy novel for children, *The Little Lame Prince and his Travelling Cloak*, was better than it sounds, and remained hugely popular for two or three decades.

Charles **DARWIN** (1809-82)

Though he was the grandson of the eminent botanist and poet Erasmus Darwin (1731-1802) who had himself written extensively on evolution, Charles Darwin would not have thought of himself as a writer, yet his books became the most important of the 19th century. He was a Christian but for atheists his books became, and still are, holy texts.

First and uncontroversially came the book whose full title is *Journal of Researches into the Geology and Natural History of the Various Countries Visited by HMS Beagle* (1839), in which he dealt with the complex inter-relationship of living forms within their environment. Meanwhile he was working, painstakingly, on another book. Realising the impact it might have, Darwin delayed publication of his belief-shattering *Origin of Species* until 1859, at the time he learnt that his rival Alfred Wallace was

68

about to publish on the same theme. Darwin's was an astonishing book of revelations – as even its full title made apparent: *On the Origin of Species by Means of Natural Selection: or The Preservation of Favoured Races in the Struggle for Life*. Out went the Garden of Eden; out went Noah's ark; out, devastatingly, went God's simultaneous creation of all animals and plants. Everything evolved, said Darwin, from a 'single progenitor', and that progenitor was not God: it was, instead, a simple organism which had developed and diverged through the aeons – to produce *us* and every other living thing. He showed the theory, he showed physical evidence, and he argued that since *artificial* selection (animal and plant husbandry practised by farmers) can improve breeds and create stable new ones within a few generations, *natural* selection, working over longer lengths of time, is easily able to do the same.

The Victorians were already agonising over the loss of faith. The Romantic poets, earlier, had promoted atheism. Pre-Victorian scientists had promoted rationalism. Lyell's *Principles of Geology* (1830-33) had shown that Earth was millions of years old and had been created through millennia of chaos. Robert Chambers's *Vestiges of Creation* (1844) demonstrated biological evolution and natural law. So did God exist? Was there any need for him? These were already deeply troubling questions before Darwin's volcano of a book erupted to lay down another layer of hard evidence.

His own faith remained unshaken. Darwin saw God's hand in all things. The Old Testament, he thought, was allegory and parable – but as such was no less true. God directed but did not intervene. Thus reassured, Darwin went on to produce more books, expanding on his earlier ones. *The Descent of Man and Selection in Relation to Sex* came in 1871, swiftly followed, less controversially, by *The Expression of the Emotions in Man and Animals* in 1872. His books only continued the controversy and overheated debate. Darwin's life was dedicated to reasonable enquiry and yet, extraordinarily, for some he remains controversial to this day.

John **DAVIDSON** (1857–1909)

While earning a living reluctantly as a schoolmaster in his native Scotland, Davidson began quietly writing plays and poetry. He was first published in 1885 when his curious novel, *The North Wall*, and a verse drama, *Diabolus Amans*, slipped into view. He continued with plays and in 1893 produced his first anthology of poems, bizarrely named *Fleet Street Eclogues*. Having pierced the poetry barrier he published *Ballads and Songs* in 1894, followed by three more volumes in the '90s. He was now contributing to the *Yellow Book* and labouring with his verse dramas (never the most rewarding medium): *Godfrida* (1898) and *Self's the Man* (1901) would be followed by four more in the Edwardian decade. In 1901 he began his philosophical *Testaments* in blank verse. Like much of his writing, these five books were satirical and rebellious. He had never been a happy man, and in 1908 he drowned himself off the Cornish coast.

J T DELANE (1817–79)

Famous, indeed feared in his day, John Thaddeus Delane was editor of the *Times* in its most glorious days, becoming editor in 1841, three years after joining as a reporter. Gregarious and phenomenally hard-working, a determined socialiser (it was said that he once dined out on a hundred successive evenings), he would work on the next day's edition if necessary until five o'clock in the morning. To garner news he did not scruple to use his contacts and the information he heard or overheard at dinner parties. He personally broke the scandalous news that without his Prime Minister's knowledge Palmerston was secretly supplying arms to the Italian insurgent Garibaldi. When Peel's cabinet finally agreed to abolish the Corn Laws, it was Delane's *Times* that broke the story. The ultimatum that launched the Crimean War was printed in the *Times* before it reached the Tsar. Delane never toadied to earn his tip-offs; on the contrary he was a renownedly independent man. He would attack the government or support it, as he saw fit. While he was at the *Times* he doubled its circulation and made it the most important voice in the land. 'We aspire, indeed, to participate in the government of the world,' he averred in 1854, and in **Trollope's** *The Warden* he was caricatured as 'Tom Towers'.

Charles **DICKENS** (1812-70)
What larks, Pip. What larks!

Joe Gargery, the honest country blacksmith, shakes his head in cheerful bemusement at the sight of his old friend Pip doing well in London. What larks, indeed. Dickens is full of larks – his characters, the scrapes they get into, their romances – what larks. Pip and Joe are the two sides of their author: Pip the serious observer, seeing life in all its grim unfairness, knowing that coincidence and abuse of power wait to thwart one's 'expectations'; Joe the simple, honest optimist. Pip, unlike Charles Dickens, has no interest in society or other people's lot; Joe Gargery puts others first. He is how Dickens would like to be, how he'd like all of us to be, though he knows we're too like Pip, too wrapped up in ourselves to see straight, too wrapped up in ourselves for larks. Dickens gives us lots of serious material: even in Pickwick he finds time to satirise the 'Rotten Boroughs' and corruption of elections, and he slams – that repeated Dickens cause – the imprisonment of debtors. *Nicholas Nickleby*, his next most light-hearted tale, exposes the vicious cruelty of 'farming schools' and the helpless vulnerability of fatherless young women (Kate). There isn't a book by Dickens in which some social evil is not revealed. Yet, in every book – even in *Hard Times* – he remembers to leaven the loaf with larks.

Hard Times has larks? It has: the villains, Gradgrind and Bounderby, are satirised so well they could have been scripted for *Spitting Image*, *Little Britain* or *The Now Show*. Listen to Bounderby on his upbringing: 'I hadn't a shoe to my foot. As to a stocking, I didn't know such a thing by name. I passed the day in a ditch, and the night in a pigsty. That's the way I spent my tenth birthday. Not that a ditch was new to me, for I was born in a ditch.' Mrs Gradgrind hopes it

was a dry ditch – but he brushes her aside: 'I was one of the most miserable little wretches ever seen. I was so sickly that I was always moaning and groaning. I was so ragged and dirty that you wouldn't have touched me with a pair of tongs.' His mother, he says, bolted, leaving him to his grandmother. 'And, according to the best of my remembrance, my grandmother was the wickedest and the worst old woman that ever lived. If I got a little pair of shoes by any chance, she would take 'em off and sell 'em for drink. Why, I have known that grandmother of mine lie in her bed and drink her fourteen glasses of liquor before breakfast!'

Larks, there are always larks. But Dickens could be serious. Hence the workhouse in *Oliver Twist* (and his most evil villains, Fagin and Bill Sikes); the perils of gambling and its Nemesis, the implacable debt-collector, in *The Old Curiosity Shop*; hypocrisy and swindlers (not to mention murder) in *Martin Chuzzlewit*; an obtuse father putting his inadequate son before his capable daughter in *Dombey and Son*; the married woman's lack of rights, another dreadful school, swindling and – his own worst memory – the bottle factory, in *Copperfield*; the interminable, self-serving legal system in *Bleak House*; the follies of Benthamism in *Hard Times*; the debtors' prison and the great financial crash in *Little Dorrit*; legacy swindles, pretentiousness and financial skulduggery in *Our Mutual Friend*; and all those essays and 'occasional pieces' where he shows us the police by night, criminals, poor lodgings and opium dens, suicides and mudlarks on the Thames, the truth behind the greasepaint...

Dickens the reformer can't escape the other Dickens, the Dickens who enjoys larks. Every book has comic interludes: Pickwick, the title character, along with the now dated Sam Weller and all their friends; the Crummles family and their travelling theatre (starring 'The Infant Phenomenon' who had been ten years old for the last ten years); Mr Micawber, for whom 'something will turn up'; Mrs Jellyby, who devotes herself to charity while ignoring her own family – including the infant Peepy: 'one of the dirtiest little unfortunates I ever saw – fixed by the neck between two iron railings'; fat Flora Finching – 'a lily had become a peony' (his cruellest caricature, as she was based on his real-life ex-sweetheart, Maria Beadnell); the drunken Mrs Gamp: 'Mrs Harris,' I says, 'leave the bottle on the chimney-piece, and don't ask me to take none, but let me put my lips to it when I am so disposed.'

He was not a 'great writer' in the way Shakespeare was, nor in the way some of his contemporaries were, but just as if one were forced to choose only one British writer one would select Shakespeare, if one could choose only one 19th century writer, one would have to select Charles Dickens.

Goldsworthy Lowes **DICKINSON** (1862-1932)

Dickinson was a beloved fellow of King's College, Cambridge – beloved by friends and students, most of whom realized that he was homosexual and that he frequently fell for his male pupils. To most of them it made no difference to the affection they felt for him. Sadly, he was always attracted to manly men, to real men, who were all too heterosexual. As a result his love remained unrequited and he went to his grave having never had a loving sexual relationship. We know this because he set it out in his 1927 autobiography, a book too frank to be published at that time. The official biography, by E M Forster in 1934, skated over it, and only in 1973 could Dickinson's own words be published. Yet he never hid his love for other men, and anyone who read his most famous book, *The Greek View of Life* (1896), ought to have suspected what was, to many, the unimportant truth. His next most famous book, *The Meaning of Good*, came out in 1901, and the rest – on the First World War, on politics, on religion, on Europe, on China, were published in the 20th century. Several earlier books, such as *From King to King* (1891), *Revolution and Reaction in Modern France* (1892) and *The Development of Parliament During the Nineteenth Century* (1895) were of their time.

Benjamin **DISRAELI** (1804–81)

The time will come when you will hear me
- Disraeli in his maiden speech

For Victorian England to elect a Jewish Prime Minister was as unlikely as for America to elect a black President – yet Disraeli's race was only part of what made his elevation so unlikely (he was Jewish by race, not religion: his father had him baptised as a Christian, but Disraeli never forsake the Jewish cause). What else stood against him? He was a Prime Minister who in a previous life had been a poet, novelist and political satirist, who had tried to found a newspaper (the *Representative*) that had failed, who had had to flee from debts, whose first novel (*Vivian Grey*, 1826) had caused a scandal, who had written half a dozen more novels, who had conducted an open love affair with the naughty Lady Henrietta Sykes, who had been blackballed from the Athenaeum, who had switched parties while trying for a seat in Parliament, and who was remembered from his youth as a Byronic dandy and acerbic wit: he won his first seat (on his fifth attempt) in the year Victoria came to the throne. Though a Conservative, he spoke out on behalf of the working class (though his working class characters could never speak believably) and he associated himself with the 'Young England' group – these were the views he expounded in his great trilogy of 'Condition of England' novels, *Coningsby* (1844), *Sybil* (1845) and *Tancred* (1847).

'When I want to read a novel I write one': Benjamin Disraeli

After a biography on Lord George Bentink in 1852 (regarded by some as the first political novel) Disraeli concentrated on Parliamentary politics, and he wrote no more novels for twenty years. He had, in a sense, chosen the wrong party: in the middle decades of the century the Conservatives remained almost permanently out of office. Disraeli, now their leader, became Prime Minister briefly in 1868, then again from 1874 to 1880. Prior to this he had broken his literary silence with *Lothair* (1870) and ten busy years later he followed it with his final novel, *Endymion* (1880, unfinished). Returning one evening from a dinner party, he caught a chill, which worsened, and bronchitis killed him. The Queen sent primroses to lie upon his coffin.

'He is full of poetry, romance and chivalry' wrote Victoria on Disraeli

Lord Alfred DOUGLAS (1870-1945)

He knew why he was famous, and for much of his life he bitterly resented it: he had been the aristocratic young lover of Oscar **Wilde**. Worse, it was his father who had brought Wilde down. Worse again, his reputation had been further besmirched by the later publication of an edited version of *De Profundis* slanted against him. Worse still, his own father-in-law had stolen away his son. He had been in and out of court on libel cases – against his father-in-law, against Robert Ross, against Arthur Ransome, against Winston Churchill – and always, the courts found against him. No one believed him when he maintained – loudly – that he was *not a homosexual*, that he detested it, that he was a practising Roman Catholic, married, with a son. And no one, he felt, paid the attention they should to his writing.

He was, in fact, quite a good one. For Wilde, he had translated *Salome*

(1894), though against Wilde he would later write two unfortunate books, *Oscar Wilde and Myself* (1914) and *Oscar Wilde: A Summing Up* (1940). He can be judged more clearly as a journalist (he edited the literary magazine, *The Academy*) and as a poet: *The City of the Soul* was his first, in 1899. He wrote a decent book of sonnets and, in 1898, a book of comic verse, *Tails with a Twist* by 'a Belgian Hare'.

Ménie Muriel **DOWIE** (1867-1945)
The granddaughter of the Scottish publisher Robert **Chambers**, she wrote up her travels in *A Girl in the Karpathians* (1891) and followed that book with a collection of travel essays, *Women Adventurers* (1893). Her first novel, *Gallia* (1895), was different: a forthright 'New Woman' story, with a frank (and therefore shocking) approach to sex. *The Crook of the Bough* (1899) tackled sex again, this time attacking the treatment of women in Turkey. *Love and his Mask* (1901) took an unblinkered look at the Boer War. (Dowie was actively involved in progressive politics.) She had also written pieces for the *Yellow Book* and, not surprisingly, for *Chambers' Journal*

(later anthologised in *Some Whims of Fate*, 1896). Society columnists loved her extravagant costumes, the most famous of which was made of leopard-skin. But her writing career stopped abruptly following a nasty divorce: her husband accused her of adultery with the mountaineer Edward Fitzgerald, and was granted custody of their child. She never saw the child again. She married Fitzgerald, and together they took to farming, breeding cattle, and extensive travelling. There were no more books.

Ernest **DOWSON** (1867-1900)

The classic *fin de siècle* poet of decadence, deeply immersed in the closeted *Yellow Book* and *Savoy* circles, he epitomised decadent behaviour, falling in love with a girl of twelve, toying with Roman Catholic exoticism, whiling away his hours between Dublin, Paris and mainly London, with its Café Royal, luxurious drawing rooms, seedy taverns and damp gutters beneath the stars. He died, in character, of excess. *Dilemmas*, a book of stories, came out in 1895; *Verses* in 1896; *The Pierrot of the Minute*, a one-act verse drama, in 1897; *Decorations* (with more experimental poems) in 1899. Two poems of his will always be anthologised: '*They are not long, the weeping and the laughter*' and '*Non Sum Qualis Eram Bonae Sub Regno Cynarae*', better known (incorrectly) as '*I have been faithful to thee, Cynara! in my fashion.*'

Sir Arthur Conan **DOYLE** (1859-1930)

Though he is a turn of the century writer, how can we leave him out? Creator of the world's greatest fictional detective, whose adventures seem to sum up the streets and fogs and miasmic mysteries of the Victorian world, Conan Doyle wanted recognition as a writer of serious historical fiction. It was a hopeless cause: Sherlock Holmes was not only his greatest creation, he was his first. While the first historical novel, *Micah Clarke*, appeared in 1889, the first Holmes story, *A Study in Scarlet*, had splashed across the cover of *Beeton's Christmas Annual* in 1887. (His second, *The Sign of Four*, came in 1890.)

THE FIRST BOOK ABOUT SHERLOCK HOLMES!

A STUDY IN SCARLET BY A CONAN DOYLE

A COMPLETE NOVEL
Presented with THE WINDSOR MAGAZINE XMAS. NUMBER

Determined to make his historical novels succeed, Doyle alternated them with Holmes. He produced *The White Company* in 1891, the same year Holmes debuted in the *Strand*. But Holmes was a smash hit – and demanding. *Strand Magazine* wanted stories, and Doyle obliged, with half a dozen at a time. The first collection, *The Adventures of Sherlock Holmes*, came out in 1892, *The Memoirs* in 1894. And after the first dozen came the famous crisis in which Doyle killed off his golden goose, plunging him and his arch enemy down the Reichenbach Falls. Holmes was dead.

Now Doyle could concentrate on historicals. *Rodney Stone* and *The Exploits of Brigadier Gerard* came out in 1896. *Uncle Bernac* bustled in the following year. But the public (and his publishers) screamed out for Holmes. Eventually, in 1902, Holmes reappeared, in *The Hound of the Baskervilles*, a novel duly followed with more short stories. These later Holmes stories (he couldn't lie down; no one would let him) were fairly good but not as good as before. But he still sold. Doyle plugged away with historicals: sound stories, still worth reading, but not what the public wanted. He interested himself in miscarriages of justice, the First World War, spiritualism – even fairies – but he couldn't shake the master: Sherlock Holmes stalked on. Holmes's adventures were concluded again in 1917, with *His Last Bow*. But he came back in 1927, with *The Case-Book of Sherlock Holmes*. And every year since, he has been reborn on film or television.

George du **MAURIER, (1834-96)**
Born in Paris, though the son of a
naturalised Englishman, du Maurier was
one of the most well-known illustrators
of the Victorian age, a mainstay of Punch
and other periodicals, and a first choice to
illustrate the novels of major authors. (It
was more common in those days for adult
novels to be issued illustrated.) From the
'60s he had been writing comic verse,
much of which appeared in the
magazines he illustrated or for which he
supplied cartoons. In 1891 he published
his first novel, *Peter Ibbetson*, and then, in

1894, the short novel which made an enormous impact and is remembered
to this day – though in some ways it was just a skit (he caricatured some of
his friends as characters in the story). The book was *Trilby*, and it tells how
young Trilby's singing voice comes to her through the aid of Svengali, the
mesmerist, and how it is lost when Svengali dies. Du Maurier's one other
novel, *The Martian*, was published posthumously in 1897. He was the
grandfather of Daphne du Maurier.

Valentine **DURRANT**
Justifiably obscure author of boys' stories who was commissioned by
Blackwood's Magazine to pen a series of monthly partwork novels, to called
the 'Cheveley Novels', the first of which, *A Modern Minister* staggered
through its twelve parts for a year (1877-8), and the second of which, *Saul
Weir*, was pulled mid-story. Reviews cannot have helped: 'Durrant's style,
when not a ridiculous reproduction of Dickens's worst, is very ponderous.
His humour is clumsy in the extreme; his incidents are melodramatic; his
characters caricatures drawn with an unintelligent hand. It is sincerely to
be hoped that the series may not be prolonged.' Thus spake the *Athenaeum*
in May 1858, and thus ended the *Cheveley Novels*. Durrant himself is
believed to have been the son of a Brighton baker. Over the rest of his story
a veil is drawn.

Pierce **EGAN**, the Younger (1814–80)
Great name, but it is really his father, the Elder, who is the more famous – being an early sports writer (especially on boxing) and for his *Life In London*. His son wrote a number of historical novels and was generally to be found in cheap – but mass-market – volumes and magazines. Typical was his *Robin Hood and Little John* (1840) which ran to 41 episodes.

George **EGERTON** (1859–1945) Pseudonym of Mary Dunne
Born in Australia, the eldest of six children, she had an itinerant upbringing until, in 1887, she eloped to Norway with the husband of a friend. While there she read many of the new-style Scandinavian writers such as Ibsen, Strindberg, and Björnsen. In 1890 she met and fell in love with Knut Hamsun, who encouraged her to write about female concerns and gender issues. She translated his novel *Sult* as *Hunger* (1899).

Back in England in 1891 she met and married a one-time gold prospector who was hopeless with money. They tried living economically in Ireland, where she wrote six stories in ten days, published as a collection, *Keynotes*, illustrated by Aubrey Beardsley, and it became her greatest success, placing her in the 'New Woman' style of fiction. She continued to write short stories, bringing out four more collections: *Discords* (1894), *Symphonies* (1896), *Fantasies* (1897), and *Flies in Amber* (1905). Her stories also appeared in the *Yellow Book* and she produced a novel, *The Wheel of God* (1898).

Her marriage ended in 1900 following her husband's adultery with a younger woman – and, unconventionally, Mary took pity on the girl and helped her financially. That same year she went back to Norway, fell in love again, published her collected love letters in *Rosa Amorosa* (published the following year, 1901), was rejected by her lover, and returned to England to marry someone else in July 1901. All her important works had now been written, though she lived on until 1945 when she died of a mild stroke.

George **ELIOT** (1819–80)
Born Mary Ann (she later changed it to Marian) Evans, she was brought up in the Midlands. As a child she was unusually interested in literature and religion, though in her twenties (to her father's disappointment) she became a free-thinker, moved to London and became a contributor to the

Westminster Review, published by the handsome and philandering John Chapman. She was its assistant editor from 1852-4 and, significantly, a paying guest at Chapman's home – though whether he ever courted her, or whether the courtship was entirely by her on him, remains a matter of some debate. Most incline to the latter – especially since, to put it kindly, Miss Evans was no looker. During this time she also met and fell for the philosopher Herbert Spencer, who remained a friend – no more than a friend – all her life. At the same time she met George Henry Lewes, whose marriage had crumbled but, because of the divorce laws at that time, could not be dissolved. She and he set up house together and, although they could never marry, lived as man and wife openly until his death. It is difficult today to imagine how truly shocking that was for ordinary Victorian society, and indeed it was a situation that some of their friends took years to accept.

Till now she had written literary pieces for journals, as well as two major book-length translations, but in 1857 she began writing fictional episodes for *Blackwood's Magazine*, episodes that would later be combined to become *Scenes of Clerical Life* (published 1858) under the pseudonym 'George Eliot'. Its favourable reception encouraged her to write *Adam Bede* (published 1859), which she followed with *The Mill on the Floss* (1860) and *Silas Marner* (1861).

These were and are major novels, and were received as such at the time. Some lesser novels followed: *Romola* (serialised in *Cornhill*, 1862-3), *Felix Holt, The Radical* (1866), then a return to greatness with *Middlemarch*, first published in instalments in 1871-2. (The parts were issued by Blackwood every two months, and were priced at five shillings a time.) She surprised many by following that huge family saga with another first-class novel (some say her greatest), *Daniel Deronda*, also published in parts, from 1874 to 6. Few argued with her status at that time as Britain's greatest living novelist.

Lewes died in 1878, after which Marian shocked just about everyone by marrying a younger man, John Cross, her financial advisor. The marriage lasted a mere seven months before she died, of kidney disease and laryngitis. Cross survived her by nearly forty-four years.

Havelock **ELLIS** (1859-1939)

The once controversial, and still doubtful, self-styled pioneer of sexual liberation, who gave up a half-hearted medical career for a more adventurous one in print. His first move was to publish (shock horror) unexpurgated versions of Elizabethan and Jacobean plays (the *Mermaid* series, 1887-1889), which he quickly followed with a *Contemporary Science* series. He then began producing works of his own, each with a more shocking or sales-inducing title: *The New Spirit* (1890), *Man and Woman* (1894), *Sexual Inversion* (1897). Then came his major work, *Studies in the Psychology of Sex* (in stages between 1897 to 1910). More would follow in the 20th century, including *The Erotic Rights of Woman* (1918). Though he positioned himself as an expert on marital relations, he himself was homosexual and married to a lesbian. Since his death his views, advice and motivation have been called increasingly into question.

Sebastian **EVANS** (1830-1909)

Largely unknown poet (also a journalist, stained glass designer, barrister and politician) whose medievalist *Brother Fabian's Manuscript* (1865) has come to be regarded by some as 'the most important forgotten masterpiece of the Victorian period' (George Macbeth, in *The Penguin Book of Victorian Verse*). He was born in Market Bosworth and from 1867-1870 edited the *Birmingham Daily Gazette*. Late in life (1898) he published *A High History of the Holy Graal*, part translated from the Welsh. Other works are hard to find but worth the quest. His sister Anne Evans (1820-70) was a less scholarly though lyrical poet, and her works were gathered in *Poems and Music* in 1880. Perhaps it's unfair to quote her *Tirlywirly*:

> *Tirlywirly, all alone,*
> *Spinning under a yew;*
> *Something came with no noise,*
> *But Tirlywirly knew.*

Julian Horatio **EWING** (1841-1885)

One of the great children's writers, little read today but avidly collected (sometimes for the accompanying illustrations by Caldecott etc.). Born into the trade (her mother, Mrs Gatty, published *Aunt Judy's Magazine*, for children) Juliana was a natural story-teller who began professionally with contributions to her mother's magazine and to Charlotte Yonge's *The Monthly Packet*. Mrs Ewing's stories were fresher and less didactic than those by many of her contemporaries. *Jackanapes* (1879), *A Flat Iron for a Farthing* (1872), *Lob-Lie-by-the-Fire*, (1873) and *The Story of a Short Life* (1885) are the most famous, though *The Brownies and Other Tales* (1870, illustrated by Cruikshank) gave its name to the cadet wing of the Girl Guide movement.

J Meade **FALKNER** (1858-1932)

An odd combination, he was a clergyman's son who spent much of his life in the armaments trade while writing children's adventure stories and some poems on the side. (Later in life he became Chairman of the Armstrong-Whitworth armaments company and honorary librarian to the dean and chapter of Durham.) *The Lost Stradivarius* (1895) was his first adventure story, but his greatest success came with *Moonfleet* in 1898.

Frederick William **FARRAR** (1831-1905)

The son of a missionary and ordained himself, a headmaster and writer of sermons and *The Life of Christ* (1871), it is hardly surprising that his works for children were of the edifying kind. His name remains alive for one of those books, rarely read now but forced down the throats of many an unwilling Victorian child: *Eric, or Little by Little* (1858). Consider Farrar's advice on swearing:

> *'Speak out, boy! Tell these fellows that unseemly words wound your conscience; tell them that they are ruinous, sinful, damnable; speak out and save yourself and the rest. Virtue is strong and beautiful, Eric, and vice is downcast in her awful presence. Lose your purity of heart, Eric, and you have lost a jewel which the whole world, if it were 'one entire and perfect chrysolite', cannot replace'.*

George Manville **FENN** (1831-1909)

Prolific writer of full-length and shorter stories, often for boys, whose work turns up frequently in Victorian magazines and cheap hardback editions. His boys' tales were in the action-filled style of the more successful G A **Henty** whose biography he wrote in 1907. But he was versatile enough for sporadic ventures into semi-factual and comic tales also. He married the writer for younger children, Annie S Swann.

A
FLUTTERED DOVECOTE

By
GEO. MANVILLE FENN,
AUTHOR OF
THE MASTER OF THE CEREMONIES,
THE PARSON O' DUMFORD

WITH
60 ILLUSTRATIONS BY
GORDON BROWNE.

WARD & DOWNEY, LONDON.

Edward **FITZBALL** (1793-1873)

Fitzball was fully established as the author of barnstorming melodramas before Victoria came to the throne – the most successful of many being *The Flying Dutchman* (1827) and *Jonathan Bradford* (1833) – though he stormed on in her reign with such gripping dramas as *The Negro of Wapping* (1838) and *The Wreck and the Reef* (1847). His free-running pen also produced four novels, some lively verse and a useful *Thirty-Five Years of a Dramatic Author's Life* (1859). This last book is still sought after.

Edward **FITZGERALD** (1809-1883)
Known mainly for introducing generations of English-speaking readers to *The Rubáiyát of Omar Khayyám* (1859) via his free but sensitive translations, Fitzgerald had what sounds a perfect life (if one ignores his unfortunate marriage – as, for much of his life, he did). Born comfortably off, he worked at little other than leisurely authorship. He filled his days with reading, writing and meeting friends (including literary lions such as Thackeray, Tennyson and Carlyle). His translations were of real value but none achieved anything like the success of *Rubáiyát* – though it was a success he had to wait for: it is claimed that the original book failed to sell a single copy in its first two years. (Presumably Fitzgerald had given a gratis copy to his mother.) Only when Rossetti and Swinburne discovered and, as leaders of advanced taste, began promoting it in 1861 was it noticed. The book then became a Victorian sensation, reissued in many forms – deluxe and miniature, lavishly or simply illustrated, bound conventionally or in expensive materials. Fitzgerald himself completely revised the book, producing an entirely fresh translation in 1868, a translation which showed how freely (or loosely) he re-presented the Persian quatrains. A third, slightly revised, version appeared in 1871. Opinions differ as to which is the better, and

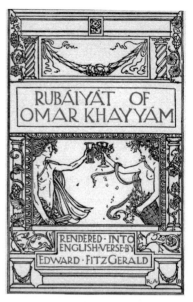

volumes containing both main versions are commonly available. Though *Rubáiyát* was his major work, his *Collected Letters* (finally brought together in 1980) give useful insights into the mid-Victorian world of literature.

John FORSTER (1812-1876)

Born in the same year as his great friend Charles **Dickens**, whose biographer he would become, Forster was a notable critic, biographer, editor and literary journalist. Apart from biographies of Dickens, Goldsmith, Landor and Swift (uncompleted) he also wrote comprehensive *Lives of British Statesmen* (1836-1839) and *Historical and Biographical Essays* (1858). The *Dickens* (1872-1874), hard on the heels of the great man's death, remains Forster's most read and permanent work, even if, out of respect both for his lifelong friend and for Victorian sensitivities, he left out some of the juicier details, such as Dickens's long-term affair with Ellen Ternan. The now familiar revelations about Dickens's childhood, however, appeared for the first time in Forster's work.

The son of a Newcastle butcher, Forster had something of the butcher about his look – bewhiskered and plump, jolly, if rather pompous, and fond (like Dickens) of parties, dressing up and rumbustious dancing.

Sir James FRAZER (1854-1941)

An anthropologist and classical scholar of Free Church upbringing, a Fellow of Trinity, he was an unlikely best-selling author – but he became one through his immense and revelatory book, *The Golden Bough* (published in two volumes in 1890, building to twelve volumes by 1915,

and issued since in abbreviated form). The ripened fruit of his detailed research, *The Golden Bough* described the religious behaviour of the primitive world, showing how, wherever one looked, early magic developed into religion, and thence on to rationalism and science. It was the vast compass of his study and his approachable language, that made his tome attractive; his interpolated studies of totemism, fetish and fertility rites were of particular interest. In the last half century the book has lost its appeal and is less often read. Frazer's other works are still read by scholars.

James Anthony **FROUDE** (1818-94)

Froude was a lifelong friend and disciple of **Carlyle** and was appointed Carlyle's literary executor. An obvious choice, Carlyle would have thought, as Froude was a notable historian. But after Carlyle had died and Froude had been through his papers, the resultant biography was not as Carlyle would have expected. Froude (almost certainly in pursuit of truth, with no thought of malice) revealed the truth about the Carlyle marriage, exposing Carlyle as a finicky and neurotic martinet who had cramped and belittled his gifted wife. Apart from his three-volume biography of Carlyle, Froude, in half a century of writing, produced a number of serious history books, giving fine and detailed accounts of Christianity, the Elizabethans, England and the Irish, the Colonies, the Knights Templar, Catherine of Aragon, the navy and the intriguingly titled *England's Forgotten Worthies* (1852).

Frederick James **FURNIVAL** (1825-1910)

There was a robustness in the Victorian gene that disappeared in the following century, but F J Furnival still had it. A muscular scholar; teetotal; agnostic, socialist and vegetarian; he was an obsessive categoriser and organiser (and strong supporter of women's rights). For the Philological Society in 1861 he edited (and oversaw the compilation) of their *New English Dictionary*, a book that developed into the *Oxford English Dictionary*. During his years of meticulous research he founded a series of learned societies: the Early English Text Society, the Chaucer, the Ballad, the New Shakspere (sic), the Wyclif (sic again), the Browning and the Shelley Societies. He helped found the Working Men's College in 1854 and taught grammar there, and in his spare time (he had some?) was a keen rower.

Richard **GARNETT** (1835-1906)

A phenomenally learned (literally: his erudition was legendary) museum scholar. For much of his life he held important posts in the British Museum Library and, although he wrote some crisp biographies and works on art and literature, he is better known for having fathered Edward Garnett (highly influential publisher's reader and husband of the translator Constance Garnett, but a post-Victorian figure) and, to his surprise, for his own book of short stories, *The Twilight of the Gods* (1888).

Elizabeth **GASKELL** (1810-1865)

Not merely one of the best women writers of the Victorian age but one of the best novelists, remembered (and still enjoyed) as author of the delightful *Cranford* (1853), the 'social conditions' novel *Mary Barton* (1848), the 'shocking' (because of its non-condemnation of illegitimacy) *Ruth* (1853), the 'condition of England' *North and South* (1855) and, perhaps the most enjoyable of her 'serious' novels, *Wives and Daughters* (not quite finished, 1866).

Gaskell was the daughter of a Unitarian minister and never strayed from her down-to-earth religious faith. She married a minister of that faith, and it was while mourning the death of their son that she wrote her first novel, *Mary Barton*. (By then she was in her mid-thirties, and had been writing shorter pieces for years; she was renowned within the family as a 'born story-teller'.) Despite her background, any 'preaching' within her novels was far from pious: she loathed social injustice and cruelty and she used her stories to speak out against them. But her stories were neither blasts of bombast nor polemical: her tone was positive, always seeking better understanding and communication between different classes – whether those classes be employers or employees, the rich or poor, or simply, the generations within a family. Like many Victorian writers, she packed detail into her stories but, where other writers padded out, she wrote with absolute clarity and made her readers see vividly how it was to live in a near but distant world.

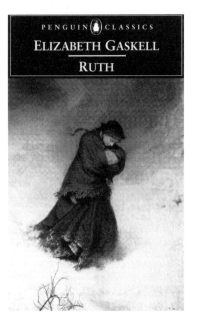

She was a journalist too, and a contributor of 'pieces' to magazines, and it is significant perhaps that her first recorded publication, although a poem, was entitled *Sketches Among the Poor, No. 1.* It appeared in *Blackwood*'s in January 1837. Only a few, random pieces came out over the next decade until *Mary Barton* in 1848, but the success of that novel (published anonymously at first) led to her being celebrated in London and having pieces taken by Dickens's celebrated *Household Words*. She swiftly became one of his principal – if often tardy –

contributors. (The first sketches for what would become *Cranford* appeared in that magazine.)

In August 1850 she met the equally celebrated (though less prolific) Charlotte **Brontë**, and the two became great friends. From that friendship grew the choice of Mrs Gaskell as Charlotte's biographer, following her early death (in 1855). *The Life of Charlotte Brontë* was a warm, readable and, at the time, controversial book – controversial because, far from painting the Brontë family in a rosy light, the book revealed many of the family skeletons: Charlotte's brother Branwell and his adulterous affair, the mistreatment of children at Cowan Bridge School, the authoritarian demands of Patrick Brontë. There were threats of libel cases, and parts of the book had to be rewritten (only after its second edition, by which time the damage was done). Yet, to this day, Mrs Gaskell's account remains a fine, and perhaps the best, Brontë biography.

In 1865, with her husband newly retired as a minister, the Gaskells moved to a new and more suitable home. They had not finished unpacking when, unexpectedly, Elizabeth Gaskell, in the middle of a happy conversation, stopped mid-sentence and died.

Margaret **GATTY** (1809–73)
Editor of the much-loved *Aunt Judy's Magazine* and mother to children's

writer Julia Horatia **Ewing**, she wrote plenty of popular children's stories for the mid-19th century generation – notably *Parables from Nature*, published in five volumes (1855-1871) and *The Fairy Godmothers* (1851). *Aunt Judy's Magazine* was named after daughter Julia, a story-teller from early childhood, and it broadened the content of children's magazines by including book reviews, fund-raising campaigns (e.g. for a sponsored cot at Great Ormond Street Hospital), educational snippets, and illustrations from top artists (Cruikshank, Caldecott, Browne, etc.). Daughter Julia joined her mother in contributing stories – as did Lewis Carroll whose 'Bruno's Revenge' was commissioned for the magazine in 1867.

W S **GILBERT** (1836-1911)

Most famous now as part of the seemingly inseparable Gilbert & Sullivan, William Schwenck Gilbert began as a barrister but whiled away the empty office hours (he was never a successful barrister; he claimed to have earned £75 in two years) by penning comic verse for magazines like *Fun*, verses which would be collected into two classic collections, both called *The Bab Ballads* (1868 & 1872). At the same time he wrote burlesque for the theatre: *Dulcamara* (1866) was his first, *The Palace of Truth* appeared in 1870, *Pygmalion and Galatea* in 1871, and three more in the '70s. At the same time again (there really was very little call for his legal services) he had begun a collaboration with Arthur Sullivan. *Thespis* (1871) was a so-so start but *Trial By Jury* (1875) was a great hit and launched the Savoy Operas. He did write other plays, both during and after the collaboration with Sullivan, but they never achieved the success of the light operas.

He was knighted in 1911 and that same year he leapt into the lake in his garden in an attempt to rescue a young schoolgirl, Ruby Preece. There was something almost Gilbertian in the concept of a man in his seventies gallantly risking his life for a maiden. But life is no comic opera: he suffered a heart attack and died. Miss Ruby Preece survived.

George **GISSING** (1857-1903)

Many writers broke the mould of how Victorian writers should be shaped, but Gissing took the mould and shattered it. Conventionally educated at a Quaker boarding school and Owens College (the precursor to University of Manchester), Gissing fell for a prostitute, stole money to help her, and was duly expelled. He spent a month in prison, a year on the bum in America, then settled in London – where he married Nell, the prostitute from Manchester, an alcoholic. Unsurprisingly, it didn't work. They split up in 1883, and in 1890 he married a second time, again 'beneath him', and again it didn't work. (They split in 1897. She entered an asylum five years later.) In the year that his second marriage failed, Gissing met and fell for the far more suitable Gabrielle Fleury – but he was married already, so he and Gabrielle went to France where they could live as man and wife.

A common theme of Gissing's novels is that of the middle class, intelligent man who falls for a woman beneath him. It occurs in his first, *Workers in the Dawn* (1880), and several others. It is one of the themes of his most famous novel, *New Grub Street* (1891), though the main theme of that book is the struggle to earn a living from writing without prostituting oneself to publishers and the public. 1892 saw the publication of his most autobiographical novel, *Born in Exile*, a story saturated in self-loathing. Bitter as Gissing's writing can be, he remained a champion of women's liberty: *The Odd Women* (1893) would be the best example of that, though the topic recurs elsewhere. *In the Year of Jubilee* (1897) subverts the idea of a man brought down by a lesser woman – though not as much as does his early and somewhat confused *Demos* (1886) in which a lower class man inherits a fortune, becomes a hypocritical capitalist and is brought down by his middle class wife. These tales are, by 19th century standards, grim – yet very readable. Polemical as Gissing can be, he is a far from one-note writer. He wrote

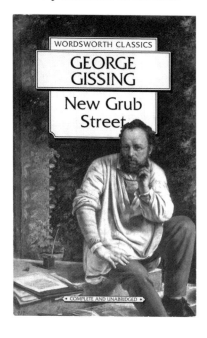

WORDSWORTH CLASSICS

GEORGE GISSING

New Grub Street

● COMPLETE AND UNABRIDGED ●

some 20 novels, sundry other works, an objective biography of Dickens and, with a surprising switch to a more benign tone, a late apparent autobiography (which it isn't) called *The Private Papers of Henry Ryecroft* (1903). He died of lung disease in France, and after his death at least half a dozen more books gradually trickled onto the market. He is one of the truest commentators on Victorian life, and he has a more secure place in the canon now than he had in his lifetime. He would have appreciated that.

Catherine Grace **GORE** (1799-1861)

Living half a century before Gissing, her writing was as different from his as could be. Where he tackled the grinding life of the struggling under-classes, she specialised in what were known as the 'Silver Fork' novels which, as the name suggests, served a pleasant (or bland, depending on one's taste) concoction of fashionable life and manners. Don't be misled by the intriguing sounding *Mrs Armytage: or, Female Domination* (1836, the year before Victoria came to the throne) – the clue is in the affected spelling of Armytage, not in the female domination. *The Banker's Wife, or Court and the City* (1843) more aptly represents her. In *Mr Punch's Prize Novelists*, Thackeray parodied her style with his *Lords and Liveries: By the Authoress of "Dukes and Dèjeuners," "Hearts and Diamonds," "Marchionesses and Milliners," Etc. Etc.* which caught her tone exactly:

> *The seventeenth Earl— gallant and ardent, and in the prime of youth — went forth one day from the Eternal City to a steeple-chase in the Campagna. A mutilated corpse was brought back to his hotel in the Piazza di Spagna. Death, alas ! is no respecter of the Nobility. That shattered form was all that remained of the fiery, the haughty, the wild, but the generous Altamont de Pentonville! Such, such is fate !*

Sir Edmund **GOSSE** (1849-1928)

Famous delineator of the autocratic Victorian family in his *Father and Son* (1907), a book still in print. The book details his dismal upbringing as the son of Philip Gosse, a member of the Plymouth Brethen, a zoologist and fearsome father who, unlike the specimens displayed in modern Misery Memoirs, is portrayed with sympathy and observation. Sir Edmund himself survived or perhaps benefited from his upbringing to become an assistant librarian at the British Museum and, ultimately, librarian of the

House of Lords. In the decades around the turn of the century he was at the centre of London literary life; he wrote a number of books of literary criticism, fine in their way, though none are read as avidly as that personal memoir.

R B Cunninghame **GRAHAM** (1852-1936)
A real-life adventurer who, perhaps in the flickering flames of a mountain camp fire, found the odd moment to jot his adventures down. The son of a Scottish Laird and a half-Spanish mother, he was, at different stages in his life, a virulently outspoken MP, a Scottish Nationalist, a rancher in Argentina, and a traveller throughout South America and Arabia. Most of his books came out in the 20th century, though a number of travel and boys' tales were earlier, as was his thrilling account of searching for the forbidden city of Tarudant in Morocco: *Mogreb-el-Acksa* (1898).

Ennis **GRAHAM** (see Mrs Molesworth)

Kenneth **GRAHAME** (1859-1932)
Grahame was a respected writer in the Victorian period, but his most famous book, *The Wind in the Willows* was not published until 1908 – and was almost not published at all. Grahame had never intended the book for publication: to him it was not a proper book but an amalgamation of caricatures, bedtime stories and once-private letters to his son; when he did submit the collection (to an American publisher) it was rejected; and when published in England it attracted little notice. The book was a slow burner, taking several years to approach classic status. It was very much an Edwardian tale, with its wistful appeal for a then-fashionable mystic paganism (yet '*The*

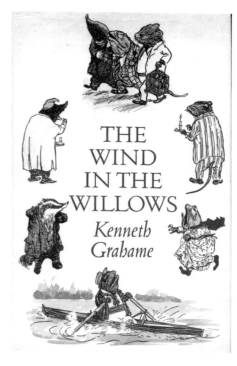

Piper at the Gates of Dawn' is a section often skipped today).

In the 1890s, Grahame had contributed to the *Yellow Book* and had published two story books, *The Golden Age* (1895) and *Dream Days* (1898), both of which painted the trials of childhood in touchingly sombre tones. Grahame's preface to *The Golden Age* is an extraordinary piece, seemingly out of place in a book for children, yet accurately berating adults as 'hopeless and incapable creatures' with neither sympathy nor understanding for their hapless offspring. (Grahame would have pointed out that the stories were aimed more at adults than at children.) But the fanciful tales in *The Golden Age* were a great success – with both critics and children – and led to the sequel three years later. The two can also be found in combined editions. So popular were they at the time that *The Wind in the Willows* was seen by Edwardian readers as a let-down. A sad footnote to all three books is that Grahame's son, to whom the later tales were first told, committed suicide when just nineteen.

George and Weedon **GROSSMITH** (1847-1912 & 1852-1919)

Remembered almost exclusively for their jointly-written *Diary of a Nobody* (1892) which Weedon also illustrated and which first appeared in *Punch*, the brothers had passed through several other careers – George as a journalist, Weedon as an artist, both men in small parts on the stage. George (seen here) went on to become a principal comic baritone with the Savoy Opera (early 78rpm records of him still exist) and Weedon to manage Terry's Theatre. George published his memoirs in two volumes, 1898 and 1910, and Weedon a novel, *A Woman with a History* in 1896, together with several plays.

Sydney **GRUNDY** (1848-1914)

Though as a playwright he was known for his cleaned-up and bowdlerised versions of wicked French plays and for his condemnation of the 'advanced' playwright Ibsen, he was, in fact, no relation to the more famous 'Mrs Grundy', a woman of even stricter morality, since she was the fictional creation of the earlier comic dramatist Thomas Morton (1764–1838) in his play, *Speed The Plow*. It was she, not he, who gave her name to 'Grundyism', meaning narrow-minded moral rigidity.

H Rider **HAGGARD** (1856-1925)
Author of 34 adventure novels, including two of the most famous of the 19th century: *King Solomon's Mines* (1886) and *She* (1887). Invincible as his heroes were, Haggard himself started out as 'the family dunce' in the view of his father – a view no doubt reinforced when Haggard failed his army entrance examination. But a good chap survives adversity, and Haggard joined the Colonial Service to embark on a successful career in South Africa (leaving long before the British were defeated there) and was knighted in 1912. Africa provided the background to his greatest tales – and Haggard's African scene and characters are less stereotyped than are those from other 19th century pens. Notable also from his African *oeuvre* are *Allan Quatermain* (1887 – the title character appears in *King Solomon's Mines*) and the Zulu trilogy written 1912-1917. Haggard strayed outside Africa with fine tales such as *Eric Brighteyes* (Iceland, 1891) and *Montezuma's Daughter* (Mexico, 1893). But it is for the set of African novels in the mid-1880s that he will be best remembered: perhaps for Quatermain, the archetypal British hero, but more likely for *She* – Ayesha, 'She-Who-Must-Be-Obeyed'.

Thomas **HARDY** (1840-1928)
Hardy is one of the least easy writers to sum up. Some things most readers know: that he was both a prose writer and a poet, and that some readers prefer his poetry and others his prose; that he came from and set his novels in Dorset which he fictionalised as Wessex; that his novels include such well-known classics as *Far From The Madding Crowd* (1874) and *Tess of the D'Urbervilles* (1891). But few have read his first published novel, *Desperate Remedies* (1871) and none his true first, *The Poor Man and the Lady*, rejected by publishers Chapman and Hall in the

late 1860s. No readers – not even his biographers – agree on the details of his upbringing or romantic life. Nor is it really clear whether he enjoyed or tolerated London.

Certainly he was a country boy, the son of a stone mason, and as a student he was both diligent and encouraged – by his mother Jemima and by his headmaster, Isaac Last. Far from book-bound, he accompanied his father from time to time both at his building work around the county and during his part-time occupation as violinist in the village band; much of this grounding is apparent in Hardy's later writing. But before he could write he needed a paying profession, and he became apprenticed as an architect. In

THOMAS HARDY
Far From the Madding Crowd

his off-time he wrote poems, that were rejected, and articles, a few of which were not. ('*How I Built Myself A House*' appeared in 1865.)

Where his first novel had been melodramatic, his second, *Under The Greenwood Tree* (1872), was as idyllic as its title suggests – and was untypical of what would follow. *A Pair of Blue Eyes* came in 1872 & 3, the love story of a young architect, assumed to be partly autobiographical, and it was followed by his first great hit, *Far From The Madding Crowd* in 1874. All the great Hardy themes were here: the heroine torn between two lovers (Troy or Gabriel Oak: no contest), death in childbirth (Fanny in the workhouse), *crime passionel* (jilted Boldwood shoots Sergeant Troy), and magnificent scenery (which few could describe as beautifully as Hardy).

He could now afford to marry (the long-suffering Emma Gifford) and to write full-time. Uncertain of his metier, he alternated three less successful novels with three good ones: *The Return of the Native* (1878), *The Trumpet-Major* (1880) and *The Mayor of Casterbridge* (1886). The success of *Madding Crowd* had made him an important literary figure, and the married couple's life became divided between London and their native Dorset. From his books one would assume that Hardy hated, or was at the

least uncomfortable in, London but he and
Emma spent 'the season' there each year and,
almost certainly, although biographers differ,
the famous author was occasionally tempted to
dally outside his marriage. *The Woodlanders*
appeared in 1887, the superb *Tess of the
D'Urbervilles* in 1891, and *Jude the Obscure* in
1895. As before, these three were interspersed
with lesser works. There were also a number of
excellent short stories.

His *Tess* had been much criticised, both for
its supposed immorality and for its bitter
conclusion. But the hostile reaction to *Jude*,
this time for its gloomy pessimism and its 'anti-
religious' stance, encouraged him to return to
poetry. His first volume (the first of eight),
Wessex Poems and Other Verses, appeared in
1898. He was now a Grand Old Man of English Letters, with a
controversial reputation (partly for his private life but mainly for his
'shocking' books). Yet his poems received a luke-warm reception. Indeed,
much that he produced in the 20th century would be poorly received. His
poems were badly under-rated; they have since come to be accepted as
among the finest English verse. His novels, though naturally they vary,
have been avidly read (and, in some cases, dramatised) for over a hundred
years. His reputation, once controversial, is now undeniable. He was a
stone-mason's son and his body lies in pomp at Westminster Abbey.

Beatrice **HARRADEN** (1864–1936)
Despite the spelling, hers was an unfortunate name for a feminist. A
suffragette, a leader of the Women's Social and Political Union, a suffragist
evangelist to America, and a feminist novelist, Miss Harraden's first was
Things Will Take A Turn (1891) but her great success (a million seller, quite
a feat in those days) was *Ships That Pass In The Night* (1893). The plot
would seem to belie her convictions, concerning as it does a consumptive
patient in a winter resort at Petershof, but it did convey her feminist
principles. Later titles include *In Varying Moods* (short stories, 1894),
Hilda Strafford (1897), *The Fowler* (1899) and others through to 1928.

Frank **HARRIS** (1856-1931)

Notorious for his imaginatively autobiographical *My Life and Loves* (published in four volumes 1922-7) his first book was a 20th century collection of short stories, *Elder Conkin*. He wrote biographies, including a notable *Oscar Wilde*, but is known now, as he was then, for his unrepentant boasting (especially about his sexual exploits) and for his fights against contemporary prudery. In Victorian times he edited *The Evening News* from 1882-86, *The Fortnightly Review* to 1886 to 94 and then *The Saturday Review* until 1898. Somehow, this outrageous figure was also entrusted with editorship of *Candid Friend*, *Vanity Fair* and *Hearth and Home*.

R S **HAWKER** (1803-75)

Eccentric priest cum poet based in Morwenstowe on the Cornish coast, he became addicted to the occult and to opium and, in his church, chose to wear a fisherman's jersey, to compare himself to Saint Francis, and to welcome animals to his services. His poems tend to reflect his Cornish background, his eclectic beliefs and his take on history; and his one prose work of note was *Footprints of Former Men in Far Cornwall* (1870). The best poetry collection was his *The Quest of the Sangraal* (1864) and his most famous individual poem 'The Song of the Western Men' includes the lines:

> *A good sword and a trusty hand!*
> *A merry heart and true!*
> *King James's men shall understand*
> *What Cornish lads can do!*
> *And have they fix'd the where and when?*
> *And shall Trelawny die?*
> *Here's twenty thousand Cornish men*
> *Will see the reason why!*

Benjamin Robert **HAYDON** (1786-1846)

Though he thought of himself – declared himself, insisted that he was – Britain's finest historical painter (which he was not), Haydon was a perceptive critic, a champion of the arts, a debtor several times imprisoned and, ultimately, a spectacular suicide. He seemed to know everyone: Prime Ministers (from whom he borrowed money), writers and artists, importunate tradesmen, and several mistresses. Along with his friend

Leigh **Hunt** he was cruelly caricatured by **Dickens** as Harold Skimpole in *Bleak House*, though when Dickens later denied that Skimpole was based on Hunt, Haydon was dead, so Dickens didn't apologise to him. Haydon's smaller artworks, especially the portrait sketches which he disdained, were far better than his mammoth oil paintings, but his greatest product may have been his very readable *Autobiography and Journals*, published posthumously in 1853, which has been pretty much in print ever since.

W E HENLEY (1849-1903)

It is ironic that his best-known poem, *Invictus* (1875) should contain the lines: 'I am the master of my fate; I am the captain of my soul' since, as a child, William Ernest Henley was struck down with tuberculosis and had to have a leg amputated. (Later, he was a friend of Robert Louis **Stevenson** who based Long John Silver on him.) Henley was a greatly respected editor of several important magazines and of a Burns collection, he wrote books of literary and art journalism, issued *Tudor Translations* (1892-1903) and, with Stevenson before they fell out, wrote four plays (1882-5). But he is remembered as a poet. His time in hospital inspired much of his finest verse (*Hospital Sketches*, in *Cornhill* magazine, 1875). Other books came out between 1888 to 1900, and he is still anthologised.

G A HENTY (1832-1902)

Prolific writer of boys' adventure tales, still much collected, as much for the illustrated book covers as for the books themselves. In his day, he was the pre-eminent figure in British boys' fiction. George Alfred Henty knew whereof he spoke: he had fought in the Crimean War and had served as a war correspondent in later skirmishes – despite having been the archetypal sickly child. His first story, *Out in the Pampas*, appeared in 1871 (though he'd written it for his own children in 1868) and he eventually wrote some 80 full-length novels, most of which were heroic, patriotic, historically accurate and approved of as much by parents as by the sturdy little British bulldog pups themselves. His themes and settings were often obvious from the titles – *Under Drake's Flag* (1883), *With Clive in India* (1884), *Redskin and Cowboy* (1892) and his final opus, *With the Allies in Pekin* (1904). For some years he edited *Boys' Own Magazine* and *Union Jack*. He also wrote a dozen books for grown-ups, but they can be ignored (as they were then).

Thomas **HOOD** (1799-1845)

At the top of his career by the time of Victoria's coronation, Hood had edited magazines such as *Gem*, the *Comic Annual*, and *New Monthly Magazine* and was an established writer of parodies and satires. (*Hood's Magazine* began in 1843.) Through his pun-filled poems he fuelled the Victorian mania for puns and word-play. (Classics to look out for – still funny today, despite or because of their appalling puns – are *Faithless Nelly Gray* and *The Ballad of Sally Brown* and *Ben the Carpenter*.) But in 1843 his poem *The Song of a Shirt*, lambasting the appalling working conditions and exploitation of seamstresses, caused a sensation and outcry for change. It came in the same year as his *The Bridge of Sighs*, mourning the emblematic suicide by drowning of a 'fallen woman'. His most anthologised poem (often parodied in its turn) is *I remember, I remember*. But these serious works were greatly outnumbered by his parodies and skits. He was, first and foremost, a humorist.

Thomas **HOOD** the Younger – 'Tom Hood' (1835-1874)

Humorous artist and writer, son of the above. Where his father's comic poems were illustrated by John Leech and others, the younger Hood usually illustrated his own (although his *Fairy Realm* of 1865 was illustrated by Doré). His first book had been *Pen and Pencil Pictures* (1857) and he worked in this vein all his life, editing *Fun* from 1865 and beginning the popular *Tom Hood's Comic Annual* in 1867. He wrote and illustrated many children's books, as well as half a dozen novels and a collection, *Favourite Poems*, in 1877. He also illustrated two books by his sister, under her married name of Frances Freeling Broderip: *Tiny Tadpole and Other Tales* (1862) and *Tales of the Toys, told by Themselves* (1869).

Anthony HOPE (1863-1933)

One of the most enjoyable Victorian adventure stories came late, in 1894. It was *The Prisoner of Zenda*, set in the splendidly named Ruritania, a romantic kingdom (not far, one assumes, from Transylvania) in which the devilish ruler discovered he had an English doppelganger. It was an immediate success and came in the same year that Hope's quite different book, the mildly amusing *The Dolly Dialogues*, culled from pieces in *The Westminster Gazette*, became a popular success also. 'Hope' had been a barrister (real name Sir Anthony Hope Hawkins; he was knighted in the First World War) but the success of *Zenda* and *Dolly* in one year was enough to persuade him give up that profession and concentrate (if that was the word) on writing. So successful had *Zenda* been that a dashing sequel, *Rupert of Hentzau* followed in 1898. None of his other novels achieved the success of that Ruritanian pair.

Gerard Manley, HOPKINS (1844-1899)

> *I wake and feel the fell of dark, not day.*
> *What hours. O what black hoürs we have spent*
> *This night! What sights you, heart, saw; ways you went!*
> *And more must, in yet longer light's delay.*
> — from *I wake and feel the fell of dark, not day.*

Would Hopkins offend God if he wrote poetry? Only a Victorian could obsess to such an extent that, believing he might offend, he must burn all the poems he had so far written. Hopkins did just that when he joined the Jesuits in 1868, having been a brilliant student of Baliol (nicknamed the 'star of Baliol'), a fervent follower of the Oxford Movement, a convert to Roman Catholicism in 1866, and a double first graduate. Throughout his life this brilliant man would be tortured by his religion. In 1875 a disaster at sea, when five Franciscan nuns drowned on the Deutschland, inspired him to take up his pen again, to commemorate their deaths. But his approach to poetry continued to be tortuous; rather than accept the usual dictums of composing, he devised his own, inventing terms such as 'inscape', 'instress' and 'sprung rhythm' to replace them. He was a 'difficult' poet, but most of those difficulties were of his own making. Inevitably, he died unhappily: posted against his wishes to Dublin to be Professor of Classics, he died of typhoid fever.

Richard Hengist (originally Henry) **HORNE** (1802-1884)
Poetry is ever undervalued: so thought Horne who, after fifteen years of seeing his poems published but unrewarded, published his epic poem *Orion* in 1843 at a mere farthing (hence his becoming known as 'the farthing poet'). Whether for this reason or for its own real merit, the poem was greatly noticed and much praised by eminences such as G H Lewes, Carlyle, Poe and the like. Horne wrote several verse tragedies for the stage, together with other books of poetry and literary journalism, notably for *Dickens's Household Words* and *Daily News*. He compiled a useful *A New Spirit of the Age* in 1844 and, after joining the gold rush in the 1850s, wrote (25 years before his life ended) an *Australian Autobiography and Australian Facts and Prospects* in 1859.

E W **HORNUNG** (1866-1921)
The brother-in-law of Conan Doyle, he countered Doyle's great detective with his own Gentleman Thief, *Raffles*, first met in *The Amateur Cracksman* (1899) and continued through three more collections of his adventures. (Raffles was not, in fact, the first gentleman thief in fiction. Guy Boothby's Simon Carne predates him by two years.) Hornung's other anti-hero, the *Australian Stingaree*, came in 1905.

Lord **HOUGHTON** see Monckton **Milnes**

A E **HOUSMAN** (1859-1936)
Housman's impact was in the 20th century, especially during and after the First World War, but the book of poems which made him famous, *A Shropshire Lad*, was published, at his own expense and to little notice, in 1896. No other poems would appear in volume form till *Last Poems* (1922) and a book of scraps, *More Poems*, in 1936. Alfred Edward Housman was an unhappy man, as can be seen from his wistful poems. At Oxford he fell in love with another (male) student and, for reasons no one quite understands, he failed his finals. An academic career thus denied him, he worked for ten mind-numbing years in the Patent Office, pining for his native Shropshire and writing scholarly pieces on classical poets. It was

only after his university friend married (1887) that Housman finally began writing poetry of his own. In 1892 his other writings led to his being given the professorship of Latin at London University, and while there he spent a decade on a definitive study of the works of *Manilus*, which was published in five volumes between 1903 and 1930.

Mary and William HOWITT (1799-1888 and 1792-1879)

A Quaker couple, married in 1822, who between them wrote some 180 books for children and were well-known figures in the Victorian literary scene. Mary was the poet of the pair, her best-known verse being ' "Will you walk into my parlour?" said the spider to the Fly'. (That's in her misleadingly titled *Sketches of Natural History of 1834*.) William preferred prose, with titles varying from the (surprisingly gruesome in places) *A Boy's Adventures in the Wilds of Australia* (1854) to the Derbyshire-based *The Boy's Country-book* of 1839. (Both were partly autobiographical.) He also edited a short-lived *Howitt's Journal*. Among Mary's many books she issued the first English translation of Hans Christian Andersen (*Wonderful Stories for Children*, 1846) which led to a quarrel with the famously unpleasant Andersen when he demanded a large share of the book's non-existent profits. Unusually, late in life, both the Howitts abandoned their Quaker beliefs: Mary to become a Catholic and William to become a Spiritualist.

W H HUDSON (1841-1922)

Though of English ancestry, he was born in Argentina and lived there till 1868 when his father died. He contracted rheumatic fever at the age of 15, became unable to live the outdoor life to the extent he wanted, but nevertheless immersed himself in nature, especially ornithology. Some of his natural history contributions appeared in Argentinean journals (they would later in British ones) and his

Argentinean upbringing is beautifully recalled in *Far Away and Long Ago* (1918). Hudson travelled for a while, then came to England, but was not naturalised till 1900. Ensconced here, he continued writing on nature, earning next to nothing from those writings. He produced two novels, *The Purple Land* (1885) and *The Crystal Age* (1887) but they do not compare to works such as *Argentine Ornithology* (1888) to which he contributed, *The Naturalist in La Plata* (1892), *Idle Days in Patagonia* (1893) or *British Birds* in 1895. He remained desperately poor, though he was helped by his publishers, Dent, and his editor Richard Garnett, and was given a Civil List pension in 1901. Later would come his most successful books, *Green Mansions* (1904) and *A Shepherd's Life* (1910). He is remembered as one of our finest writers on the natural world.

Thomas **HUGHES** (1822-1896)

To have written one of the most famous, yet now largely unread, classics of schoolboy literature, *Tom Brown's Schooldays* (1857), ought to have been enough, but Hughes, a Liberal MP, Christian Socialist, keen amateur boxer and exponent of 'muscular Christianity', worked tirelessly for good causes such as a widened franchise, the Co-operative Movement and improved education for the working man. A satirist couldn't have chosen a more typical Hughes title than his *The Manliness of Christ* (1879) – and one hesitates to read his *The Scouring of the White Horse* (1859) until one learns it's actually about the Berkshire Vale of the White Horse. Mock him as we may, we cannot deny that Hughes was a profoundly decent man. His Rugby School sequel, *Tom Brown at Oxford* (1861), can be avoided.

Leigh **HUNT** (1784–1859)

Though he is little read now, Leigh Hunt was at the centre of 19th century literary society. Taught as a charity boy at Christ's Hospital, he went on to become a respected critic, poet, essayist and editor. In this role – as editor of the *Reflector* – he had in 1811 been sentenced, along with his brother John, to two years' imprisonment for libel on the Prince Regent. Before Victoria came to the throne he had, in the *Reflector*, the *Examiner* and other journals, championed many who were or would become major literary figures (he was especially supportive of the Romantics), and in her coronation year his anthology, the *Book of Gems*, included his two most famous poems, 'Abou Ben Adhem' and 'Jenny Kissed Me'. More anthologies would follow – full of amiable, well-informed essays and of poems – and of these books, perhaps *Table Talk* (1851) is where one should begin.

It is hard to see such a man, as we are always told we must, as the basis for the leech-like Harold Skimpole in **Dickens**'s *Bleak House* (Dickens strongly denied it, and the two men were good friends.) Certainly he spent time in jail – for better reasons than might have occurred to Skimpole – and certainly he was often out of funds, but the high regard with which he was regarded by so many contemporaries suggests that, for once, Dickens's denial contained the truth.

Thornton Leigh **HUNT** (1810-73)

Son of the above and included here only to distinguish between them. He was a journalist, joint founder of the *Leader* and a senior writer for the newly created *Daily Telegraph*. His greatest claim to fame today comes from his having 'stolen away' and four times impregnated the wife of G H **Lewes** who, in her turn, would not divorce her husband, causing him, in his turn, to 'live in sin' with 'George **Eliot**'.

Violet **HUNT** (1866-1942)

Wonderfully entitled 'An Immodest Violet' in the biography by Joan Hardwick, this passionate feminist and long-time lover of the writer Ford Maddox Ford began her novel writing in the 1890s. (Some would say her greatest works of fiction were her 20th century reminiscences of the Pre-Raphaelites.) But in the period that this book covers, her novels are *The Maiden's Progress* (1894) – an odd novel, written entirely in dialogue; *A Hard Woman* (1895) – which contains the splendid line: 'Men hate to find a woman's husband sitting about when they call'; *The Way of Marriage* (1896) – copies of which seem to have totally disappeared; *Unkist, Unkind* (1897) – about a determined governess; *The Human Interest* (1899) – about a landscape painter; and a collection of short stories, *The Affairs of the Heart* (1900). Violet was the daughter of the artist Alfred Hunt and not, as some have thought, the more famous Holman Hunt.

T H HUXLEY (1825-1895)

Famous for his 'God v Darwin' exchange with Bishop Wilberforce in 1860, Huxley invented the word 'agnostic' to describe his own beliefs. (Others called him 'Darwin's Bulldog'.) Whatever some Victorians thought of him, Huxley was a paradigmatic self-taught man. Having had a mere two years formal schooling, the teenage Huxley read textbooks in bed by candlelight and taught himself German solely from a dictionary. After winning a Free Scholarship to Charing Cross Hospital he trained in medicine and specialised in comparative anatomy, before joining the navy and travelling the world. (He met his wife in Australia.) He left the navy to become a lecturer, became a Fellow of the Royal Society in 1851 and began a series of books on natural sciences. *On the Educational Value of the Natural History Sciences* (1854) was followed by the controversial *On Races, Species and their Origin* in 1860. Books that followed ranged from ethnology to (the lion's den) *The Evidence of the Miracle of Resurrection* (1876). Unafraid of controversy, his later books included *Social Diseases and Worse Remedies* (1891) and *Evolution and Ethics* (1893). Yet, despite the hostility shown towards him by some religious opponents, he himself was no evangelical anti-religionist: sitting on the London School Board in 1870 he supported the inclusion of Bible Study in the curriculum, on the grounds that it taught an excellent code of conduct. His was a clear, dispassionate mind, and much of what he taught resounded long after he had gone. He was the grandfather of Aldous Huxley.

Jean INGELOW (1820-97)

Sentimental poet and author of some children's stories (notably *Mopsa the Fairy*, 1869). Of her many collections, *Jean Ingelow's Poems*, Longman's

1867, is now greatly sought after for its accompanying wood engravings. (The first edition, without illustrations, was in 1863.)

W W JACOBS (1863-1943)

Known mainly for his humorous short stories, William Wymark Davies was a contributor to both the *Idler* and *Strand* magazines in the 1890s; it is from those magazines that many of his stories were collected for reissue in book form. One of his more macabre stories, a Gothic piece entitled '*The Monkey's Paw*', became a popular play. Jacobs was also wrote a small handful of novels.

Anna JAMESON (1794-1860)

A name hardly remembered now, but in the early years of Victoria's reign Mrs Jameson was at the centre of London's literary society, both as a critic and as a writer. Very much a self-made woman, she first earned her living as a governess (*Diary of an Ennuyée*, 1826), then as a critic (beginning with *Loves of the Poets*, 1829), while dabbling in travel writing (*Winter Studies and Summer Rambles*, about Canadian Indian tribes, 1838), moving later to art criticism. (*Memoir of the Early Italian Painters*, 1845 and *Sacred and Legendary Art*, 1848 are two of her collections.) Early in this hard-won career she separated from her husband, who had found the attractions of the West Indies more to his taste. (Their marriage, it is said, was never consummated.) Early in her career came perhaps her finest book, originally called *Characteristics of Women* (1832) but later changed to *Shakespeare's Heroines*. As if her range of talents wasn't wide enough already, she also illustrated this book, in which, bizarrely, she called Shakespeare 'the Poet of Womankind.' (Mrs Jameson was a promoter of women's rights.)

She was never rich, and could afford to live no nearer the heart of literary London than far-off Ealing; she earned her position through hard work and a fine brain. When young she had been something of a beauty but as she aged she grew more formidable in appearance. Carlyle (hardly a looker himself) sneered at this 'little, hard, broad, red-haired, freckled, fierce-eyed, square-mouthed woman', but it has never been easy, and it certainly wasn't then, for a woman to be judged for her mind rather than her looks. Mrs Jameson did so, and it is greatly to her credit that, against considerable odds, she became so highly regarded (if not by Carlyle) within

London's literary world. Further clues to her character may be gleaned from her *Memoirs and Essays* of 1846.

Richard JEFFERIES (1848–87)

Jefferies was the restless son of a Wiltshire farmer, yet – curiously when one thinks of his later life – never wanted to be a farmer himself (perhaps because the farm was close to Swindon?). He left home at 16, returned, and began writing for the local newspaper, *The North Wiltshire Herald*. But his rural sketches were too good not to be published elsewhere; some were published in the *Pall Mall Gazette* (later reissued as *The Gamekeeper at Home*, 1878) and from then on his meticulous but accessible observations found an ever-widening readership. *Wild Life in a Southern County* (Wiltshire) and *The Amateur Poacher* (a title guaranteed to alarm gamekeepers) were both published in 1879, along with *The Gamekeeper at Home* in 1880 and two other titles. *Wood Magic* followed in 1881, and one of his most famous, *Bevis, The Story of a Boy*, in 1882. His next (very fine) book, *The Story of my Heart* (1883) was, in part, a late entry to the God Debate and ruffled some parsons' feathers, while the 1885 volume, *After London*, was a grim futuristic fable that alienated others, though it's a decent work that could be enlisted into the Green debate today. But these late wanderings from the meadowland were soon forgiven and Jefferies continues to be remembered as one of England's greatest writers on the open fields and the world of nature.

Jerome K JEROME (1859–1927)

His *Three Men in a Boat* (1889) has eclipsed his other works – indeed, most readers are completely unaware of them. *On the Stage and Off* (1885) came first (Jerome was both an actor and a theatre journalist) and *Idle Thoughts of an Idle Fellow* (1886) remains a pleasant read. The great 1889 title, about three young clerks who take a decidedly amateur rowing holiday on the Thames, was an immediate success and has never been out of print since. There had to be a sequel, but Jerome took his time, and it wasn't until 1900 that *Three Men on the Bummel* saw the three men attempt a similar trip in Germany. Part of the reason for Jerome's procrastination was that in 1892 he had founded *The Idler* magazine, and an Idler, you know, can never hurry.

Douglas and Blanchard **JERROLD** (1803-57 and 1826-84)
There were two, father and son, both called
Jerrold and both with a 'William' that they
dropped. Douglas William Jerrold (father) was
a journalist and playwright (plays include *Paul
Pry*, a farce of 1827; *Fifteen Years of a
Drunkard's Life*, a melodrama of 1828; *Black-
Eyed Susan*, the big hit of 1829; *Mutiny at the
Nore*, another melodrama in 1830; *The Prisoner
of War*, 1842; and *Time Works Wonders* in 1845).
His Men of Character (1838) was illustrated by
Thackeray. He was a founding writer on the
new *Punch* periodical (1841), where he stayed
for years (writing as 'Q') with series such as
'*Story of a Feather*' and '*Punch's Letters to his
Son*'.

He wrote one enormously successful comic book (largely collected
from his Punch contributions), *Mrs Caudle's Candlelight Lectures*,
published in book form in 1846. (Mrs Caudle was the archetypal nagging
housewife, and lived on under various names through Music Hall, Variety
and the seaside comic postcard. Les Dawson must have known her well.)
During these fruitful years he ran Douglas Jerrold's *Shilling Magazine* and
Douglas Jerrold's *Weekly Newspaper*. The last years of his life were as
editor of *Lloyd's Weekly Newspaper*.

His son, William Blanchard Jerrold, to confuse matters, took over as
editor of *Lloyd's Weekly Newspaper* and also wrote plays (including *Beau
Brummel*). It is his text, not his father's, that accompanies Doré's
engravings in *London: A Pilgrimage* of 1872.

Geraldine **JEWSBURY** (1812-80)
We have to take her partly by repute. Known by her friends as a great wit
and conversationalist, little of which is recorded, and an intimate friend of
Jane Carlyle, between whom many illuminating letters were exchanged and
half of which were destroyed at the wish of both parties, we are left with
little more than her frequent mention in literary biographies. (She was at
the heart of literary circles in Manchester and later, London.) But there are
some novels. *Zöe*, a 'sensation' novel mixing religious doubt and female

passion, came first, in 1845; *The Half Sisters* in 1848; her robustly feminist *Marian Withers* in 1851; along with three more adult and two children's novels through to 1859. The 1892 collection of letters from her to Jane Carlyle is interesting but suffers from the lack of letters from Jane to her. (Those were the ones destroyed.) Though never a well woman she sported, at her prime, a mass of Pre-Raphaelite red hair and smoked cigaritos.

Lionel JOHNSON (1867-1902)

Well-born, well educated, reasonably successful, but his life was not happy. He left New College, Oxford to begin as a reviewer and contributor to various journals and, in his mid-twenties, converted to Catholicism. Around the same time he began researching into his Irish past (editing *The Irish Home Reading Magazine* in 1894) and promoting Irish literature in London – though his first major work was a useful *The Art of Thomas Hardy* (1894). *Poems* appeared in 1895, *Ireland and Other Poems* in 1897 and *Post Liminium* posthumously, in 1911 – for he died young, a self-confessed alcoholic, though the cause of death was a fractured skull, following a fall.

Henry Arthur JONES (1851-1929)

A now forgotten playwright, contemporary with and, in the 1890s, almost as successful as **Pinero**. A melodrama, *The Silver King* (1882), was his first real success (though not his first play) and among the plays that followed were *Saints and Sinners* (1884), *The Dancing Girl* (1891) and *The Case of Rebellious Susan* (1894). His *Michael and the Lost Angel* created the biggest stir, though it survived a mere ten performances and the loss of its leading actress, Mrs Patrick Campbell, who walked out on it. She, like most members of its few audiences, objected to its theme of an adulterous priest. Jones continued in the theatre all his life.

Benjamin JOWETT (1817-93)

Few literary or religious biographies of the 19th century fail to mention him somewhere. A legendary Oxford Fellow from as early as 1838, subsequently Regius Professor of Greek and eventually Master of Balliol, he taught or influenced a great many famous men. In 1855 he entered the long-running religious war between the Tractarians, the Broad Church (Jowett's), the High Church, the Roman Catholics and Rationalists with his, by comparison, sensible *Epistles of Paul* in which, among other recommendations, he urged the abolition of religious tests (and thus religious belief) from university degrees; Jowett pressed for the use of reason rather than blind faith in interpreting the scriptures. So outraged were the Tractarians and his Vice Chancellor that Jowett was almost charged with heresy – a charge he defended in *Essays and Reviews* (1860). (Religious tests were finally removed in 1871.) Jowett's Greek translations and commentaries were widely read – the most popular versions with the public, though not, of course, with his critics – and helped make his name nationally known. Many who had never met him knew of his thin piping voice, his long silences and his shock of white hair. There was a rumour, never confirmed, that he proposed marriage to Florence Nightingale.

Julia **KAVANAGH** (1824–77)

Novelist who did much to improve the image of the French in John Bull's island. Though born in Ireland, she spent much of her youth in France and fell in love with it. Her admiration fills the pages of novels such as *Madeleine* (1848), *Nathalie* (1850) and *Adèle* (1858) and, as if to show that her France was no fiction, she produced *Woman in France During the Eighteenth Century* (1850) and a fine *French Women of Letters* in 1862 (then an *English Women of Letters* in 1863). A British-based *Bessie* appeared in 1872 and a book of short stories, *Forget-me-nots* in 1878.

Annie **KEARY** (1825–79)

Though she wrote several other books for children she (with her sister Eliza) is best known for *The Heroes of Asgard* (1857), the first version of the Norse myths for English-speaking children.

John **KEBLE** (1792–1866)

A quiet, unambitious but academically brilliant man, initially a tutor at Oriel but later the vicar of a country parish, his first work was an anonymous book of sacred verses, *The Christian Year* in 1827. The book achieved enormous success, running into 92 editions. But it was his *Assize Sermon on National Apostasy* in 1833 that is generally considered to have engendered the Oxford (or Tractarian) Movement, whose ideas caused so much religious ferment in the mid-century. Keble's sermon led directly to the new movement's *Tracts for the Times* (1833) to which he contributed nine tracts. Keble then rather withdrew from the fray, producing an unremarkable *Lyra Innocentium* in 1846. For almost 30 years of Victoria's reign he lived modestly, a happily married and popular vicar, although the debate that he started ran and ran.

Fanny KEMBLE (1809-93)

Daughter of the actor Charles Kemble, niece of Sarah Siddons and famous as an actress, she remains alive through her writings – especially her letters, though there is a volume of poems (1844) and several interesting autobiographical works. *Journal of a Residence on a Georgian Plantation in 1838-9* (published 1863) blew the gaff on her earlier, tamer Journal of a *Residence in America* (1835). *Records of a Girlhood* appeared in 1878, *Records of a Later Life* in 1882, and *Further Records* in 1890 (just after her one novel, *Far Away and Long Ago*, 1889). Hers was no ordinary actress's life – but then, whose was in the 19th century? Her famous family was practically bankrupt; they used her deliberately on stage, and the gamble paid off. After a tour of America she stayed behind to marry but, given that he was a slave-owner and she an ardent abolitionist, the marriage did not succeed (though it did last more than decade). Her return to the English stage was billed as a triumphant response to public demand but was, in truth, a hand-to-mouth existence. We cannot know for ourselves how she was on stage, but we can savour the vigour of her writings.

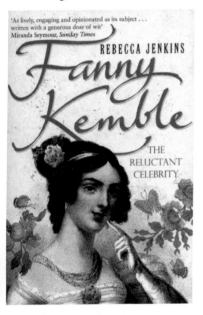

'As lively, engaging and opinionated as its subject . . . written with a generous dose of wit'
Miranda Seymour, *Sunday Times*

REBECCA JENKINS

Fanny Kemble

THE RELUCTANT CELEBRITY

Robert Francis KILVERT (1840-79)

The author of the 19th century's most enduringly popular diary began his clerical career as a curate in Wiltshire and Radnorshire before becoming vicar of Bredwardine in the border county of Herefordshire. His diaries were never intended for publication and are therefore entirely honest and free from cant. They are also one of the clearest accounts we have of Victorian rural life – from the poverty of his poor parishioners to the comfort of the gentry; from the joys of rugged walking to the beauties of young girls. Delightful and frank as the notes appear, we can only regret their expurgation, first by his wife (a wife of only five weeks, as he died of peritonitis soon after their marriage) and second by his niece (who destroyed 19 volumes!). All were long dead by the time the remains were published, between 1938 and 40 (and in a further abridged volume in 1944) having been found and edited by William Plomer.

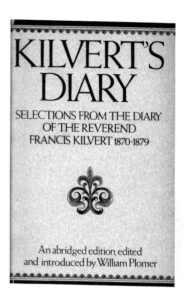

KILVERT'S DIARY

SELECTIONS FROM THE DIARY OF THE REVEREND FRANCIS KILVERT 1870-1879

An abridged edition, edited and introduced by William Plomer

Alexander **KINGLAKE** (1809-91)

Historian, barrister and travel-writer, famous for one book, *Eothen* (1844) relating in simple language his travels and adventures in Arabia and the Holy Land. Some twenty years later he would write a comprehensive history of the Crimean War, clear and thorough, longer than *Eothen*, but marred a little by its unquestioning admiration for the stumbling Lord Raglan.

Charles **KINGSLEY** (1819-75)

Today's readers associate Kingsley with *The Water Babies* (1863), though that book is untypical of his output or his mission. For Kingsley was a man with a mission: to reform. His first novel, *Yeast* (serialised in *Fraser's Magazine* in 1848) and his second *Alton Locke* (1850) were both campaigning novels – for (and at times, against) Chartism, for education, for improved sanitation, for the working man. (The working woman was seldom noticed then; Kingsley cannot be blamed for that.) His historical *Hypatia* (*Fraser's* again, in 1851) told of a philosopher torn to pieces by early Christians, and outraged sturdy Victorians more than had his socialist stories. Then came his spirited (and today, his second most famous book)

Westward Ho! (1855), another historical novel, set in Elizabethan times, which again upset many (though not most) of his readers with its lip-smacking violence. He continued to alternate historical with political novels: *Hereward the Wake* (1866) was more approved of (a frequent 'school prize') and *The Heroes* (1856, about Perseus) inspired or was presented to young readers also. *The Water Babies* was unambiguously aimed at them, although its exposure of the plight of chimney-sweeps (a relatively short part of the novel as a whole) tugged at

the heartstrings of more adult readers, and changed the law.

Kingsley was one of the 'great names' of the Victorian book-world, despite the number of times he gave offence to readers (attacking exploitative employers one day, Roman Catholicism the next) and despite the paradoxes of his nature – viz: he was a staunch churchman whose writings show he enjoyed sex (with his wife); he was a 'Muscular Christian' although he stammered and suffered from breakdowns; he was a fierce patriot who attacked the establishment; he attacked slavery yet would descend to racism. He was himself the son of a clergyman, and in 1844 he became the rector of Eversley (Hants), a village in which he lived for the rest of his life. A prolific writer (he believed in cramming every minute with things well done) his collected works would fill some 28 volumes.

Henry KINGSLEY (1830-76)

Younger, less famous brother to Charles, and no mean author himself (though his scenes are better than his plots). A remarkably physical man – a 'Muscular Christian' rumoured with scant proof to have been homosexual and, in later life, to have become an alcoholic – he spent five years in Australia as a policeman and gold-digger in the 1850s, thus gaining plenty of colourful material to enliven his *Geoffrey Hamlyn* (1859) and *The*

Hillyars and the Burtons (1865). Other novels (he wrote some 20 altogether) – including his fine *Ravenshoe* (1862) with its splendid scenes of the Crimea, and *Mademoiselle Mathilde* (1868) – were well received but not enough to secure his living. He spent some time as editor of the *Edinburgh Daily Review* and served as its correspondent in the Franco-Prussian War and, when times were hard, he turned with limited success to his more successful brother for loans. It did not improve their relationship.

Mary **KINGSLEY** (1862-1900)

In an age of great Victorian travellers, Mary Henrietta Kingsley (niece of Charles Kingsley) should stand out. A self-educated, self-sufficient young woman, she spent much of her adult life looking after her ailing parents, and it was only after their death that she was able to start living for herself. She was now in her thirties and, almost as if there was nothing else for her to do, she travelled to Africa to tidy up her father's affairs. In less than a year there, she undertook two hazardous journeys (to Angola and to Gabon) in which she faced perils such as swamps and rapids, crocodiles and leeches, cannibals and an aggressive gorilla, and during which she climbed the awesome Mount Cameroon. Out of these experiences came her *Travels in West Africa* (1897, a book every girl of pluck should seek out. In the Boer War she returned to Africa as a nurse, but caught enteric fever and died.

Rudyard **KIPLING** (1865-1936)

To some he is the archetype of Jingoism and Empire, to others the author of *The Jungle Book* (1894) and *Just So Stories* (1902), while to others he is one of our finest writers of short stories. Edward Burne-Jones was his uncle by marriage and Stanley Baldwin his cousin but, more famously, the young Rudyard, after an idyllic early childhood in India, was sent with his sister to a day-school in England and placed in the far from tender care of the Holloways. Kipling called their

Southsea home 'The House of Desolation', and wrote of his experiences in *The Light That Failed* (1890) and a short story, 'Baa, Baa, Black Sheep'. (Kipling's schoolboy tales in *Stalky & Co*, 1899, relate to his later years in the United Services College.)

Education in Southsea was mainly in the hands of Mrs Pryse Agar Holloway who, through her distorted Calvinistic religious practices, took delight in harsh discipline, rote-learning and cruelty to children. She also allowed her own older son to bully young Rudyard. 'I had never heard of Hell, so I was introduced to it in all its terrors,' he wrote later. He and his young sister stayed with this family for five and a half years, at the end of which Rudyard had changed from an outward-going life-loving confident child to a cowering boy with weak eyesight. Then, at the age of eleven, in a scene straight out of Victorian domestic drama, he was rescued: his mother came to England to see her children and when, the first night, she went to his bedroom to kiss him goodnight, the boy instinctively raised an arm to ward off the customary blow. Only then did his mother realise what she and her husband had put them through, and the two children were swiftly removed to live with her.

Out of hardship can come strength, and it could be argued that one of Mrs Holloways's frequent impositions – enforced rote-learning from the Bible – equipped Kipling with both a thorough knowledge of it and, more usefully for a writer, and instinctive tendency towards a biblical turn of phrase. He even acknowledged (in his autobiographical *Something of Myself*, 1937) that his time with the Holloways helped shape his personality in ways that benefit an artist: 'It demanded constant wariness, the habit of observation, and attendance on moods and tempers.' For the rest of his life Kipling mourned the loss of his sunny childhood in India, and it was that country – often seen through the eyes of a child – that informed much of his most popular writing. Another legacy from that scarred childhood might be found in his adult character: he remained a secretive, wary man – paradoxically supportive of discipline and strong government. His adult precept might have come from one of his own poems, in which he advises:

Lock your heart with a double lock / And throw the key away.

From 1882-89 Kipling worked as a journalist in his beloved India, and his works from that time combine his respect for India with that for the servicemen he knew there. Books include *Departmental Ditties* (1886), *Plain*

Tales From The Hills (1888), *Soldiers Three* (1890) and the enormously popular *Barrack-Room Ballads* of 1892. (This is the book that includes 'Mandalay', 'Gunga Din', 'Tommy', etc.) He spent four years of married life in Vermont and, although he and his wife returned to England in 1896, they continued to travel widely, travels which took in South Africa and the Boer War. So popular were his books in his day, and his ballads especially, that he seemed an inevitable choice for Poet Laureate, but he refused that and other honours – although in 1907 he did become the first English writer to win the Nobel Prize.

The last year of Victoria's reign saw one of his best, perhaps his greatest book, *Kim*, which told of the adventures of the orphaned Kimball O'Hara, a child in India. But Kipling's reputation began to tarnish – in critical circles, if not with the populace – and his brazen enthusiasm for the Empire and the white man's rule began to pall. His poetry was seen as too simplistic and Victorian (though it continued to sell) and the critics ignored his 20th century children's books (*Puck of Pook's Hill*, 1906; *Rewards and Fairies*, 1910). For a hundred years since, Kipling has been regarded with suspicion and unease, but the books – both prose and poetry – remain colourful and passionate. His love and respect for India is less patronising than patriarchal, his pride in the Empire speaks of his day, and his understanding of, and his ability to articulate the common soldier has never been bettered.

> *When you're wounded and left on Afghanistan's plains,*
> *And the women come out to cut up what remains,*
> *Jest roll to your rifle and blow out your brains*
> *An' go to your Gawd like a soldier.*
>
> – the last verse of *The Young British Soldier*

Henry LABOUCHERE (1831-1911)

One of the most colourful Victorian journalists, Labouchere was also an independently minded Liberal MP (for Northampton, 1880-1906: his constituents recognised a good 'un). Following his education at Eton and Trinity, the Diplomatic Service was unwise enough to offer him a post in St Petersburg. They should have spotted their mistake when he stayed at home, claiming he couldn't afford the fare. Later they offered him a post in Argentina, which he said he would accept only if he could live in Germany.

He was dismissed. He then became Paris correspondent for the *Daily News* during the 1870 siege, from where his press pieces included a recipe for ragoût of cat. Back in London he founded the sensational paper *Truth* in 1876 and aimed it squarely at gossip and controversy, attacking the cost of the Royal Family, the waste of jingoistic wars, and the perquisites of privilege and politicians. 'It is the business of a newspaper,' he once declared, 'to create a sensation.' So he did.

'LEL' – Letitia Elizabeth **LANDON** (1802-38)

Though she died in the year Victoria was crowned, LEL was an archetypal Victorian writer, the epitome of acceptable good taste: anodyne, unchallenging and perfectly suitable for well brought up young ladies. Her novels range from her first, *The Fate of Adelaide* (1821) through to *Duty and Inclination* (1838) with *Ethel Churchill* (1837) as her best. Her poems (collected later in 1850 and 1873) appeared in numerous polite periodicals, and for several years an annual selection appeared, decorated with full-page line engravings, as *The Drawing Room Scrap-Book*. Typical were the first four lines to '*The Snowdrop*':

> *Thou beautiful new-comer,*
> *With white and maiden brow;*
> *Thou fairy gift from summer,*
> *Why art thou blooming now?*

Her private life was less sedate: while unmarried she supported herself through writing, and was rumoured to have had affairs with the Irish writer William Maginn and the aristocratic Bulwer Lytton. These rumours killed her engagement to John Forster (biographer of Dickens) and when she finally did marry she travelled with her husband (George Maclean) to West Africa where, in circumstances never explained, she swallowed prussic acid and died.

William Savage **LANDOR** (1775-1864)

The best parts of his life were over by the time Victoria came to the throne: he had been sent down from Oxford, had volunteered for Spain against the French, had published most of his poetry, had had a work attacking Fox suppressed, had emigrated and lived in Italy for 20 years, had separated from his wife, and had become increasingly interested in classical literature.

His commentaries on the classics and contemporary authors were published from his return to Britain (1835) until his death. Titles include *The Hellenics* (1847) and *Imaginary Conversations of Greeks and Romans* (1853). In 1858 Landor, always an angry, intemperate man, was accused of libel and fled back to Italy, where he was cared for by Robert Browning.

Edward William LANE (1801-76)

Remembered mainly for his respectable translation of *The Thousand and One Nights* (1838-40) – a version traduced by Burton as 'garbled and mutilated, unsexed and unsouled' – Lane was a knowledgeable scholar of Arabic and Egyptian ways, old and new. He produced *Selections from the Kur-an* (sic) in 1843 and was working on an Arabic Lexicon when he died.

Andrew LANG (1844-1912)

If Lang had joined the immortals on whom he wrote, he would look down with surprise and sadness upon his legacy – for he is now known mainly as the compiler of *The Blue Fairy Book* (1889) and its 11 successors in other colours, still in print. Yet he was a serious scholar and prolific writer. A Scot who settled in London in 1875, his output included poems, essays, reviews, criticisms, plays, biographies and novels, few as light-hearted as his *Fairy Books*. (These, incidentally, were co-written with his wife Leonora and, it is said, a bevy of her friends, to increase their popular acceptability.) *Ballads and Lyrics of Old France* appeared in 1872, *Ballades in Blue China* in 1880, *Helen of Troy* in 1882, *Grass of Parnassus* in 1888, along with biographies and anthropological works such as *Custom and Myth* (1884), *Myth, Ritual and Religion* (1887, with a much updated edition in 1899) and *The Making of Religion* in 1898. He was a co-translator of *The Odyssey* (1879) and *The Iliad* (1883) and wrote several novels no longer worth tracking down. His version of *Arabian Nights' Entertainments* (1898) was, like the *Fairy Books*, firmly edited (some would say emasculated) by his wife, though his *Nursery Rhyme Book* (1897) remains one of the best of the Victorian era.

Edward LEAR (1812-88)

His many friends would have echoed his own wry words, 'How pleasant to know Mr Lear', yet he considered himself a depressive; his epilepsy made him solitary and shy; and he was a restless and inveterate traveller. He was also, as one wants to believe from his limericks, delightful company. And, of course, hugely talented – a prolific and superb artist, possibly the finest topographical artist of his day. He was the twentieth of a stockbroker's twenty-one children and, in an unsettled childhood, was brought up by his grown-up sister Ann. His artistic ability – and his love of nature – was soon evident, and at the age of nineteen he published his *Illustrations of the Family of Psittacidae, or Parrots* (the or Parrots, one feels, is a typical Lear touch) and John Gould's magnificent *Birds of Europe* (published from 1832 to 37) contains many Lear paintings. Lear's work earned him the sponsorship of Lord Stanley and it was for Stanley's grandchildren in 1846 that Lear produced *The Book of Nonsense* with its limericks and quirky illustrations. The book was largely unnoticed. By then he had turned from animal painting to landscape and in that same year, 1846, he published a travel book, *Illustrated Excursions in Italy* – a book noticed by the Queen, who asked him to Osborne House to give her drawing lessons.

But London high-life was not for Lear, and he set off on his travels – through Europe, Arabia and eventually to India and Ceylon. He was still epileptic, and frequently unwell. On his travels he wrote more travel books, and a copious amount of letters to his friends. An enlarged edition of *The Book of Nonsense* was issued by Routledge in 1871 (who bought the copyright outright for a mere £125) and in 1871 his *Nonsense Songs, Stories, Botany and Alphabets* was published, containing 'The Owl and the Pussy-Cat' and 'The Jumblies' etc. He had settled in San Remo, but by now his sight was failing and his final years were sad. Two more Nonsense books were published (plus other compilations after his death). His travel books include works on *Sicily* (1847), *Albania* (1851), *Calabria* (1852), *Corsica* (1870) and his *Italian Journal* of 1873-5.

W E H **LECKY** (1838-1903)

William Edward Hartpole Lecky was born and educated in Dublin and had to wait till his third book for real success – though it came when he was still young and full of spirit. The title of his *History of the Rise and Influence of Rationalism in Europe* (1865) was enough to split potential readers into opposing camps. Predating **Frazer's** *Golden Bough* (1890) Lecky's book traces the change in belief from early magic and witchcraft through into religious dogma and on into contemporary rationalism. This and his later histories include philosophical and theosophical commentary, supporting argument and investigation against dogma and intolerance, and show how the less dogmatic a society is the more it can make progress. Mankind, he notices with wry amusement, does not reason itself out of wrong beliefs but simply finds it no longer holds them. He notes also the role of accident and the way events can be changed by seemingly irrelevant or minor people or events (a famous example is his discussion on the length of Cleopatra's nose). Other worthwhile books include his *History of European Morals from Augustus to Charlemagne* (1869) and his magnificent *History of England in the Eighteenth Century* published in stages from 1878 to 92. From 1895 he was MP for Dublin University where, with typical perversity, he opposed Irish Home Rule.

Vernon **LEE** pseudonym of Violet Paget (1856-1935)
A much thought-of intellectual essayist of her time whose works seem less interesting today, and whose first novel, *Miss Brown* (1884) was unwisely dedicated to Henry James – who hated it and may have re-used its theme (of an ingénue actress taken up and 'improved' by a clever man), along with that of Mrs Ward's *Miss Bretherton*, as the basis for his own *The Tragic Muse* (1889-90). Much of Lee's writing was on art, literature and Italy. (See also Amy Levy.)

Sheridan **LE FANU** (1814-73)
Though he began as a successful journalist and minor novelist, it was as a writer of tales of mystery and the supernatural that the Irish Le Fanu found his fame. Early novels (properly forgotten) include *The Cock and Anchor* (1845) and *Torlogh O'Brien* (1847), and his journalistic work of the '40s and '50s has largely disappeared, but in the 1860s Le Fanu found his metier, from what may have seemed an unimpressive start – for when *The House by the Churchyard* was serialised in 1861 it was in the *Dublin University Magazine* which Le Fanu owned. The tale was enthusiastically

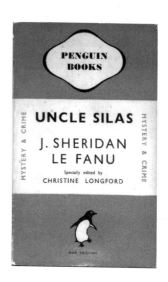

received. *Wylder's Hand* followed in 1864, along with his classic and very readable *Uncle Silas* that same year. For the next two decades Le Fanu continued to sell in large numbers, until his popularity waned. Other than *Uncle Silas* the best of his books was *In a Glass Darkly* (1872), a collection of five short stories which introduced *Carmilla*, the female vampire, who manifested herself, you will notice, some 25 years before *Dracula*.

Richard **LE GALLIENNE** (1866-1947)

Though a poet, journalist and novelist, it is as a chronicler of his age that Le Gallienne serves best. He was born in Liverpool of Channel Islands descent (hence his name) and his first book, *My Ladies' Sonnets and Other 'Vain and Amatorious' Verses* (an awful title) was printed privately in Liverpool in 1887. The following year he moved to London, where he met and mingled with the fin de siècle group around Beardsley and the Decadents. He contributed to the *Yellow Book*, wrote some novels (*Young Lives*, 1889, describes London well), married thrice, and in 1926 summed up his era in *The Romantic '90s*.

Mark **LEMON** (1809-70)

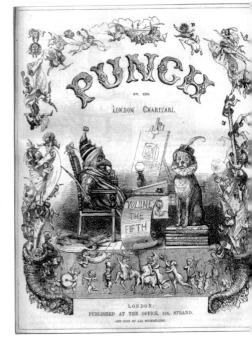

The first joint-editor of *Punch*, a magazine he founded with Henry Mayhew, subsidised through its early years and edited till his death. He helped found *The Field* also. Very much a working journalist, he contributed to other magazines, wrote many pieces for the theatre, produced five novels and some collections of short stories, and was a friend and colleague of most in literary London. (In 1851 he co-wrote a farce with Charles Dickens, *Mr Nightingale's Diary*, in which they both acted.)

In a short poem looking back on his life in 1870, he wrote:

Round about the world we went;
Ne'er were such free lances
Victors, in each tournament
Winning beauty's glances.

William **LENNOX** (1799-1881)

Lord William Pitt Lennox (godson of William Pitt) wrote some 13 novels in the 1840s through 1860s that, although fashionable in their time, seem feeble now (and are practically unlocatable) but he did leave a useful legacy in his *Celebrities I Have Known*, his surprisingly lively memoirs published in three volumes in 1857, two more volumes in 1863 and a final four volumes in 1877. Packed with anecdote, they include the tale of his having been baptised not from a font but from a dog's drinking bowl. His mother threw the famous 'Eve of Battle Ball at Waterloo', celebrated in *Vanity Fair*, in Byron's *Childe Harold*, and in Lever's *Charles O'Malley*. Lennox was at the ball but missed the battle, having previously fallen from his horse.

Charles **LEVER** (1806-72)

Famed in his time for his *Confessions of Harry Lorrequer* (1837) which he called 'a notebook of absurd and laughable incidents', Lever was a better writer than that book suggests. *Charles O'Malley, the Irish Dragoon* (1841) is less well-known but better. Lever's stories are crammed with drink and scuffles, drink and women, riding and duelling – just the stuff for the desk-bound Victorian male confined indoors. The books usually began as magazine serials, though one of them, *A Day's Ride* (in *All The Year Round* in 1863) was such a flop that Dickens had to replace it with the hastily-done *Great Expectations*. Lever's early successes helped gain him the editorship of the *Dublin University Magazine* but he couldn't stick it and before long was off around Europe, gathering material on the way for novels such as *Con Cregan* (1849) and *Maurice Tiernay* (1852). Later books, like *Lord Kilgobbin* (1872) are quieter.

Amy **LEVY** (1861-89)

A short life and a precocious talent. Her teenage writing included a review of Elizabeth Barrett Browning's *Aurora Leigh* and at seventeen, in full flood of feminism, *Xantippe*, in which she let Socrates's maligned wife tell her side of their marriage. This poem was reissued in 1881 in *Xantippe and other Verse*. Levy's Jewishness was important to her, though she doesn't appear to have had much religious faith; she was the first Jewish woman to attend Newnham College at Cambridge, and some of her writings at that time, notably her story *Leopold Leuniger: a Study* (1880), attack anti-Jewish prejudice. Other pieces, both published and private, show a young woman's fascination with suicide.

She was active among women writers sidelined in a male world: she was one of the first to demand access to the British Museum's Reading Room; she campaigned to improve woman's lot; and in *A Minor Poet and other Verse* she made little attempt to hide her lesbianism (several poems were about her love for another woman). In 1886 she fell in love with the writer Vernon **Lee** (real name Violet Paget), with whom she remained close for the rest of her short life, and she continued to produce good and, within intellectual circles, well-regarded writing. Her novel *Romance of a Shop* appeared in 1888 but its successor *Reuben Sachs* (also 1888) offended Jewish critics, who thought it attacked the Jewish lifestyle, and gentile critics, who thought it stereotypically Jewish. Levy was disheartened by the strength of criticism (which with modern hindsight is seen as unjustified) and poured much of her angst into her third novel *Miss Meredith* which she completed in just six weeks. The story has an obvious autobiographical basis in its telling of a writer (disguised, in that he is gentile) whose book is unacceptable to the dominant culture. After her last book of poetry, *A London Plane-Tree and other Verse*, she became increasingly depressed – and hypochondriacal – and committed suicide in September 1889 by asphyxiating herself with charcoal fumes. In a final tiny act of trail-blazing she became the first Jewish woman in England to be cremated.

George Henry **LEWES** (1817-78)

A gifted professional writer, Lewes is remembered as the long-term partner of 'George **Eliot**' (Marian Evans). In 1851, when they met, he was the more established: a dramatist, essayist, historian, biographer and editor of the *Fortnightly Review*. They did not live together until 1854: Lewes was married but his wife, who had run off with the writer Thornton Leigh Hunt, refused to grant Lewes a divorce. Lewes and Miss Evans lived

together openly as 'man and wife' until his death, a situation accepted by most in literary circles, though by some more hesitantly than by others. (Lewes was not only a respected writer he was, as editor, an influential man.) Almost certainly, he influenced George Eliot's work. But his own work should not be overlooked: two novels (*Ranthorpe*, 1847 and *Rose, Blanche and Violet*, 1848); a *Life of Robespierre* (1849); of *Goethe* (perhaps his finest book, 1855) and, among several theatrical appreciations, *Actors and the Art of Acting* in 1875. He wrote several books on philosophers and philosophy, together some biological studies.

Sir George Cornewall **LEWIS** (1806-63)

'A methodical, pigeon-holing man, who begins with the alphabet, defines and sub-defines without mercy, multiplies polyglot illustrations, and plods surely towards conclusions of unmistakeable value.'
  – Lewis assessed by Oliver Elton in his *Survey of English Literature*

A dry historian, but with occasional flashes of dry humour, he became a barrister in 1831 and showed a strong inclination towards politics. Interested also in dialect and the use of language, he published his splendidly titled *Remarks on the Use and Abuse of some Political Terms* in 1832. In 1833 he became a Commissioner in the Enquiry into the Poor of Ireland and, as a result, in 1836 produced his *Local Disturbances in Ireland*, and the *Irish Church Question*. He was made a baronet in 1846. In 1849 he wrote what may be his most enduring work, his *Essay on the Influence of Authority in Matters of Opinion* (saying that neither the church nor state should attempt to control intellectual conviction). His political career suffered a setback in the 1850s when Lord Russell resigned, and from 1852-5 he served as editor of the *Edinburgh Review*, publishing in 1855 his incisive *Enquiry into the Credibility of the Early Roman History*. Once back in Parliament he was immediately made Chancellor and four years later became Home Secretary (both positions under Palmerston). From 1861 he headed the War Office (in which role he helped keep Britain out of the American Civil War) but found time nevertheless to write a *Socratic Dialogue on the Best Form of Government* in 1863 (concluding that there is no best form; all are relative). A statue of Cornewall Lewis can be seen outside the Hereford Shirehall, his bust is at Westminster Abbey, and another monument is in New Radnor, Powys. Had he lived longer, wrote the historian J P Parry, he would have led the Liberal Party in the place of William Gladstone.

Eliza Lynn **LINTON** (1822–89)

By no means all successful women were feminists. Miss Lynn, as she then was, daughter of a Keswick clergyman, set out in her early twenties to earn her living from writing: *Azeth the Egyptian* appeared in 1846. She wrote regularly for *All The Year Round*, *The Saturday Review* and was a staff member for *The Morning Chronicle*. Her next two novels failed, as did her brief marriage to the engraver William Linton, but her later novels succeeded. They included *The True History of Joshua Davidson* (1872), *Patricia Kenball* (1874) and *Rebel of the Family* (1880). Despite her success she was an anti-feminist, as her collection of *Saturday Review* articles in *The Girl of the Period* (1883) made clear. Her last work was a strident posthumous memoir, *My Literary Life* (1899), which contained a famous attack upon George Eliot.

David **LIVINGSTONE** (1813–73)

The Scottish missionary and explorer has become most famous for having been 'found' by Stanley and greeted with the words, 'Doctor Livingstone, I presume?' Yet he had spent some 30 years exploring Africa for the London Missionary Society, producing books on South Africa, the Zambesi and its tributaries and the lakes of Shirwa and Nyassa. (In these later journeys his wife accompanied him, but she died there of malaria.) In 1871 he was feared lost during his search for the source of the Nile (that eternal Victorian quest; he had set out to look for it in 1866) and was almost dead when rescued by Stanley in Ujiji. (Livingstone later denied he'd needed rescuing.) His final book, *Last Journals*, was published posthumously in 1874, and he was given a national funeral in Westminster Abbey. He died as he would have wished, exploring what is now called Zambia.

Robert **LYTTON** (1831-91)

The son of Edward **Bulwer-Lytton**, and confusingly similar in name, Edward Robert Bulwer Lytton (note the missing hyphen) sheltered at Harrow (and later, in Bonn) from his parents' acrimonious separation before slipping away into the diplomatic service, where he became Viceroy of India from 1876 to 80. He found time to publish some books of verse in the 1850s (under the name 'Owen Meredith') and a later work, *Chronicles and Characters* (1868) which contained a poem he titled ironically: 'Last Words of a Sensitive Second-Rate Poet'. The title invited ridicule. A later work occupied him for many years: *King Poppy* was privately printed in 1875 under his own name, and properly published in an extended version in 1892. It was an obscure and rambling allegory. 'His style,' wrote Oliver Elton, 'may be too diffuse for a long poem, and too little assured for a very short one.'

Thomas Babington **MACAULAY** (1800-59)

Many thought him the pre-eminent historian of his day. He began in the legal profession, but attracted notice with his 1825 essay on Milton, the first of many – on many subjects – for the *Edinburgh Review*. He became a Whig MP in 1830 (for Calne in Wiltshire, then for Leeds), was a strong proponent for Reform, and in 1834 secured a post on the Supreme Council of India, where he instituted major reforms in education. After four years there he returned to begin his most famous work, a *History of England*, commencing with the 1688 revolution and designed to continue to 1830 (the death of George IV). The book was eventually published in four volumes, two in 1849 and a second two in 1855 (with a posthumous volume in 1861). By then he was already famous, having been Secretary at War, Paymaster General and author of *Lays of Ancient Rome* (another great success, 1842) and a sturdy collection of *Essays Critical and Historical*

(1843). Macaulay's literary style was – and still is – much admired, both for its clarity (reminiscent of the best 18th century prose) and for its confident 'positivism', its belief that progress was continual and for the best, and that it was exemplified by Britain and British history. His great account of that history – a history which has never gone out of print – was a greater labour than he anticipated: when he died he had covered only the years 1688 to almost 1700. Yet within that short period his scope encompassed much that appealed to Victorian readers, on the British constitution, its Crown and Parliament, the British character and the eminence of Britain in the world.

> *Thus our democracy was, from an early period, the most aristocratic, and our aristocracy the most democratic in the world.*
>
> from his *History of England*

George **MACDONALD** (1824-1905)

MacDonald's individual take on magic and religion is obvious from his writings; less obvious is that he was, for a short while, a minister too individualistic for his church (to him, heathens were not necessarily doomed). He turned to writing and became one of the foremost novelists of his time – especially for children (he had eleven). His first book was a long dramatic poem on marriage and misunderstanding: *Within and Without* (1855) which was well received. The adult novels, often with Scottish settings and prominent in what was derided as the 'Kailyard school' of writing, were decent enough but of little interest now: they include *David Elginbrod* (1863 and very popular in its day) and *Robert Falconer* (1868, perhaps the best of these), along with two extraordinary adult fantasies, the early *Phantastes* (1858, reissued at the turn of the century with Arthur Hughes illustrations) and *Lilith* (1895).

His children's books are a different matter, and must be rated among the most important of the Victorian age. The great ones are the allegorical fairy stories, *At The Back of the North Wind* (1871), *The Princess and the Goblin*

(1872) and *The Princess and Curdie* (1883), all three of which can be found in editions hauntingly illustrated by Arthur Hughes. *Dealings With the Fairies* (1867) is a fine collection of tales, also illustrated by Hughes. *Ranald Bannerman's Boyhood* (1871) and *Gutta Percha Willie* (1873) stand out among his other children's books. MacDonald remains one of the more 'collected' children's writers.

William McGONAGALL (1830-1902)

Britain's most derided poet displayed his appalling wares in *Poetic Gems* (1890), a volume which contains many unintentionally hilarious odes including his famous 'The Tay Bridge Disaster'. Born in Edinburgh, the son of an Irish weaver based in Dundee and, for a while, a weaver himself, he let his ambition carry him back to Edinburgh where he read his verses in public houses and sold them in broadsheet form.

> *I must now conclude my lay*
> *By telling the world fearlessly without the least dismay,*
> *That your central girders would not have given way,*
> *At least many sensible men do say,*
> *Had they been supported on each side with buttresses,*
> *At least many sensible men confesses,*
> *For the stronger we our houses do build,*
> *The less chance we have of being killed.*

Wise words from his *The Tay Bridge Disaster.*

Arthur MACHEN (1863-1947)

Welsh occultist, cataloguer of diabolistic books and keen member of Cabbalistic societies such as 'The Order of the Golden Dawn' (Aleister Crowley and Yeats were fellow members), his books include translations of *The Heptameron* (1886) and *Memoirs of Casanova* (1894), along with original works such as *The Great God Pan* (1894), *The Three Imposters* (1895) and others in the 20th century. One of his 20th century stories ('*The Bowmen*') inspired the First World War legend of The Angel of Mons.

Fiona MACLEOD (see William Sharp)

Lucas **MALET** (1852-1931)

This was the pseudonym of Mary St Leger Harrison, nee Mary Kingsley (daughter of Charles), whose 12 novels, including *The Wages of Sin* (1891) and *The History of Sir Richard Calmady* (1901) were popular in their day.

Captain **MARRYAT** (1792-1848)

Frederick Marryat, though he was to become hugely popular in his day, wrote like writers of the previous century – vigorously, roughly, unambiguously. Marryat's men were men. He had been a sailor – indeed, had run away to sea – and he wrote about the navy that he knew, not flinching from its floggings and boozing, its hard battles, its cruel punishments and sometimes equally cruel practical jokes. The books came after he had left the service: *Frank Mildmay* came first, in 1829, followed by several others until *Mr Midshipman Easy* in 1836, then two more adult books before *Masterman Ready* (1841) established him as a boys' writer. The plots are unexceptional, but the dialogue is lively and the action full of spirit.

Philip Bourke **MARSTON** (1850-87)

As a poet, how could he not be melancholy? Blind from childhood, he attended the funerals of his beloved sister, his dear fiancée and his best friend (Oliver Madox Brown, son of the painter). Between 1871 and 87 he produced four sad books of poems: *Song-Tide*, *All in All*, *Wind-Voices*, and *Garden Secrets*. Two more appeared posthumously.

Harriet **MARTINEAU** (1802-76)

Victorians would be amazed (some would be relieved) at the extent to which Miss Martineau's reputation has receded. In her day she was one of the foremost woman thinkers, considered – then – an intellectual feminist, while today she is seen as little more than a frequently recurring footnote to other people's biographies. Then she was shocking; now she can seem dull. She was born in Norwich, daughter to a man who made and sold army cloth, and whose business wore out after the Napoleonic War. Never a well woman, her plight worsened when at the age of nineteen she became deaf. Thereafter she cut a striking figure with her ear-trumpet.

In that year (1823) her *Devotional Exercises* was published, a book which, together with an 1826 follow-up, espoused the Unitarianism of her youth (a faith she would later forsake). Her brother James, three years younger, advised her to 'leave it to other women to make shirts and darn stockings,' and she began earning money from reviews. In 1832 she had an unlikely success with a series of 24 didactic stories, combined under the forbidding title *Illustrations of Political Economy* and issued as 25 'improving tracts' in monthly 'parts' (one was a summary) each comprising 125 small pages and selling at one and sixpence. Her grave pen produced *Poor Law and Paupers Illustrated* in 1833 and *Illustrations of Taxation* in 1834. By the time the *Political Economy* series ended (1834) she had become a literary celebrity and was able to travel to America in support of the abolitionists. From this hazardous trip came her commercially successful *Society in America* (1837) and *Retrospective of Western Travel* (1838). Her first novel, *Deerbrook*, appeared in 1839.

As her career progressed in the 1840s she lost her religious faith, and shared her new beliefs with readers in *Laws of Man's Social Nature* in 1851. (A radical *History of the Thirty Years' Peace* preceded it in 1849, and an admired *Philosophy of Comte* came in 1853.) Through all this time she remained unwell. By the mid-40s she had, to the bemusement of her friends, become a near convert to the healing powers of Mesmerism, and had retreated from noxious London to the healthier climes of Tynemouth and Ambleside. Her reputation was sufficient to draw many of the leading figures of the day (and some lesser ones) to her home at Knoll where, if they were lucky, they could shout to her down her ear-trumpet.

She continued to promote her own qualified version of feminism, her scientific and political theories, her opposition to slavery and her militant agnosticism. She refused a Civil List pension, fearing it would compromise her independence, and she worked on an *Autobiographical Memoir* which was published in the year after her death. It remains a useful commentary on the personalities of her day.

Henry **MAYHEW** (1812-87)

Mayhew's most famous book (never since out of print, in one version or another) is *Mayhew's London*, a book he himself never issued under that name but which, in its various versions, has been compiled from his extensive social surveys, *London Labour and the London Poor* (1851), *The*

Criminal Prisons of London (1862) and *London Children* (1874). The books themselves were compiled by Mayhew from his numerous journalistic exposés, mainly in the *Morning Chronicle*. He was foremost a journalist; his various novels and pieces for the theatre have barely survived. In 1841 he helped found *Punch* (briefly he was joint editor).

L T **MEADE** (1854–1914)
Pseudonym of Elizabeth ('Lizzie') Thomasina Meade
Prolific author, mainly of girls' stories and crime novels, though she could turn her hand to fiction of many kinds. From her reputed total of some 300 books one might choose the campaigning *Great St Benedict's* (1876), *A World of Girls* (1886), or *The Sorceress of the Strand* (1903) – or, indeed any you can find in the pulp pile. Her vast output encouraged her to collaborate – with Robert Eustace on science fiction novels and 'Clifford Halifax' (actually Edgar Beaumont) on crime stories.

George **MEREDITH** (1828–1909)

Kissing don't last: cookery do!

If only all Meredith's utterances could have been as succinct as that from *Richard Feverel*. Then could his sales have matched his reputation, then could the keen middlebrow reader have enjoyed his splendid books. For they are splendid, encrusted with splendour, ornate, bejewelled and weighted down – heavy, intricate and gorgeous. Meredith was a poet, and the poet's love of sonority suffused and drenched his later fiction. He began as a poet: 'Chillianwallah', a battle poem, appearing in *Chambers's Journal* in 1849, the year he married Mary Ellen, the widowed daughter of the humorous writer Thomas Love Peacock. Meredith funded his first book, *Poems* in 1851, a book praised by Tennyson and Kingsley but disparaged by its author. His oriental fantasy, *The Shaving of Shagpat* (1856) was clever and amusing but did not sell. What else could he do wrong?

He sat, in 1856, as model for one of the century's most beautiful paintings: *The Death of Chatterton* by Henry Wallis. Meredith posed as the delicate and lovely young poet Chatterton, a suicide beneath an attic window. The following year his wife ran off with Mr Wallis.

I expect that Woman will be the last thing civilised by Man

he wrote, in *The Ordeal of Richard Feverel*

In 1859 Meredith's first great novel, *The Ordeal of Richard Feverel*, appeared, shocking many of its (initially) few readers with its subplots of adultery, child abandonment and, worst of all, benevolent prostitution. Critics admired it; Mudie's Library refused to take it. Meredith continued to scrape a living with contributions to the *Fortnightly Review* etc., in which his next novel, *Evan Harrington*, was serialised in 1860. (It was published in 1861.) Something like a secure income came from his then being employed by Chapman and Hall, with whom he remained a reader until 1894. His much-praised book of poems, *Modern Love and Poems of the Roadside*, came out in 1862, and in 1864 he remarried. Four novels later came the first of his books to achieve reasonable sales: *The Adventures of Harry Richmond* (1871, by no means his finest work). *Beauchamp's Career* came in 1876, followed by the acclaimed *The Egoist* in 1879.

But commercial success eluded him. His 1883 volume, *Poems and Lyrics of the Joy of Earth*, contains some of his finest verse, and only in 1885, with

Diana of the Crossways (a tender tale, but rather too close to the real-life story of Caroline **Norton**'s failed divorce) did one of his books run to three editions. Nothing later would sell as well. His reputation grew; his sales did not. Was the public wrong? As he grew older – and more deaf – his books became increasingly dense and convoluted; he would not compromise on his style. He was admired by fellow writers, awarded the Order of Merit, became president of the Society of Authors, but the public refused to love him. Nor, to be honest, have they loved him since.

As Oliver Elton said: 'The public was outstripped by the reach and novelty of his vision, and still more by his swift strange pen.'

Owen **MEREDITH** (see Robert Lytton)

Alice **MEYNELL** (1847-1922)
Much respected in her day for her volumes of religious verse (she was Roman Catholic, not an advantage at the time) and well-liked in literary circles, it is for her essays and prose that she is valued now. Volumes of poetry include *Poems* (1893) and *Later Poems* (1902). Essays and criticisms were gathered in *The Rhythm of Life* (1893), *The Colour of Life* (1896) and *The Spirit of Place* (1899). Many of her essays had first appeared in the *Pall Mall Gazette*, the *Tablet* and the *National Observer* as well as in *Merry England*, a periodical she helped found with her husband Wilfred in 1883. Yet her poetry bears re-reading:

> *The Lady Poverty was fair:*
> *But she has lost her looks of late,*
> *With change of times and change of air.*
> *Ah slattern, she neglects her hair,*
> *Her gown, her shoes. She keeps no state*
> *As once when her pure feet were bare.*

from *The Lady Poverty*

John Stuart **MILL** (1806-73)
One of the most influential thinkers of his day, though he himself was much influenced by others, he underwent a famous reversal in his views when he recanted his early espousal of Benthamite philosophy. Those early views were inculcated in part by his strict father James, who started him in Greek at the age of three, in Latin and political economy at eight, and who encouraged him to form the Utilitarian Society in 1823. In 1825 Mill edited *Bentham's Treatise Upon Evidence*. But in 1826 Mill suffered a form of mental breakdown, during which he swung from Utilitarianism to a more romantic view (Wordsworth and Coleridge were now his influences).

In 1836 he met the next great influence on his life, Harriet Taylor, a highly intelligent and gifted woman with views very different from James Mill or Jeremy Bentham. Unfortunately she was married. Not until her

husband died in 1849 could she and John marry, two years later. In the interim she helped him with works for which he remains famous: his *System of Logic* (1843) and *Principles of Political Economy* (1848). Some say she should be listed as co-author of these works. Undoubtedly, and as Mill always acknowledged, she was an active contributor to both his thought and writing. But in 1858 she died suddenly. Like him, she was consumptive and, after a carriage accident in 1842, Harriet's back injury had left her virtually unable to walk. He grieved her mightily. Perhaps he poured his energies into his work, for in 1859 he produced his famous essay on *Liberty* (1859) and two volumes of *Dissertations and Discussions*. Harriet's hand has been detected in these pieces.

Weighty works continued: *Thoughts on Parliamentary Reform* completed that crowded year, followed by *Representative Government* (1861), *Auguste Comte and Positivism* (1865). Then came one of his most famous works, *The Subjection of Women* in 1869. An *Autobiography* appeared in 1873. He has always been regarded as one of the great political theorists (not just of the 19th century), though he was an MP himself for only a brief period (1865-8) and was rejected for re-election. More than half of his life (35 years) was spent in the service of the East India Company. Influence again: his father's influence won him the job. This cannot detract from the huge influence Mill himself has had on political thought since his day. As Roger Ellis wrote: 'Wherever there is injustice or oppression it is still to Mill that people turn for the most rational, often the most eloquent of arguments for freedom, toleration, and the decencies of public life.'

Hugh MILLER (1802-56)

Evangelical stonemason turned poet and later journalist, he moved from his *Poems Written in the Leisure Hours of a Journeyman Mason* (1829) to palaeontological and religious writing. Editor of the *Witness* from 1840, author of a fine *The Old Red Sandstone* (1841) and his autobiographical *My*

Schools and Schoolmasters (1854), he was determined enough to attack the redoubtable evolutionary classic *Vestiges of Creation* (Chambers, 1844) with his own creationalist *The Footprints of the Creator* (1849). After recording in his diary 'a fearful dream' he shot himself on Christmas Eve 1856, thus perhaps destroying his chances of meeting with his God.

Richard Monckton **MILNES** (1809–85)

Less famed for his literary output than for his literary friends (he knew everybody and was wealthy enough to have everyone who mattered call at his house; his breakfasts were legendary) and famed also for his fine collection of pornography, Milnes (aka Lord Houghton) published several books of verse: *The Brookside* (1830), *Past Friendship* (1844), his best-known *Strangers Yet* (1865), and some appreciations of other poets.

Mary Russell **MITFORD** (1787–1855)

Remembered – and mainly known at the time – as author of the delightfully undemanding collection of sketches of rural life, *Our Village* (1832), she also wrote *Belford Regis: Sketches of a Country Town* (1835, which unlikely as it sounds was a portrait of Reading); *Country Stories* (1837); a novelised rural collection, *Atherton, and Other Tales* (1854); *Recollections of a Literary Life* (1852) and, before all these, some stage dramas, successful at the time but no longer staged. She was a copious letter-writer and, in her youth, something of a poet. One would not guess from her pleasant writings that it was her father's gambling debts that pushed her into writing for money.

Mrs **MOLESWORTH** (1839–1921)

One of the most prolific Victorian children's writers, Mary Louisa Molesworth benefited from having some of her books illustrated by Walter Crane and by the decision of her publishers, Macmillan, to issue a Molesworth book each Christmas. From many titles one might select her first collection, *Tell Me A Story* (1875); her first full-length children's novel, *Carrots* (1876); her most popular, *The Cuckoo Clock* (1877); the mawkish *A Christmas Child* (1880); *Two Little Waifs* (1883) or any of the prettily illustrated volumes. She wrote a few less successful adult novels (under the pseudonym 'Ennis Graham') in which could be detected traces from her real-life unhappy marriage to Major Richard Molesworth, a Crimea veteran whose head wound had left him with 'a very violent temper'.

George **MOORE** (1852-1933)
One of the self-created bad boys of the Victorian literary scene, the Anglo-Irish Moore used his father's racing stables as background to his most successful novel, *Esther Waters* (1894) but preferred to base himself in London and to import progressive European ideas into his books. (He had studied painting in Paris for several years.) Two volumes of poems (*Flowers of Passion*, 1878, and *Pagan Poems*, 1881) preceded his more important work, and his first novel, *A Modern Lover* (1883), laid out his true manifesto: a racy tale set in bohemian circles, telling of a 'nice girl' who posed nude, it was immediately banned by circulating libraries. His second novel, *A Mummer's Wife* (1885), told of an actor's wife ruined by drink, and was also banned by Mudie's. In ensuing titles Moore maintained his progressive challenge while gossiping, contributing to journals and making himself well known. His supposedly autobiographical *Confessions of a Young Man* appeared in 1888 and, while being a good read, did nothing to clean up his image. Two later volumes of autobiography in the 20th century were even less reliable.

They cannot detract from *Esther Waters* (1894), one of the century's most beautifully told tales of seduction: a religious girl (Esther), seduced by a footman, sacrifices much for her illegitimate son. 'One doesn't do the good that one would like to do in the world,' she says. 'One has to do the good that comes to one to do.' His critical work, *Modern Painting* (1893), was well received in advanced circles but, in 1899 in protest against the Boer War, he returned for a decade to his native Ireland and involved himself in the Celtic revival there. From 1911 until his death he lived in London's Victoria, in Ebury Street: hence the name of the collected edition of Moore, the Ebury Edition.

William **MORRIS** (1834-96)

Say the name William Morris today and it will conjure different images to different people. To some he was a craftsman/artist, to others he was part of the Pre-Raphaelite/Arts and Crafts Movement, to a few he was a campaigning socialist, to yet more he designed trendy wallpaper. Here we will look mainly at his literary work – though it all stemmed from his first meeting Burne-Jones at Oxford and his being drawn into the Pre-Raphaelite circle. It was with Rossetti and Burne-Jones that Morris moved into design, and it was at Oxford that he met his future bride, Jane Burden, with whom Rossetti later had a long affair.

Morris published his first verse collection, *The Defence of Guenevere and Other Poems* in 1858 and his second, *Poems By The Way* much later in 1891. In between he achieved public success with a poem in heroic couplets, *The Life and Death of Jason* (1867) and an epic poem, *The Earthly Paradise* between 1868 and 70, hugely popular in its day. He made some classical translations before taking himself away from his agonising marital problems on a trek to Iceland, a country with which he became fixated. Out of these journeys came a partly therapeutic but surprisingly successful *Sigurd the Volsung and the Fall of the Niblungs* in 1876. This unhappy period also sparked a less successful novel, *The Novel on Blue Paper* (written in 1872, published 110 years later). The 1880s saw him increasingly involved in radical politics; he leafleted, spoke in public, and wrote major political pieces such as *A Dream of John Ball* (1886-7) and *News From Nowhere* (1890).

Though Burne-Jones, Rossetti, Ford Madox Brown and Philip Webb were all board members of his design company (Morris, Marshall, Faulkner & Co., founded in 1861) Morris was, in every sense, its driving force. Most of the seemingly immortal designs were his alone. His Kelmscott Press produced, in limited editions, some of the most ornately beautiful books of the 19th century, notably the 'Kelmscott Chaucer'. He continued writing (cramming it into all his other activities) and in his last few years produced several more books, each published by the Kelmscott Press, of which the most important may be *The Well at the World's End* (1896). (I say 'may be' because his writings, unlike his fabric designs, have not survived the test of time; revered in their day, they now seem mannered and unconvincingly archaic.) His last completed work was *The Sundering Flood*, published in 1898. Never a fit man, he worked frantically, some would say manically, until he died. The cause of death, according to one doctor, was simply 'being William Morris'.

Arthur **MORRISON** (1863-1945)

A curiously neglected writer. Born in Poplar, he set most of his stories in the East End. He had been clerk there to the trustees of the magnificent People's Palace (for the improvement of working people) and he sub-edited the *Palace Journal*. Another paper, *The National Observer*, first serialised his *Tales of Mean Streets* (1894), and this work led to his other great accounts of the East End, *A Child of the Jago* (also 1894 – the Jago is, effectively, Bethnal Green) and *The Hole in the Wall* (set around a pub in the East End, 1902). Along with these fine realistic tales Morrison wrote a number of the best early detective stories, whose straightforward hero owed little to Sherlock Holmes: *Martin Hewitt, Investigator* (1894), *Chronicles of Martin Hewitt* (1895) and *Hewitt: Third Series* (1896). Most had appeared earlier in magazines. He also wrote a historic novel about a smuggler, *Cunning Murrell*, in 1900.

A J **MUNBY** (1828-1910)

Arthur Joseph Munby is, if truth be told, better known for his love life than for his verse. He lived for almost two decades with 'a woman beneath him' – a general maid called Hannah Cullwick – until he married her secretly in 1873. She continued to live with him as his servant. He had first met Hannah on one of his habitual explorations of London streets, on which he would approach working women and ask them about their lives and work. He would sketch them and note details about their clothes and dialects in his journals. His copious notes on this obsession and his secret marriage were retrieved by Derek Hudson and used as the basis of *Munby: Man of Two Worlds* in 1972. This much later book casts a new light on Munby's own *Verses New and Old* (1865), *Vestigia retrorsum* (1891), *Vulgar Verses* (1891, under a pseudonym: Jones Brown) and *Susan* (1893).

Sir James A H MURRAY (1837-1915)

The literary equivalent of a self-made man, Murray was born in Hawick, a tailor's son and, while working as a casual labourer, set about self-improvement. He became a teacher, a member of the Philological Society, a medieval text expert for the Early English Text Society, headmaster of Mill Hill School and finally, in 1878, editor of the new *Oxford Dictionary*. His drive and enthusiastic scholarship did much to make it what it is today. He also wrote *The Dialect of the Southern Counties of Scotland* (1873).

John Henry NEWMAN (1801-90)

Newman's writings in his day were of enormous importance to the schisms in the Church of England – few signs of which could be seen in the 1820s, when as a leading figure in the 'Oxford Movement' his sermons were reported and praised widely, or early in 1833 when, among a good many other hymns, he wrote 'Lead Kindly Light'. Yet that same year he issued the first of his *Tracts for the Times*, arguing for tradition and the doctrine of apostolic succession, and beginning a controversy almost impossible to imagine today. He was seen as too close to the Church of Rome, and in 1845 he joined it, leaving behind the other great figures of the Oxford Movement, Keble and Pusey. It was as if a leader had abdicated and joined the enemy. Welcomed

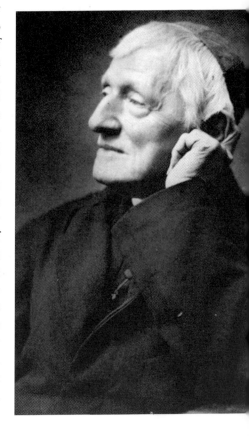

in Ireland, he continued to issue theological – and controversial – pieces, each of which was seized upon by both sides of the divided church at home. That this man of brave and honest belief should raise such rage and opprobrium says much for the strains within the Victorian church, assailed on the one side – as it believed – by science and agnosticism, and on the other by reformers and Roman Catholics.

Though unlikely to find themselves on the reading list of the modern general reader, most of Newman's writings are of high quality. He wrote the poem *The Dream of Gerontius* (1865, later set to music by Elgar). His *Apologia pro Vita Sua* (1864, a reply to Kingsley) made an enormous impact, not only among those who agreed with him. His *The Idea of a University Defined and Illustrated* (1873) would make an important contribution to the same debate today. He wrote two novels, *Loss and Gain* (1848, on the Oxford Movement) and *Callista* (1856, a historical tale), and was made a cardinal in 1879.

Caroline NORTON (1808-77)

Though the granddaughter of the playwright Richard Sheridan and an author and poet in her own right, it is for her notorious divorce case that she is remembered. In 1836 her husband sued for divorce on the grounds that her affections had been alienated from him by Lord Melbourne. The jury dismissed his case, but it left Mrs Norton robbed of her children and close to financial and social ruin. She was already a professional writer, with a book of poetry, *The Sorrows of Rosalie* (1829), and two novels, *The Undying One* (1830) and *The Wife and Woman's Reward* (1835). The unjustness of her situation led her to campaign for improved marital rights (specifically on custody and a married woman's property rights) while she continued to earn money from poetry (often radical in its theme) and novel-writing. She helped bring about the Infants' Custody Act of 1839 and, in 1855, long after her own failed divorce case, campaigned for a divorced woman's right to her own property. Her pamphlet included the challenge: 'Why write? Why struggle? It is the law! You will do no good! But if everyone lacked courage with that doubt, nothing would ever be achieved in this world.' Full rights under the Married Woman's Property Act did not come until 1882.

Novels include *Stuart of Dunleath* (1851), *Lost and Saved* (1863) and *Old*

Sir Douglas (1867). In 1877 she remarried. She was the model for Meredith's *Diana of the Crossways*.

Laurence **OLIPHANT** (1829–88)

After a peripatetic childhood he became a barrister in Ceylon and produced two travel books, *Journey to Khatmandu* (1852) and *The Russian Shores of the Black Sea* (1853). As secretary to Lord Elgin he travelled with him to America and China, then became a *Times* correspondent before returning to London, from where he wrote his satirical *Piccadilly* (1866). By now he had become an MP and all seemed rosy – except that in 1867 he fell under the influence of an American 'prophet' Thomas Lake Harris, joined his Brotherhood of New Life, and gave Harris most of his property. He didn't free himself from these delusions till the 1880s, after which he wrote his second novel, *Altiora Peto* (1883) and the weirder *Sympneumata* (1885), a book apparently dictated by a spirit to his wife, and reading little better.

Margaret **OLIPHANT** (1828–97)

Cousin to Laurence above, she was the Scottish author of some one hundred books. She had been widowed early in life and saw writing as a means of income. *Mrs Margaret Maitland* was her first novel, in 1849, and off she set: contributing to *Blackwood*'s and other magazines and turning out the books which, if usually undemanding, were of a decent standard. *The Athelings* (1857) and *Miss Marjoribanks* (1866) stand out. Her non-fiction works include a biography of Laurence, a well-received *Literary History of England* (1882), an interesting *Annals of a Publishing House: William Blackwood and His Sons* (1897) and her own revealing autobiography in 1899.

W E **O'SHAUGHNESSY** (1844–81)

He had a relatively short life, the adult part of which was largely spent in the Department of Printed Books and the Natural History Department at the British Museum. Arthur William Edgar O'Shaughnessy produced four romantic verse collections: *An Epic of Women* (1870), *Lays of France* (1872), *Music and Moonlight* (1874), and *Songs of a Worker* (1881). From the 1874 collection came 'We are the music-makers', subsequently set to music by Elgar. Melancholy was his watchword, though together with his wife he did produce a poetry book for children: *Toyland* (1875).

OUIDA (1839-1908)

A risible figure today, Ouida's life was a life of contrasts. Her real name was Marie Louise de la Ramée, she was daughter to a French teacher working in Bury St Edmunds, and her adopted name came from a childhood mispronunciation of 'Louise'. Early contributions to *Bentley's Miscellany* were praised by its editor Harrison **Ainsworth** and her first novel, *Held in Bondage* (1863) was likewise praised. Several novels later, her *Under Two Flags* (a tale of the Foreign Legion, 1867) was a great success as, a little later, were *Folle-Farine* (1871) and *Two Little Wooden Shoes* (1874).

An established novelist, she was able to indulge her love of travel and high living, spending much time in Italy and finally settling in Florence in 1874. Her lavish lifestyle, her absence from this country (and, it must be said, her relatively humble upbringing) in part explain the unreality of her high society settings and her many factual errors. But her heroes were men and her beauties beautiful, which was what her readers wanted. But readers are as fickle as lovers, and after a while they tired of her. As the novels failed, she turned to society journalism (in which her snobbery and lack of real knowledge was exposed) and her income fell far below her expenditure. She left Florence for more modest accommodation in Lucca, and then from 1904 saw out her years in destitution in even poorer quarters in Viareggio.

Francis **PALGRAVE** (1824-97)

If he'd had a penny for every copy... The Palgrave poetry anthology first appeared in 1861 and was reprinted in many forms and revisions for more than a century. The first edition was *The Golden Treasury of Best Songs and Lyrical Poems in the English Language* and although the spines of subsequent editions

used snappier titles they were mainly called the '*Golden Treasury*'. Palgrave himself compiled the first major revision: that Second Edition, in 1897, abandoned the restrictions of his first, limited to poems published before 1850 and to poets no longer alive in 1861. 20th century revisions added later poets.

Palgrave himself was the son of a barrister, a Cohen who converted to Christianity, and, partly as a result of his book, he became Professor of Poetry at Oxford in 1885. Far less common than his anthology (can there be a second-hand bookshop without one?) are the few volumes of his own verse: *Idylls and Songs* (1854) was the first, *Amenophis* (1892) the last, together with a few prose works and his early, part autobiographical work, *The Passionate Pilgrim* (1858).

Walter **PATER** (1839-94)

Pater was the high priest of aestheticism, a controversial Oxford don (controversial both in his views and, on at least one occasion, in his over-friendly relationship with a male student) whose motto could have sprung from his best book, *Studies in the History of the Renaissance* (1873): 'To burn always with this hard gem-like flame, to maintain this ecstasy, is success in life.' From the same book comes his almost infamous 'art for its own sake' doctrine, taken up in the late 19th century as an axiom by the Decadents and aesthetes. Pater taught that a man should treat his own life as a work of art, rather than be a slave to society's rules. As well as his authoritative writings on art and philosophy (much of it in journals, later anthologised) he wrote some literary fiction including *Marius the Epicurean* (1885) and *Gaston de Latour* (1896, unfinished). Of the various collections, *Plato and Platonism* (1893) is perhaps the most interesting today, with its bold (for the time) defence of Greek philosophy and homoeroticism.

Coventry **PATMORE** (1823-96)

> *Let those love now, who never loved;*
> *Let those who have loved love again*
> from his *Nunc Amet Qui Nunquam Amavit*

A poet of substance in his day but less so since. His collection, *The Angel in the House* (1854-63), was compiled from four separate long poems and was emblematic of the idealised Victorian family in which the dutiful wife was the eponymous Angel and the woman's 'priceless gift', as he called it, 'made brutes men, and men divine.' He himself married three times (his first two wives died) and in later life he converted to Roman Catholicism. He had been associated with the Pre-Raphaelites, contributing to their short-lived magazine *The Germ* in 1850 and having one of his poems inspire a Millais painting, 'The Woodman's Daughter', but he parted amicably from them to continue with his poetry. His day-job was as an assistant librarian in the British Museum.

> *Who is the happy husband? He*
> *Who, scanning his unwedded life,*
> *Thanks Heaven, with a conscience free,*
> *'Twas faithful to his future wife.*

from his *Prospective Faith*

Mark **PATTISON** (1813-84)

The presumed model for George Eliot's dessicated Casaubon in *Middlemarch* – he who wasted his years and his wife's patience in an uncompleted work of scholarship – Pattison wrote the biography *Isaac Casaubon 1559-1614* in 1875 and spent many years on a biography of Scaliger (himself a medieval scholar) which he never completed. Eliot's *Middlemarch*, oddly, was published earlier, in 1871, and the Casaubon coincidence is such that Eliot must have known of Pattison's lifework and been convinced he would never finish it. Pattison's own married life was rumoured to have been as loveless and sexless as that of Casaubon and Dorothea in *Middlemarch* – for much the same reasons: he was a dry old academic, locked in his study, and she was 27 years his junior. (Soon after Pattison's death she married Sir Charles Dilke who was, at the time, accused of seduction in someone else's scandalous and very public divorce case. But that's another story.) Pattison himself spent his life much concerned with education, religious debate and the Oxford Movement; his writings were mainly on these subjects, although his *Memoirs* (1885, published by his widow) give a useful picture of 19th century Oxford.

Sir Arthur Wing **PINERO** (1855-1934)

From gilded youth to disillusion, Pinero lived long enough to see his reputation soar and fall. Besotted with the theatre, he became an actor, wrote for the stage, and had his first one-act play, *Two Hundred a Year*, put on in 1877. He continued to act and write and had a hit with his first farce, *The Magistrate*, in 1885. He then gave up acting to concentrate on writing plays, having equal success in farce and the 'problem play'. Over the next decade he became Britain's most successful playwright, at least two of his plays (*The Second Mrs Tanqueray*, 1893, and *Trelawny of the 'Wells'*, 1898) becoming mainstays of the West End and repertory theatre. When his knighthood came in 1909 it climaxed a career which had already peaked.

James Robinson **PLANCHÉ** (1796-1880)
One of the best-known dramatists of the Victorian stage, he incorporated spectacular effects into his plays. He is credited with some 176 plays, libretti, and other entertainments, including translations, comedies, farces, burlesques, musical revues, and fairy-tale extravaganzas. Apart from these he wrote a lively autobiography, *Recollections and Reflections: A Professional Autobiography* (1872) as well as a few history books, some children's books and many articles and reviews for magazines and newspapers. Despite his name (he was of Huguenot descent) he was born in London. At the age of 24 he married Elizabeth St George (also 24), a skilful playwright herself: she was best at sentimental and melodramatic scenes while he excelled at amusing dialogue and banter.

After his wife died at the age of 50 (of a series of strokes) Planché never remarried. Of their two daughters, Katherine and Matilda, Katherine died young, and it was left to her ageing father to bring up her children. Matilda married a rector and in her spare time, often using the pen name Susie Sunbeam, wrote moral tales for children. When her husband died she too moved in with her father, bringing another seven children in her wake. Planché was, unsurprisingly, dogged by debt much of his life (though 'Susie Sunbeam' did earn a modest income from her works) and in 1871, 15 years after he had left the theatre, he was granted a civil list stipend of £100 a year to add to what he could earn from books and articles.

Thomas **PREST** (1810-1879)
One of the great writers of Penny Dreadfuls, a plagiariser, careless of facts and, characteristically, about whom little is known, Thomas Peckett Prest claimed to have invented one of the great villains of street literature,

Sweeney Todd. Certainly Prest wrote the long serial about him. He was also at the forefront of the band of hack writers who not only stole their stories from other authors but shamelessly rode on their backs to sell their work. Prest and others working for the publisher Edward Lloyd emblazoned the covers of his partworks with titles such as *Oliver Twiss, Penny Pickwick, Nickelas Nicklebery, Martin Guzzlewit* et cetera – written, in the case of Dickens rip-offs in the name of 'Bos' rather than 'Boz' which was

Dickens's pen-name. His first success came with *Ela the Outcast*; or *The Gypsy of Rosemary Dell* (1838), a story so successful that Lloyd reprinted it in 1856. Prest was an editor too, having overseen an edifying journal entitled *The Calendar of Horror*s, and serials under his own name included *Fatherless Fanny, Phoebe the Peasant's Daughter* and *The Maniac Father, or The Victims of Seduction.*

But the greatest of all was *Sweeney Todd* or, as it was first called, *The String of Pearls* (1840). In 1842 Todd first appeared on stage (in a version drafted by George Dibdin Pitt and staged at the Britannia Saloon, Hoxton) and in 1846 the entire story was rerun in *Lloyd's People's Periodical* and *Family Library*. The various dramatisations and retellings all added to the story but the basis was Prest's, as were many of the best lines. ('You go off for a walk around the block, Tobias – while I finish off this gentleman.')

> *And well did they deserve their reputation, those delicious pies! There was about them a flavour never surpassed and rarely equalled; the paste was of the most delicate construction and impregnated with the aroma of a delicious gravy that defied description.*

Though Prest is credited with 100 book-length stories they brought him no great fortune. He turned to drink and died alone and penniless in a lodging house. A fitting end, dramatically, but undeserved.

Adelaide **PROCTER** (1825-64)

Her most famous poem, 'The Lost Chord' – set to music by Sir Arthur Sullivan and sung in a million drawing rooms – is but one of her enormous output. She was the poet most often published in Dickens's *Household Words*, and among her collections were two volumes of *Legends and Lyrics* (1858 & 61), *A Chaplet of Verses* (1862) and *The Message* (1892). Though a good deal of her poetry was devotional and all of it conventional, she was reasonably feminist for her time, and she allowed this to show at times in her work. She was the daughter of the poet B W Procter, who wrote as Barry Cornwall.

Sir Arthur **QUILLER-COUCH** – "**Q**" (1863-1944)

Best known as a compiler – he edited the first *Oxford Book of English Verse* in 1900 – he was an author, poet, critic and parodist in his own right. His first novel was *Dead Man's Rock* (1887) – not a cowboy book, as it sounds, but the first of his Cornish tales (he was born in Bodmin). Others of these include *Troy Town* (1888), *The Splendid Spur* (1889) and *The Ship of Stars* (1899). *Verses and Parodies* appeared in 1893 and *Poems and Ballads* in 1896. A good deal more followed in the 20th century, and he was knighted in 1910. He almost always wrote as 'Q'. In *Punch*, earlier in the century, 'Q' was Douglas **Jerrold**.

Sir Walter **RALEIGH** (1861-1922)

He did not lay down his cloak for the queen to walk on. This Sir Walter was a respected critic and biographer whose *Style* (1897) was a writers' bible in its day, though it reads fustily today. He wrote *The English Novel: From the Earliest Times to the Appearance of Waverley* in 1891, a biography of Stevenson in 1895 and another of Milton in 1900. More were to follow in the 20th century.

Charles **READE** (1814-84)

Prolific playwright and reforming novelist, at times too reformist for his own good. He didn't begin writing till in his thirties but, once he started, he plunged right in. He first dramatised Smollett's *Peregrine Pickle* (1851), then switched direction by converting his own play *Masks and Faces* into a novel, *Peg Woffington* (1853). With successes both in the theatre and in print he began on the first of his reforming novels, *Christie Johnstone* (1853) urging the reform of prisons. *It Is Never To Late To Mend* (1856) beat louder on that same drum (he would later convert the novel into a play) just as another of his plays that year, *Gold*, became the novel *Foul Play* in 1869. Meanwhile he had moved in with the actress Mrs Seymour, with whom he would live some 15 years until her death, while he continued writing, writing. *The Autobiography of a Thief* and *Jack of all Trades* both appeared in 1858; *Love Me Little, Love Me Long*, in 1859; and his most famous novel, *The Cloister and the Hearth*, in 1861. Then came *Hard Cash* (1863), a novel scheduled for publication in 1862 but delayed, perhaps due to illness but more likely because the over-committed Reade had got into a tangle with the story. When it did appear, serialised in Dickens's *All The Year Round*, the novel turned out to be a shocker – not shockingly bad but shocking in its reformist scenes and propaganda. Reade had turned his attention to the abuses of patients in private asylums, writing of forcible incarceration and showing in great detail the cruelties inflicted on inmates by callous staff. Not only was his tale too hot – too uncomfortable – for Dickens's readers, but it was far too long. Reade had the bit between his teeth and was heading for the horizon. Cut it short, cried Dickens, and Reade reluctantly agreed. He scrambled together a hasty ending, only to find his final episode accompanied by a large-print paragraph from Dickens disavowing editorial responsibility.

In 1866 Reade was again in hot water. His fine novel, *Griffith Gaunt*, exposed marital fault lines: a young wife dallies with her priestly advisor and her husband abandons her to contract a bigamous marriage. For this novel Reade found himself in court and, when he turned to Dickens for help, Dickens turned aside. But Reade was tough enough to defend himself – as he had to on other occasions. His *Put Yourself In His Place* (1870) attacked dubious practices in trade unions (for whom he normally had sympathy). *The Simpleton* (1873) provoked a libel trial. His play, *The Wandering Heir* (1873) was clearly based on the Tichborne affair of 1871. His epistolary *Hang in Haste, Repent at Leisure* (1877) led to the reprieve of four people condemned to death for murder. In short, he was a trouble-seeker – irascible, hot-tempered and, although he over-wrote and loaded his pages with too much evidence, he was a far more incisive and informative writer than one would assume from the near absence of his novels in bookshops now.

William Winwood **READE** (1838–75)

The nephew of Charles Reade above. A real-life explorer, he would have been a shining moral example were it not for his attacks upon religion. His explorations were detailed in *Savage Africa* (1863), *The African Sketchbook* (1873) and *The Story of the Ashanti Campaign* (1874). But his unwelcome atheism in *The Matyrdom of Man* (1872) horrified many – though not all and certainly not H G Wells, who would later describe it as an 'inspiring presentation of human history as one consistent process.' Reade died young, not from anything caught in Africa, nor from a bullet in the Ashanti War, but in Wimbledon, of consumption.

Talbot Baines **REED** (1852–93)

Writer of boys' stories, normally set in healthily masculine schools (though he never went to a private school), and a contributor to *Boy's Own Paper*. (Many of his books began life as serials in BOP.) A pure-minded man, he gave the copyrights of his stories to the Religious Tract Society, with which he was involved. Books include *The Fifth Form at St Dominic's* (1881), *Cock House at Fellsgarth* (1891) and (in a different vein) *History of the Old English Letter Foundries* (1887). He was an expert on the history of typography.

Captain T Mayne **REID** (1818–83)

His boys' adventure stories had a grounding in personal experience. The son of a Northern Ireland minister, he emigrated to the States when he was 19, where he fought in the Mexican-American War and was badly wounded. On his return to Britain in 1849 he began writing stories. *The Rifle Rangers* (1850) was swiftly followed by *The Scalp Hunters* (1851) – in which the hero sinks in quicksand, is stabbed in the back, almost dies of thirst in the desert, and meets the eponymous scalp-hunter. But it was his third book, *The Desert Home* (also 1851) which was the first to be aimed specifically at boys. Published in time for Christmas that year, it would be followed by a similarly well-timed novel practically every year thereafter, with titles such as *The Boy Hunters* (1853), *The Cliff-Climbers* (1864) and *The Headless Horseman* (1866). His earlier 1856 novel, *The Quadroon*, was dramatised by Boucicault as *The Octoroon*. Reid's adventure stories were occasionally interspersed with books on natural history and even a book on croquet. But despite all his success he died in debt.

Anne Thackeray **RITCHIE** (1837-1919)
Often the children of the famous are justifiably sneered at and condemned for trading on their parent's name. Not so with Mrs Ritchie, nee **Thackeray**, beloved daughter of one of the century's greatest authors. Losing her mother to an asylum and her sister to a mortal illness, Annie remained close to her father, acting as his confidant, succour and secretary – eventually as editor of the *Biographical Edition* of his works – while quietly laying the groundwork for her own literary career. Her first novel, *The Story of Elizabeth*, came out in the year her father died (1863), and was followed by seven others, each of them light and airy, sweetly gentle, if wavering in plot. She was on stronger ground as a literary biographer: she covered Mrs **Gaskell**, **Tennyson**, **Ruskin** and the **Brownings**, and contributed to periodicals and magazines. Popular, it seems, with everyone who knew her, Anne's sweet if absent-minded nature was legendary (she once turned

up for a meeting with Tennyson a week early – to no one's great surprise). Her niece Virginia Woolf wrote of her affectionately and used her as the basis for 'Mrs Hilbery' in *Night and Day*.

Thomas William **ROBERTSON** (1829-71)

Influential playwright and director in his day whose plays began a shift towards a more naturalistic form of domestic drama ('cup and saucer drama' it was called at the time). He reached his peak in the 1860s with a series of six comedy hits at the Prince of Wales Theatre, of which *Caste* was the greatest. Pinero portrayed him as 'Tom Wrench' in his *Trelawny of the Wells*.

Robert **ROSS** (1869-1918)

A journalist and critic famous mainly for having been the close friend, confidant and literary executor of Oscar **Wilde**, a role which set him strongly against Wilde's more notorious confidant, Lord Alfred **Douglas**, who felt that Ross had betrayed him – and Wilde – by publishing Wilde's *De Profundis*, intended by Wilde (said Douglas) as a private and certainly very personal letter. Ross (who claimed to have initiated Wilde into homosexual practices when Wilde was sixteen) devoted his later years to the Wilde literary legacy, and a biography he commissioned from Arthur Ransome in 1912 spurred the intemperate Douglas into one of his many court actions. Though unsuccessful, as Lord Alfred's's actions usually were, costs were awarded against Ross and he lost his art advisory post with the Board of Trade. This encouraged an extraordinary Testimonial to be signed by some 300 well-known supporters. Signatories from the Asquiths (he was Prime Minister) to H G Wells told Ross that he had 'long been distinguished for the justice and courage of your writings ... Your work as a Man of Letters, however, is but a small part of the useful energy which you have shown in many directions...' The praise seems wildly overblown today.

Christina **ROSSETTI** (1830-94)

When I am dead, my dearest,
Sing no sad songs for me;
Plant thou no roses at my head,

Nor shady cypress tree:
Be the green grass above me
With showers and dewdrops wet:
And if thou wilt, remember,
And if thou wilt, forget.

For long in the Rossetti household she was overshadowed by her colourful brother Gabriel and even, to an extent, by the industrious William. She suffered from erratic health – perhaps having a mental breakdown when fourteen – and lived a quiet domestic life in the approved Victorian fashion (though her Italian immigrant family led a more artistic and political life than was normally thought proper), helping her ageing mother look after her almost blind father and run the house. She was deeply religious (sometimes scorned as such by Gabriel) and was a follower of the Tractarian movement. (Her sister Maria became a nun.) Christina's adherence to this Protestant sect contributed to the ending of her engagement to the lesser Pre-Raphaelite artist James Collinson in 1850 when he became a Roman Catholic. (She never married, though she had one or two other wistfully unconsummated romances.)

Where sunless rivers weep
Their waves into the deep,
She sleeps a charmed sleep;
Awake her not.

She had been writing poetry since childhood (some of which had been privately published by her father) and in that sad 1850 she contributed five poems to her brother's short-lived *Germ* magazine under the pseudonym 'Ellen Alleyn'. (One of them, *Dream Land*, begins as above.) It was not until the following decade that her poems began to be noticed: *Macmillan's Magazine* published her in 1861 and her brilliant *Goblin Market and Other Poems* came out in 1862. Further books followed slowly, as poetry will. *The Prince's Progress and Other Poems* came in 1866, *Sing-Song* in 1872, *A Pageant and Other Poems* in 1881 and *Time Flies: A Reading Diary* in 1885. (There was also a less interesting *The Face of the Deep: A Devotional Commentary* in 1892.) Incidental poems, often of a religious nature, appeared in periodicals, and she wrote the famous carol *In the Bleak Mid-Winter*. The first collected edition of her works, with biography, was published in 1904 under the editorship of her brother William. 'Her life,' he wrote, 'had two motive powers – religion and affection – hardly a third.' She had died of breast cancer.

When she was young her brother Gabriel would sometimes use her as a model for his paintings: perhaps the best-known is his *Ecce Ancilla Domini* in which she features as the Virgin. In her later life she became less housebound, working through the church for the poor, and she helped provide a refuge in Highgate for the reclamation of prostitutes. To anyone unfamiliar with her name this summary of her life would suggest that she was a typically over-religious and forgettable Victorian 'poetess' but she has, in fact, written some of the best loved poems in the national repertoire.

Dante Gabriel **ROSSETTI** (1828–82)

With his easy talent, louche good looks and cheeky Cockney-Italian manner, Gabriel Rossetti naturally stood out. He was considered the poet in the family – despite the presence of his sister, Christina, who became arguably the country's greatest female poet. He would be the bread-winner, despite having a brother William who held down a respectable job with a comfortable salary all his life. Outside the family, Gabriel founded (he claimed) and led (perhaps) the Pre-Raphaelite art movement – despite being outclassed, outsold and certainly outlived by Hunt and Millais. He was the great lover – perhaps, again: his presumed mistress, Fanny, cuckolded him and his wife Lizzie was a drug addict who may have committed suicide. He himself suffered from a testicular complaint which some say precluded him from having much sex at all.

And yet. His best paintings are incomparably beautiful; the late ones and the lazy ones are poor, but what of that? Not even Hunt and Millais could match the beauty of his best work. His poems were erratic, yet some were very fine. He could be bold: his *Jenny* shocked many by being a clear paean to a working prostitute. If Rossetti didn't found the Pre-Raphaelites (Hunt claimed he did, and we will never know) he certainly brought them much publicity. Rossetti probably didn't found their famous but unsuccessful magazine *The Germ* but he contributed and perhaps helped his brother edit it. He was revered by many who knew him – and this should perhaps count most of all, since we can only guess and try to make him out from their accounts. Those who knew him praised him.

He wasn't the first or last young man whose flame blazed brightly but flickered out – though in Rossetti's case he wasn't granted an especially early death. He drank hard, did drugs harder, behaved more and more bizarrely, yet lived into his fifties – dying a recluse. Among his best-known oddities were his obsessive collecting of antiques and bric-a-brac, the animals he let roam his house (including his favourites, the wombats), and the trust he placed in Fanny Cornforth (an ex-prostitute his family were

convinced was stealing from him) and in the conman Charles Augustus Howell. More famously, when his wife Lizzie died of a presumed laudanum overdose, Rossetti had the manuscripts of his poems cast into the coffin with her. Some years later he changed his mind, and had his erstwhile love exhumed.

His poems aren't greatly read today, though his great sonnet sequence *The House of Life* repays perusal. It was put together over the years, the first part appearing in his *Poems* (1870) and the second in *Ballads and Sonnets* (1881). It is possible but probably a mistake to read them as a commentary on his own tangled love life (to the doomed Lizzie Siddal and to William **Morris**'s wife Jane). Notable among his other poems are *My Sister's Sleep*, *Sister Helen*, *Eden Bower* and his early poem *The Blessed Damozel* which appeared first in *The Germ* (along with *My Sister's Sleep*) and inspired one of his finest paintings.

He was born Gabriel Charles Dante Rossetti but, in homage to his idealised Dante, switched the order of his names to give emphasis to the Dante. He painted a number of pictures on Dante themes and translated him in *The Early Italian Poets* (1861), later reissued as *Dante and his Circle* in 1874. He translated works and edited editions of many other Italian poets.

W M **ROSSETTI** (1829-1919)

William Michael was the level-headed one in the family, beavering away at his Inland Revenue office while undertaking administrative chores for the Pre-Raphaelites (note William's own spelling below). But that sentence disparages his contribution. He helped found and he edited their student magazine *The Germ*, he wrote many intelligent articles about the exciting new movement and art generally, he produced a life of Keats in 1887, he edited editions of his sister's and his brother's poems, he edited some poems by Lizzie Siddal, and he put together collections of Shelley, Blake and Whitman. His late works left us an invaluable source of biographical data: *D G Rossetti, His Family Letters, with a Memoir* appeared in 1895; *Ruskin, Rossetti, Preraphaelitism* in 1899; *Preraphaelite Diaries and Letters* in 1900 and *Some Reminiscences* in 1906. *Family Letters of Christina Rossetti* appeared in 1908. Keeping clear of the wilder excesses taking place around him, he cared for his mother until her death in 1886, and he married Lucy, the daughter of the painter Ford Madox Brown. He had known her since her childhood.

John **RUSKIN** (1819-1900)

If a book is worth reading, it is worth buying

from *Sesame and Lilies*

There were several John Ruskins; he was a complicated man. A rich child, spoilt and crammed with education, prodigious and kept too sheltered from the world. A bold young critic who championed both Turner and the Pre-Raphaelites but who, in old age, lost touch with modern art. An enthusiastic traveller who ended a recluse. A much-read and lauded teacher of how to live, whose own emotional life was a tragedy. One of the wisest writers of the Victorian age, yet who can astound with his naivety; at times so right, at times so wrong.

All travelling becomes dull in exact proportion to its rapidity

from *Modern Painters*

He was born to a stern and religious family of Sherry importers (Domecq), and was schooled at home. When he went to university, as he naturally would, he lived not in halls with other students but in comfortable lodgings with his mother. By then he had already contributed poems and essays to serious magazines. From childhood he had shown a great talent for drawing, a formidable talent he retained all his life; he was notable, in fact, as a critic who could practise what he preached.

Fine art is that in which the hand, the head, and the heart of man go together

from *The Two Paths*

His first book on art, *Modern Painters* (1834), established him at the forefront of art criticism. The second in his five-volume series (*Modern Painters II*, 1846) followed a tour of Italy and launched his long campaign against the careless destruction of fine old buildings and for the re-evaluation and recognition of medieval and Gothic work. Part of this campaign was his *The Seven Lamps of Architecture* (1849) and the massive *The Stones of Venice* (1851-3) – and surely the best 'taster' to Ruskin for one who has not read him is the essay extracted from *The Stones* on 'The Nature of the Gothic': like much of Ruskin's writing it sounds, but turns out not to be, a subject too dry to hold one's interest. Volumes III and IV of *Modern Painters* did not appear till 1856. That same year saw his commentary on Turner's marine paintings: *The Harbours of England*. (Turner had appointed him his executor.)

The purest and most thoughtful minds are those which love colour the most

from his *The Stones of Venice*

By then Ruskin had been famously married and divorced (for non-consummation). His delightful *King of the Golden River*, a fantasy for children, had been a gift for his wife and, though written in 1841, was not published until 1851. She divorced him in 1854. (More details about this and Ruskin's involvement with the art world will be found in my *Pocket Guide to Victorian Artists and Models.*) The 1850s saw Ruskin deeply involved in art and architecture; some of the lectures he gave nation-wide were collected in *Lectures on Architecture and Painting* (1854) and *The Two Paths* (1859). His final *Modern Painters* appeared in 1860, and in that book he strayed further than in previous volumes to attack greed and philistinism and to preach a finer way of life. These themes came to the fore in the then controversial *Unto This Last* (appearing in 1860 in *Cornhill* magazine and in 1862 as a book), and in *Essays on Political Economy* (1862 & 3), re-issued as *Munera Pulveris* in 1872.

> *Nothing that is great is easy*
>
> from *The Two Paths*

He was now one of the most listened-to voices in the movement against utilitarianism and mass production. He championed both the artist and the skilled working man (seldom, alas, the working woman), and among various books of the 1860s his *Sesame and Lilies* (1865 and 71) and *The Crown of Wild Olives* (1866 & 73) stand out. They, especially, show him at his most inspiring and his worst. The very worst was his winsome set of pseudo-dialogues with young ladies entitled *The Ethics of the Dust* (1866) in which he appears to lose all contact with the adult world as we know it. Another curious but much larger work, *Fors Clavigera* (letters 'To the Workmen and Labourers of Great Britain'), came out, again in two forms, in 1871 and 78.

> *Wealth is simply one of the greatest powers which can be entrusted to human hands*
>
> from his *Political Economy of Art*

The subjects of Ruskin's books, with their odd and sometimes Latin titles, suggest a dry über-intellectual approach and style far removed from the common reader but they are, in fact, as they certainly were in his time, invigorating, intelligible and persuasive. He was read and listened to by vast audiences (which is why second-hand copies of his books are so easy to come by today) and his name was well-known throughout the land. When he lectured he packed the halls. Lectures from the 1870s fill several volumes and some, including *The Eagle's Nest* (1872) and *Love's Meinie*

(1873-81) are sound, but as the decade progressed his writings became increasingly off-beam. His private life (which, sadly for Ruskin, was never kept private enough) became even more erratic; his celibacy was disturbed by a long infatuation with the young (and also disturbed) Rose La Touche. (She died, insane, in 1875.) 1878 saw his disastrous involvement in the Whistler libel trial (details again in my *Victorian Artists and Models*) and marked the end of his eminence as an art critic. The 1880s were a terrible period. He worked on his autobiography, *Praeterita* (*Things Past*), but failed to complete it, and spent the last decade of his life in near solitude at his house on Coniston Water.

> *Whatever bit of a wise man's work is honestly and benevolently done, that bit is his book, or his piece of art*
>
> from *Sesame and Lilies*

So should one read Ruskin? Does he have relevance today? Certainly. No one with an interest in Victorian literature or art should miss the chance to engage with a man who, at his best, was one of the most beguiling, provocative, incisive and authoritative voices of the age, a master of Victorian prose. He is the perfect companion for a leisurely sunny afternoon in the garden sipping English tea or, perhaps even better, sipping coffee at a quiet table beside a Venetian canal.

> *Races, like individuals, can only reach their true strength, dignity, or joy, in seeking each the welfare, and exulting each in the glory of the other.*
>
> from *Modern Painters*

William Henry RUSSELL (1820-1907)

Inscribed on his bust in the crypt of St Paul's Cathedral are the words: 'The first and greatest of war correspondents.' In the 19th century he was the greatest press reporter, and it was the Crimean War that made him famous. Reporting for the *Times* he exposed the awful conditions, the incompetence of generals, the even worse incompetence of the War Office and military bureaucracy. His reports, brought to Britain by courier (this was before the days of telegraph, and each 6,000 word report took ten days to arrive) carried such a woeful indictment that they brought down a government (that of Aberdeen). Though remembered for his Crimean reporting, Russell went on to cover the Indian Mutiny, the American Civil War, the Prussian Wars and the Zulu War – and again he reported unflinchingly, revealing the cruelty of the British in India and the inhumanity of slave-owners in America. He reported from the front, from among the soldiers, escaping narrowly with his life on at least two occasions. (In America a soldier aimed at him from close range, pulled the trigger, but the gun did not go off.) To us today his reports read as overblown and florid; to the Victorians they were as clear as television.

Mark **RUTHERFORD** (1831-1913)

Mark Rutherford was the pseudonym of William Hale White, and some of the books he wrote appeared as autobiographies of the fictional Rutherford. White used the books to reveal and discuss the intellectual struggles of religious dissent; he himself had abandoned the ministry (in 1854) because of both his own religious doubts and his revulsion from church hypocrisy. (He had previously, in 1851, been expelled from college for challenging religious orthodoxy.) Years later, in 1881, he published his *Autobiography of Mark Rutherford, Dissenting Minister* and the book caught the attention of a public struggling to keep up in the debate between faith and rationalism. White followed it with several more books, all as Rutherford, although in 1905 he did produce a biography of Bunyan under his own name. The Rutherford books remain important as windows into 19th century dissent.

James Malcolm **RYMER** (1804-84)

One of the great 19th century writers for Penny Dreadfuls, whose full-length stories (and full-length with Rymer could mean 1,000 pages) include

The Black Monk (1844), *The White Slave and Amy* (1844) and *Varney the Vampire* (serialised, it seemed, for ever in the mid-1840s). His prodigious output was as unbelievable as were his plots. Rymer not only wrote for the Penny Dreadfuls, he edited *Lloyd's Penny Weekly Miscellany*. Later, in the '50s and '60s he wrote for *Reynolds' Miscellany* and the *London Miscellany*. Hackwork as it is, there is something hypnotic about Rymer's rapid prose:

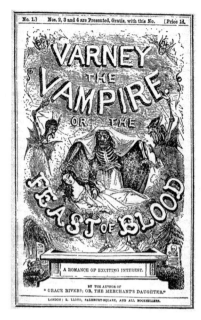

> *The storm has ceased – all is still. The winds are hushed; the church clock proclaims the hour of one: a hissing sound comes from the throat of the hideous being and he raises his*

long gaunt arms – the lips move. He advances. The girl places one small foot from the bed on the floor. She is unconsciously dragging the clothing with her. The door of the room is in that direction – can she reach it?

from Rymer's *Varney the Vampire*

Rymer also wrote under the pseudonyms (anagrams of his name): M J Errym and Malcolm Merry.

George Augustus **SALA** (1828-96)
One of the best-known Victorian journalists, beginning his career as editor of *Chat* in 1848, working for Dickens at *Household Words* in the 1850s, moving on to the *Daily Telegraph* and writing several travel books and novels on the side. A man of wide interests who could, it seemed, write on anything, Sala had, before his literary career, trained as an artist – again encompassing the entire field, as he worked both as a miniaturist and a scene painter in the theatre. (Inevitably, he was a book illustrator too.) As a journalist he followed in the wake, but without the glory, of W H **Russell**, reporting from both the Crimea and the American Civil War, but his scope was wider than Russell's. His books include *A Journey Due North* (about

Russia, 1858), *Twice Around the Clock* (about the London social scene, 1859), *My Diary in the Midst of War* (about the Crimea, 1865), and *Things I Have Seen and People I Have Known* (reminiscences, 1894).

William Bell SCOTT (1811-90)

A better artist than he was a writer (he painted *Iron and Coal* in 1862) he moved from friend to foe of the Rossettis over several decades. He had contributed to the putative Pre-Raphaelite magazine *The Germ* in 1850 and his poetry was enthusiastically praised by D G Rossetti, but his subsequent poetry turned out to be of varied quality. He has been romantically linked with Christina Rossetti, though again that appears to have amounted to little. Scott published a *Memoir of David Scott* (his brother, another painter) in 1850, *Poems by a Painter* in 1854, *Poems* in 1875 and *A Poet's Harvest Home* in 1882. But it was his *Autobiographical Notes* of 1892 that offended those still alive from the Rossetti clan. By then Scott, who had always just failed to be there, was dead, so to him it didn't matter.

Anna SEWELL (1820-78)

In her fifties she wrote *Black Beauty*, her only novel and one of the 19th century's most famous children's books, and she saw it published a few months before she died. For her efforts she was paid £20 – but she at least had the thrill of publication. Miss Sewell had been an invalid since a childhood accident – not from falling from a horse, which would have had an ironic aptness, but from an unhealed sprained ankle. (It is likely that she suffered from a bone disease.) Among her belongings was a note:

I have for six years been confined to the house and to my sofa, and have from time to time, as I was able, been writing what I think will turn out a little book, its special aim being to induce kindness, sympathy, and an understanding treatment of horses.

William **SHARP** (1855-1905)

Though a novelist in his own right he is more famous through other people. He wrote (not very good) biographies of Rossetti (who he knew) in 1882, Shelley (in 1887), Heine (1888) and Browning (1890), then in 1893 produced *Pharais*, a book of Celtic poetry and prose 'written by' one Fiona **Macleod**. The book achieved such immediate success that Sharp meticulously maintained the double identity, supplying and updating a bogus entry for *Who's Who*, and issuing more books 'by' her until his death. Fiona Macleod was regarded as a leading, if regrettably reclusive, figure in the 'Celtic Twilight' movement (named after a Yeats collection of 1893). Novels under Sharp's own name include *The Sport of Chance* (1888) and *The Children of Tomorrow* (1889). He also published four volumes of his own poetry, but kept the secret of Miss Macleod until he died.

George Bernard **SHAW** (1856-1950)

He lived and remained at the top of his profession for so long that it is a shock to think of him as Victorian. He is almost timeless. Britain's greatest dramatist, arguably, after Shakespeare, and our greatest popular polemicist. He was Irish, born in Dublin, but came to London in 1872. For some years a literary career seemed unlikely: he himself claimed that in his first nine years of writing he earned less than £10 from his pen. But the pen kept flowing; after five unsuccessful novels he found a more secure niche as an arts and literary critic, and it was as a critic that he began to make his name. He was, of course, in favour of the 'new' dramatists, preferring Scandinavian to home-grown, and he became a leading, if at times uncomfortable figure in the Fabian Society. He lectured for them extensively and in 1889 edited and contributed to *Fabian Essays in Socialism*.

The first of his plays, *Widowers' Houses*, was produced in 1892 but, though typically aggressive in its topic, it aroused little interest. *The Philanderer* aroused less. *Arms and the Man* followed in 1894, along with *Candida*, and his less often revived *The Devil's Disciple* was first staged abroad, in New York, in 1897. Meanwhile *The Man of Destiny* had been given an inauspicious launch at the Grand Theatre, Croydon. *You Never Can Tell* came in 1898, along with *Mrs Warren's Profession*, though this simple but shocking play took four years to be staged – and then only in America; Britain's Lord Chamberlain didn't lift the ban on it until 1924. (Yet I studied it at school when I was twelve.)

> '*Do you expect me to turn my back on thirty-five per cent when all the rest are pocketing what they can, like sensible men? No such fool! If you're going to pick and choose your acquaintances on moral principles, you'd better clear out of this country, unless you want to cut yourself out of all decent society.*'
>
> from *Mrs Warren's Profession*

Shaw's other plays, despite achieving only moderate initial success, were collected in *Plays Pleasant and Unpleasant* in 1898 and *Three Plays for Puritans* in 1901. The collections included the long and eminently readable 'Prefaces' for which Shaw quickly became known. (Some readers prefer the prefaces to the plays.) Though known for his wit, Shaw never hid his intellectualism; books issued around this time include his *The Quintessence of Ibsenism* (1891) and *The Perfect Wagnerite* (1898). In the 1890s he began to build his reputation as a brilliant debater and indefatigable arguer (curiously, he had begun as a nervous speaker, but he schooled himself to improve) and he set out to provoke, to amuse, to tantalise and to irritate on whichever platform he could find. Paradox became his watchword. Attacking orthodoxy was his game. His success arrived quite gradually, and his real fame was achieved in the early years of the 20th century.

Mary Wollstonecraft **SHELLEY** (1797-1851)
Mary Shelley's great claim to fame is, of course, *Frankenstein*, written long before the Victorian era, in 1818. But the wife of Percy Bysshe Shelley did write other books. *Valperga* (1823) and *The Last Man* (1826) are again before our period, as is *Lodore* (1835), *Faulkner* (1837) and her various short stories. It is her non-fiction which creeps into the first part of the Queen's reign. *Rambles in Germany and Italy, 1840, 1842 and 1843* was published in 1844, and her edition of her husband's essays and letters appeared in 1840. (She had issued an edition of his *Poems* in 1830.)

M P **SHIEL** (1865-1947)
In his day and now, Shiel has been a cult writer, sought out for his bizarre and imaginative stories. Born in the West Indies (Montserrat) he came to London to study medicine but moved into the fringes of fin de siècle fiction. *Prince Zaleski* (1895) was his most famous collection, and he followed it with *Shapes in the Fire* (1896). *Zaleski* shows all the signs of having been created at the height of the Decadent movement: he is a languid, permanently stoned amateur detective, living in a darkened castle and attended by a black servant, and he stirs himself enough to solve, by intuition alone, three mysteries. Shiel was interested in Nietzsche and contemporary ideas of eugenics and racial purity, and his imagination took an unhealthy turn with *The Yellow Danger* (1898). In 1901 he produced the book generally regarded as his best (most critics cavil at calling it his masterpiece): *The Purple Cloud. The Lord of the Sea* came out that same year, and a number of other fantasies, science fiction and detective stories continued until the Second World War.

J H **SHORTHOUSE** (1834-1903)
Famous for only one of his few books, *John Inglesant* (privately printed 1880, then 'properly' in 1881), Shorthouse caught the mood of the many Victorians obsessed by the religious squabbles around the Oxford Movement. Shorthouse himself was born a Quaker and converted to Anglicism. John Inglesant mixes 17th century religious intrigue with a more lively tale of Inglesant's quest to avenge his brother's murder. Shorthouse wrote some other less successful and now forgotten novels and, in 1882, *The Platonism of Wordsworth* which, to be honest, was never likely to set the world alight.

Francis Edward **SMEDLEY** (1818-64)

His own life was a Victorian tale of triumph over adversity, as he forged a decent literary career despite having been crippled from childhood. Nor did he sit at home and write in private: for three years he edited *Cruikshank's Magazine*, and the great illustrator provided the pictures for Smedley's popular book, *Frank Farleigh* (1850). Smedley followed this with *Lewis Arundel* (1852) and *Harry Coverdale's Courtship* (1855). Each of his books was a lively tale of sport and adventure.

Samuel **SMILES** (1812-1904)

One thinks of Smiles as an early 19th century pontificator, and it is a small shock to find that he outlived Queen Victoria. Before embarking on his crusading life of change and reform, Smiles (the son of a Scottish shopkeeper) had been a surgeon, editor of the *Leeds Times* and secretary to a railway company. Thus, unlike some amateur philosophers, he had experience of the real world. His advice, emphatically Victorian as it is, retains its appeal to some today, and his famous book, *Self-Help* (1859), has been in print most of the time since. (Its full title was *Self-Help: With Illustrations of Character and Conduct*.) That book, more than any other, preached the message summed up by its title: that by hard work, thrift and education any man in Britain could pull himself up and be rewarded with a place in the highest echelons of the bourgeoisie. It's ironic to recall that in his life in business, Smiles himself had worked so hard that he suffered a stroke.

Self-Help's huge success spawned several follow-ups: *Character* (1871), *Thrift* (1875) and *Duty* (1880). Other books praised famous men: *Life of George Stephenson* (1875), *Lives of the Engineers* (1861-2), *Josiah Wedgwood* (1894).

Alexander **SMITH** (1830-67)

Short-lived Scottish poet who was first singled out by William **Aytoun** as being a member of the 'Spasmodic School of Poetry' and later accused of having plagiarised no less than Alfred Lord **Tennyson**. Other critics praised Smith's *Poems* (1853), were moderately keen on his *Sonnets on the War* (the Crimean, 1855), and were more enthusiastic about *City Poems* (1857). His 1861 collection, *Edwin of Deira*, brought the claims of plagiarism. Smith then produced several works of prose, the best of which were his lovely *Dreamthorpe* and *A Summer in Skye* (1865).

Edith **SOMERVILLE** and Martin **ROSS** (1858-1949 and 1862-1915)

Somerville and Ross were second cousins, and 'Martin' was Violet Florence Martin. They wrote some books separately but are remembered for those on which they collaborated – most famously, *Some Experiences of an Irish R.M.* (1899). Their first book had come a decade before: *An Irish Cousin* (1889), followed by *Naboth's Vineyard* (1891), though perhaps their most satisfactory was the now less well-known *The Real Charlotte* in 1894. *The Silver Fox* came in 1897 before their huge success. *Some Experiences* is an amusing collection of stories about 'Major Yeates', a Resident Magistrate in rural Ireland. The pair wrote a number of other books, including travel books, and after Martin died Edith continued to publish under their dual name.

John Hanning **SPEKE** (1827-64)

His discoveries of Lake Tanganyika and the lake he named Lake Victoria were followed by his books *Journal of the Discovery of the Source of the Nile* (1863) and its swift follow-up *What Led to the Discovery of the Source of the Nile* (1864). The books led to an almighty row with his fellow explorer Sir Richard **Burton**, as Speke had broken his word not to publish before Burton was back in Britain to share the praise. A debate was arranged between himself and Burton, but on the eve of it Speke was killed, at his own hand while he was out shooting partridges. Was it suicide? The jury's verdict was accidental death.

Herbert **SPENCER** (1820-1903)

An optimistic if Godless philosopher (self-taught) who believed that evolution led inevitably to progress, and that progress, therefore, was good. Progress relied on science, and he deplored the tendency for philosophers and cultural leaders to ignore it. Everyone should learn science – including girls, who should learn 'bodily training' also – and everyone should make science a part of their everyday existence. **Darwin** was his exemplar (in return, Darwin called him 'our great philosopher'); much of Spencer's writing was on lessons drawn from what Darwin had shown – though Spencer's first, admired, book predated Darwin: *Social Statistics: or, The*

Conditions Essential to Human Happiness Specified (1851) set out its own theory of evolution. (It was Spencer, not Darwin, who coined the phrase 'survival of the fittest.') His works sound like textbooks – *First Principles* (1862), *Principles of Biology* (1864-7), *Principles of Ethics* (1879-93), et cetera – and, to be honest, they are not the easiest books to read. (Asquith said in his memoirs: 'Spencer's "Autobiography", a work of portentous size, covering 1,000 pages, is too long for readers of only average patience, but is well worth skimming and skipping.' Asquith's own memoirs, though, took up two volumes.)

Spencer was a strong defender of individualism (shades of Mill here) and his first principle was that everyone had the right to behave as they wanted, as long as it did not interfere with or injure others. He was a staunch defender of *laissez faire* and believed that the state's role in our lives should be as small as possible. He criticised learn-by-rote teaching and advocated learn-by-enquiry in its place (a lack of regard for authority was, he said, 'the principle cause of what success I have had in philosophical enquiry.'). He defended happiness also (happiness needed defending at that time), though for Spencer work was, or certainly led to, happiness. 'Life is not for work, but work is for life,' he maintained.

Though he had many critics (and he still does) he was much admired in 'advanced' literary and intellectual circles. Marian Evans (George **Eliot**) loved him, though he could not return her love, and they remained friends during the years she lived with G H **Lewes**. She was 'the most admirable woman, mentally, I have ever met,' he wrote to Lewes after her death. He died a bachelor.

Henry de Vere **STACPOOLE** (1863-1915)

His most famous book, *The Blue Lagoon*, was written in 1908, after our period, but he had been a member of the *Yellow Book* set in the 1890s, and their influence can be seen in his early novels such as *The Intended* (1894) and *Pierrot!* (1896). Other early works include *Death, the Knight, and the Lady: A Ghost Story* (1897); *The Doctor: A Study from Life* (1899); *The Rapin* (1899) and *The Bourgeois* (1901). Almost forgotten now apart from *Lagoon*, he was a fluent writer (sometimes of 'trash' novels) and a prolific one: he wrote some 50 books. Stacpoole was Irish, though educated at Malvern. He studied medicine and was a ship's doctor for over 40 years – signs of that and his expert knowledge of the South Pacific Islands can be traced in some of his stories. He also wrote under the pseudonym Tyler De Saix.

Sir Henry Morton **STANLEY** (1841-1904)

Stanley's life could have been written by Rider Haggard – or perhaps by no Victorian author, since he crossed too many boundaries. For a start, he was illegitimate, born in North Wales to Elizabeth Parry but named Rowlands after his presumed father. Sent to a workhouse at the age of seven, he stayed until the day a sadistic master tried to flog him with a birch. Young Rowlands grabbed the birch and flogged the master with it instead. Rather than face the inevitable consequences the lad ran away to sea, serving as a cabin boy till he was adopted by a New Orleans cotton broker – Mr Stanley. Henry took his name (just as he would later assume the middle name Morton). But the broker died, Henry became embroiled in the Civil War, became a merchant seaman – and his ship went down! Henry, unbelievably, was the only person to survive.

In his next incarnation, as a reporter for the *New York Herald*, he had his splendidly named editor Gordon Bennett send him on a mission to Africa to find the lost British explorer David **Livingstone**. Stanley found him, uttered the immortal line, 'Doctor Livingstone, I presume?' and wrote a book: *How I Found Livingstone* (1872). Now Stanley caught the exploring bug. His 1874 expedition saw him circumnavigate huge lakes, convert heathens to Christianity, team up with an Arab slave trader, map the Congo river, fight with cannibals, pythons and puff adders – and survive again, this time with less than half his original team.

The British had always spurned him (they thought him American, way too brash, and perhaps they didn't believe all his stories) so he led a mission for King Leopold of the Belgians. It was not one of civilisation's more glorious enterprises, but by the end of it Stanley had claimed 800,000 square miles of territory for what was to become 'the Belgian Congo'. (Perhaps Britain should not have spurned him.) In 1877 he led another expedition, probably his least successful, to rescue Emin Pasha from Equatoria and, while he was at it, to extend Leopold's kingdom further. (Pasha was reluctant to be rescued but was 'persuaded'.) These adventures were related in Stanley's *Through the Dark Continent* (1878) and *In Darkest Africa* (1890). Finally, in true boy's adventure fashion, he 'returned' to England a hero, married the beautiful Dorothy Tennant, became an MP and was knighted. She edited his autobiography after his death.

W T STEAD (1849-1912)

'Sensational' journalist and editor, much criticised, sent to jail, but who achieved notable changes in the law. Born in Northumberland, he went to school in Silcoates with George Newnes who was to found the *Daily Mail*, *Tit-Bits*, *Strand* magazine and other big-selling titles. William Thomas Stead was the more outrageous; he wore a shaggy red beard and bizarre clothes, and he delighted in shocking the rich and well-born people that he moved among. After the Siege of Paris he began cooking and eating mice ('Very tasty on a piece of toast'). What his wife felt we do not know: she was probably too busy looking after their six children.

He had become editor of the *Northern Echo* when just twenty-two. In 1880 he moved to London and took over the editorship of *Pall Mall Gazette*, a paper which, until his arrival, had been aimed at 'gentlemen'. Stead took it downmarket into profit and pioneered a new form of tabloid journalism. As with the best tabloids, Stead radicalised the look of the paper and launched 'crusades'. His most famous, a true 'sensation', was his exposure in 1889 of widespread child prostitution in the story he called '*The Maiden Tribute of Modern Babylon*' – a title which might not suit today's *Sun* but whose methodology could not be bettered. Stead arranged with a 'retired' brothel madam to buy a thirteen year old girl from her mother for sex, the whole story being set up and reported by his paper. The story created his greatest furore (he'd exposed too much). Stead, astoundingly, was jailed (for abduction of a minor) and while he served three months in Holloway Jail his *Gazette* sold out every day. The law had to be changed, he railed – and it was: the age of consent was finally raised, from thirteen to the sixteen that it is today. Stead used his three months confinement to write a book: *Government by Journalism*.

Released, he continued to mount crusades – against slums, corruption and an under-resourced Navy. He forced more government change (including the re-equipping of the Navy with Dreadnought battleships). Not all his crusades were triumphant; he supported whacky ideas such as the extraction of gold from sea water, a cure for cancer, the adoption of Esperanto, and the division of Britain into self-governing regions in which journalists would become 'interrogators of democracy'! He opposed the Boer War too soon, while support for it was at its height. He left *Pall Mall Gazette* in 1890 to start the *Review of Reviews*, a paper which grew rapidly in influence, with editions in Australia and America. A 'journalistic civil church', he thought, could run the world better than could politicians. On his way to America to promote this idea, he ran into his last 'sensation'. He had chosen to sail on the *Titanic* and it is claimed that, when it went down, it was at his request that the band on deck played 'Nearer My God To Thee'.

Sir Leslie STEPHEN (1832-1904)

Sir Leslie sits at the heart of a profoundly literary family. His father, Sir James, while serving as Under-Secretary of State for the Colonies and as professor of modern history at Cambridge, wrote critical studies and serious books; his brother Sir James Fitzjames (ah, those splendid English names) was chief writer for the *Pall Mall Gazette* in its pre-Stead days and author of several erudite but now obsolete works; his nephew James Kenneth was a journalist and parodist who died young and is one of the many names suggested as having been Jack the Ripper (unlikely, but ...); his first wife was Thackeray's daughter (she too died young) and one of his daughters was Virginia Woolf. Stephen was active in the God Debates (a sceptic – see his *Essays on Free Thinking and Plain Speaking*, 1873, and *Agnostic's Apology*, first issued 1876), he was editor of *Cornhill* magazine from 1871 to 1882, and from then until 1891 painstaking editor of the *Dictionary of National Biography*, a work which might never have gained its unassailable status without his industry and devotion. (He wrote 378 of the entries – 1,000 pages – himself.) One of his greatest works was his *History of English Thought in the Eighteenth Century* (1876). A keen mountaineer also, he showed his love for the sport in *The Playground of Europe* (1871). The best of his critical essays were collected in the then much respected *Hours in a Library* (three volumes, 1874, 76 & 79). A driven man, he was an archetypical Victorian father, stern and demanding – ultimately, in his old age and widowhood, plaintive and demanding – and much of our view of him comes from the portrait drawn by Virginia Woolf who showed him as Mr Ramsay in *To The Lighthouse*.

Robert Louis **STEVENSON** (1850-94)

Those who mis-spell his surname may console themselves with the knowledge that, as a young man, he changed the spelling of his other name from Lewis to Louis. He was the son of an engineer on the board of Northern Lighthouses in Edinburgh (his grandfather had built a number of them). Had he not been a sickly child (and an only child; he was brought up largely by his nurse since his mother, too, was seldom well) he would almost certainly have vanished into his father's profession, but his ill-health forced him to abandon the course at Edinburgh University. After a brief tilt at the law he turned to his first love, writing (and, it should be said, to a bohemian lifestyle). It was, perhaps, Sir Leslie **Stephen**, more than his father who put him on the straight path, by setting him to work with W E **Henley** as joint playwrights. The plays were indifferent but Stevenson could now call himself a professional writer. Unfortunately, he was also a

semi-invalid (his chronic bronchitis was presumably tuberculosis). This did not stop him travelling. He wrote short pieces on his walking tours in the Lake District and Switzerland. He took a canoe trip through France and Belgium (*An Inland Voyage*, 1878), a donkey trip through southern France (*Travels With a Donkey in the Cevennes*, 1879), then California (*The Silverado Squatters*, 1883, and posthumously, *The Amateur Emigrant*, 1895) where, in 1880, he married the woman he had first met in France in 1876, Fanny Osbourne (an American divorcee, ten years older than him, and his ideal companion).

On their return to Europe Stevenson was established as a writer, and many of his contributions to magazines and journals were reissued in book form (*Virginibus Peurisque*, 1881; *Familiar Studies of Men and Books*, 1882; *New Arabian Nights*, 1882; *The Merry Men*, 1887; *Memories and Portraits*, 1887, et cetera). By now his children's classic, *Treasure Island* (1883) had been published, to acclaim. *Kidnapped* followed in 1886, along with *The Strange Case of Dr Jekyll and Mr Hyde* the same year. A poorer but, at the time, successful children's book, *The Black Arrow*, came in 1888, *The Master of Ballantrae* in 1889, and *Kidnapped*'s less well-known sequel, *Catriona*, in 1893. His much-loved, still loved *A Child's Garden of Verses* appeared in 1885. (The less familiar *Underwoods* followed in 1887.) His output in these years (for I have not listed all of his works) seems frantic.

By now he and Fanny were in the South Seas (*Island Night's Entertainments*, 1893). Young and ailing himself, he made a point of visiting (at length) a leper colony and of writing a paean to the priest who ran it and who would eventually die of the disease (*Father Damien: An Open Letter to the Reverend Dr Hyde of Honolulu*, 1890). Stevenson was more political than his popular image suggests: he involved himself in several campaigns on the islanders' behalf, and the original text for *The Beach of Falesá* was so forceful it had to be bowdlerised for inclusion in the original *Island Night's Entertainments*. But RLS was less of a children's writer than his popular image would have it: Dr Jekyll and stories such as *Markheim* and *Thrawn Janet* have modernistic underpinnings of symbolism and psychological mystery.

Settled with Fanny in his beloved Samoa in the hope that he might defeat his condition, Stevenson began on his *Weir of Hermiston*. But he died suddenly of a brain haemorrhage, and the uncompleted *Weir* was published in 1896. He was buried in Samoa, where he is remembered as 'Tusitala', or The Teller of Tales.

Bram STOKER (1847-1912)

Best known as the creator of *Dracula* (1897), Abraham Stoker was born in Dublin and educated at Trinity, after which he set out on a conventional career as a civil servant. The theatre beckoned, and he began submitting dramatic criticism to *The Dublin Mail*. This led to his being appointed

editor of *The Penny Press*, before he switched to what seemed to him his proper calling – not as an actor; that wasn't the aspect of the theatre which appealed to him most – but as personal manager to the famous actor-manager Sir Henry Irving, a post he would hold for 27 years. He was far from a mere servant to Irving: Stoker directed and advised him, argued with him, defended him – and wrote a useful *Personal Reminiscences of Henry Irving* (1906).

He was an assiduous manager. When Irving played Don Quixote, Stoker scoured the country to find a suitably run-down horse, and had one brought by train from the north-east for the first night. Irving was in his dressing-room but the horse had not arrived. A telegram told them the horse had got to Euston and was on its way. Curtain-up approached. 'Where is it?' demanded Irving. It had managed as far as Bow Street, Stoker explained: 'Then the police stopped them.' The knackered horse was shot, and the horseman arrested for cruelty to animals. Stoker hired a cab-horse instead.

Deeply immersed in the theatre, Bram Stoker wrote some 15 works of fiction, of which *Dracula* is by far the most famous, a deserved classic, invigorated by Stoker's theatrical eye. Readers of a nervous disposition might prefer his *The Duties of Clerks of Petty Sessions in Ireland* (1879) – if they can find it.

R S **SURTEES** (1805-64)

Like many Victorian authors he was trained for the law but, in his twenties when a thriving sporting journalist, he helped found the *New Sporting Magazine* (in direct rivalry, it must be said, to the *Sporting Magazine* that he'd worked for). The new magazine benefited from Surtees's comic stories about Mr Jorrocks, a cockney grocer turned huntsman (expect many impenetrable jokes about class). Jorrocks soon had his stories reissued in *Jorrocks's Jaunts and Jollities* (1838), a book embellished with drawings by 'Phiz', and a likely inspiration for Mr Pickwick. More tales appeared in *Handley Cross* (1843, reissued in 1854 with illustrations by Leech). *Hillingdon Hall* added some feebler stories in 1845.

Surtees came up with a good second comic character, Mr Soapey Sponge (who 'sponges' on his acquaintances) in *Mr Sponge's Sporting Tour* (1853) and a less effective third, Mr Facey Romford, for *Mr Facey Romford's Hounds* (1865, posthumously). A handful of other collections came also. For many modern readers (other than fox-hunters) the humour has dated almost to the point of alienation, although the author (who ended his days hunting endlessly, managing his estates and serving as high sheriff of Durham) is celebrated by the R S Surtees Society which has issued excellent near facsimiles of a number of Victorian comic classics.

Henry **SWEET** (1845-1912)

It is given to few to find fame as a phonetician but Sweet achieved his on two counts, both of which would have surprised him. First, he had the

OUP publish the Philological Society's new dictionary – which became the *Oxford English Dictionary*. Second, he was used by Shaw as the basis for Henry Higgins in *Pygmalion*. Sweet might have hoped his fame would arise from his fine *History of English Sounds* (1874) or his *Anglo-Saxon Reader* (1876), or even his *Handbook of Phonetics* (1877), but 1877 was the year he approached the OUP, and the rest has become history.

Algernon Charles **SWINBURNE** (1837-1909)
Poets, even more than prose writers, glide in and out of fashion, and Swinburne is currently in, though not at the bottom of, a trough. He is so 19th century – lyrical, metrical, classical in theme – yet to the Victorians he was the epitome of modernity, exhibiting much that many of them did not like. Then there was his private life (not private enough to many) with his agnosticism, his attacks upon authority, his love of decadence and his barely concealed homosexuality. Though technically a Northumbrian, he spent most of his childhood on the Isle of Wight – when he was not at Eton, or at Balliol as a young man – though he never forgot his bracing holidays on the Northumberland coast. His love for the sea (he was a reckless swimmer) would be seen later in his poetry. And he was the son of an admiral.

Reaching adulthood in the years he did, it was inevitable that he would become associated with, though never a full member of, the Pre-Raphaelite movement. Later, he would stay in the **Rossetti** household at Cheyne Walk and battle with Rossetti's housebound wombats as to who could be the most bizarre. He was striking to look at: short, slight, with a shock of red hair crowning an apparently large head. He was loud, caustic and often camp, the poet's equivalent of the artist Whistler. Swinburne's first plays displayed him in a classical garb: *The Queen-Mother* and *Rosamund* (both 1860) were almost Elizabethan in tone, while his *Atalanta in Calydon* (1865) moved back to ancient Greece, blew fresh breath into old forms, blew up a storm of praise, and made his name. (It was to be read rather than staged.) At this early high point in the flamboyant young man's career it is no surprise that his next work, *Poems and Ballads* (1866), alarmed the more staid among his readers. A rapidly notorious collection, it combined his best traits with his worse, his sweetest with his outrageous, and was withdrawn by its publisher.

He showed signs of private fetishes and desires: flagellation, masochism, sadism, and antagonism towards God. When the middle classes rose against him, their howls alarmed him not one jot. Swinburne had throughout his life a fascination for subjects normally restricted to pornography. He shared also in the contemporary young's support for Mazzini and Italian Independence, to which young intellectuals ascribed the same romance as did their 1930s equivalents for the Spanish Civil War. *A Song of Italy* (1867) and *Songs Before Sunrise* (1871) showed where he stood. In the following year he publicly defended Rossetti against **Buchanan**'s 'Fleshly school of poetry' attack; Swinburne's reply was *Under The Microscope*. He continued with drama and a more careful *Poems and Ballads: Second Series* (1878), but was less careful with his private life – drinking hard, doing drugs and experimenting with sexuality. He was not a fit man (it appears he was epileptic). In 1879 he collapsed and may well have died, had it not been for the intervention of his friend Theodore **Watts-Dunton** who scooped him up, took him into his house in Putney, ministered to him and looked after him for the remaining three decades of his life. Watts-Dunton cloistered him. In the late years of the century Swinburne would occasionally emerge to be 'sighted' as he wandered vacantly about Putney Heath. He was regarded as a true rara avis.

Watts-Dunton had freed Swinburne to continue writing – most would say he wrote less vigorously, though no one could say he wrote badly. *Mary*

Stuart came in 1881, *Tristam of Lyonesse and Other Poems* in 1882, *Marino Faliero* in 1885, and the third series of *Poems and Ballads* in 1889. He found himself championed by the Aesthetic Movement (many of whom tried, with little success, to mimic his limpid verse) and he showed, to those who hadn't already realised, that he was a perceptive critic of other people's work. Fine and delicate as his published writing usually was, there lay behind it an unpublished seam of vituperative gossip and some lewd and frankly obscene material, much of which we know of only by repute. If only he could have imbued his poetry and verse drama with the same degree of meat. But he was an aesthete; his art was for art's sake, not its subject's; indeed, there often appeared to be no subject. But this shouldn't take away from his reputation as an intelligent and perceptive critic, a beautiful verse-maker, and a fearless opponent of massed propriety.

> *I am tired of tears and laughter,*
> *And men that laugh and weep;*
> *Of what may come hereafter*
> *For men that sow to reap:*
> *I am weary of days and hours,*
> *Blown buds of barren flowers,*
> *Desires and dreams and powers*
> *And everything but sleep.*

from *The Garden of Proserpine*

John Addington SYMONDS (1840-93)

A consumptive who took on one of the hardest fights of all in the Victorian age: the acceptance of male homosexuality. (An indication of how implacable the world was against homosexuality can be seen in Symonds trying to 'repress' his homosexuality in 1864 by marrying.) His weak lungs caused him to spend part of his adult life in the more congenial Switzerland and Italy, where he wrote unambiguously on platonic love, male beauty, Hellenism and the Renaissance, and rigid Victorian attitudes to God. (In Horatio Brown's biography of him, Symonds recalled God in his childhood: 'I was persuaded that the devil lived near the doormat, in a dark corner of the passage by my father's bedroom. I thought that he appeared to me there under the shape of a black shadow, scurrying about on the ground, with the faintest indication of a swiftly whirling tail.' He spoke there, one feels, for many Victorians.)

His longest book was *Renaissance in Italy*, published in stages from 1875 to 86. He wrote critical biographies, some volumes of verse including the unexpectedly titled *Wine, Women and Song* (1884) and two key pamphlets on the law and homosexuality: *A Problem in Greek Ethics* (1883) and *A Problem in Modern Ethics* (1891). His essays were collected in *Essays Speculative and Suggestive* (1890) and *In The Key of Blue* (1892).

Arthur **SYMONS** (1865-1945)

Though the son of a Methodist minister, he became a colourful figure among London-based Decadents, editing the *Savoy* in 1896 and publishing **Beardsley, Dowson**, Lionel **Johnson**, *et al*. He wrote favourable studies of Baudelaire, Blake, **Pater** and **Wilde** but, it is said, took the decadent life a little too far, causing his collapse in 1908 from which, although he recovered, he drifted into a quiet and long old age with the help of the Royal Literary Fund. His own rather good 'decadent' poems can be found in *Days and Nights* (1889) and *London Nights* (1895).

Tom **TAYLOR** (1817-80)

Playwright, editor and prolific journalist who began as a teacher, went into law, and progressed to become secretary to the London Board of Health, a post he held for nearly 20 years until 1871. He became editor of *Punch* in 1874, having previously submitted many pieces to the magazine. A thriving dramatist since the 1840s, he became 'house dramatist' at the Olympic and Haymarket theatres. He wrote farces, plays, melodramas and pantomimes, and his *Ticket of Leave Man* (1863) introduced the first stage detective, 'Hawkshaw'. Among the tasks entrusted to him was editorship of the voluminous diaries of Benjamin Robert **Haydon** (issued in 1853), a task few other writers would have had the time or editorial competence to perform.

Alfred Lord **TENNYSON** (1809-92)

The quintessential Victorian poet who deservedly became Laureate in 1850, he was one of eight children to a gloomy Lincolnshire vicar who provided much of his education privately at home. He began auspiciously at Cambridge but, when his father died in 1831, he left without taking his

degree. In 1832 he explored Europe with his university friend Arthur Hallam, who died there suddenly the following year. Tennyson was shattered at the death of his young friend and poured his grief into the long poem *In Memoriam* – a poem he would not complete and publish until 1850 (when it was widely acclaimed). Two early works that had been published were of little merit: *Poems by Two Brothers* (1827) and *Poems, Chiefly Lyrical* (1830). His *Poems* of 1833 was the first collection to show real quality. It contained a number of his finest pieces but was savaged by several critics – leading the ever-neurotic Tennyson to begin what has been called his 'Ten Years' Silence'. His 1842 collection reprised a number of his early poems, together with new ones, and was a treasury of sonorous, rolling verses, seemingly recalling a magical bygone age of glory, and wonderfully suitable for reading aloud on Victorian evenings. *A Dream of Fair Women*, *The Lotos-Eaters*, *The Lady of Shalott*, *Morte d'Arthur* and others captivated and inspired thousands of romantic readers including, notably, the young Pre-Raphaelite artists and poets. 1847 saw *The Princess*, another fine work, in which he brilliantly argued for the rights of women. In 1850 he married, became Poet Laureate and married the woman he'd first proposed to in 1833.

But he mistrusted his success. He shared his father's gloom – speaking often of the 'black blood' of melancholy in his family. **Carlyle**, indeed, thought him solitary and sad, 'carrying a bit of Chaos about him, which he is manufacturing into Cosmos.' He and his wife Emily moved to the Isle of Wight, but their new home was too easily accessible to stop people pestering him. The famous and the would-be famous flocked to

Faringford, his island home (Prince Albert called once, in 1856). He hated people recognising him in the street, yet was furious if they passed him by. Living, as he did, close to the photographer Julia Margaret Cameron, Tennyson and his family posed for her, and from those sessions we have some superb portraits, though: 'I can't be anonymous by reason of your confounded photographs,' he told her later. He made a habit of accepting membership and then resigning from London clubs, and he exhibited confusing signs of excessive shyness mixed with vanity.

The literary lion continued to produce major works. *Maud* appeared in 1855, as did *The Charge of the Light Brigade*. *Idylls of the King* came in 1859. He was made a baron in 1884 (as Alfred, Lord Tennyson, he was the first English poet to be ennobled for his poetry alone) but, perhaps inevitably, in his later years he began to be criticised by the new generation. (The waspish **Swinburne** sneered at 'Morte d'Albert, or Idylls of the Prince Consort'.) Tennyson has continually been faulted, even dismissed, by critics – but to the public he remains one of the most quoted and most loved Victorian poets.

Charles **TENNYSON TURNER** (1808-79)

Elder brother to Alfred Tennyson, but a far lesser poet. He contributed to the early work *Poems by Two Brothers* (1827) – actually the work of three brothers, Alfred, Charles and Frederick – and he published (quietly) four volumes of his own pastoral sonnets at long intervals. He took the name Turner on succeeding to his great uncle's property – a small sacrifice for prosperity.

William Makepeace **THACKERAY** (1811-63)

It would be harsh to call Thackeray a one-hit wonder but since the late 19th century this one-time rival to Dickens has never regained his early eminence. Only one of his novels is widely read – one novel and one children's story. The novel was Thackeray's first: *Vanity Fair* came out in parts through 1847 and 8, when it both shocked and delighted its readers – shocked, because this 'novel without a hero' has a clear heroine, Becky Sharpe, who is an adulterous opportunist adventuress; and delighted, because the novel is a brilliantly enjoyable satire, pillorying recognisable members of society – though not oneself! Randy old roués, lecherous swains, arch adventurers of either gender, blusterers, flusterers, milksops, snobs, swindlers and seducers throng its lively pages, and the plot rattles along like an unstoppable charabanc crammed with bustling passengers. Plus – the great overlooked joy of Thackeray – each chapter is enlivened with the author's drawings. Thackeray has been criticised as a lazy writer and as an illustrator who couldn't draw. Both these criticisms miss the point: he is a deliberately amiable writer, chatting to you, one to one, from his armchair in the club; and he doesn't try to be an artist, he draws cartoons. The kindly old uncle he purports to be spins his stories out affectionately; he drifts, digresses and discusses the text as if you and he were companion readers.

The cartoons – he was generous with illustrations – lack the competence of the professional illustrators brought in to decorate his later books, but they show the characters and the settings as the author conceived them, they complement the text and, above all, are great fun.

Vanity Fair in an edition without his pictures is only half the book. *Pendennis* (1848-50), Thackeray's

second and perhaps most autobiographical novel, contains some full-page plates and a wealth of more amusing decorated initials. *Esmond* (1852) was unillustrated and for his fourth, *The Newcombes* (1853-5), the artist Richard Doyle was used instead. For *The Virginians* (1857-9) Thackeray drew his own (to get the historical details right). He always wanted to decorate his stories, but publishers continually persuaded him not to. When he himself published (the not very good) *Lovel the Widower* in his own *Cornhill Magazine* (which he founded in January 1860) his story ran alongside **Trollope**'s *Framley Parsonage* for which the celebrated John Everett Millais drew the pictures: even Thackeray knew the battle was hopeless and he engaged Fred Walker to do the *Lovel* pictures instead.

Much of Thackeray's early work – and there was a great deal before *Vanity Fair* – was punctuated with his sketches. He had been a prolific contributor to *Fraser's Magazine* and *Punch*, and many of his skits and satires were reissued in volume form. The *Yellowplush Papers* were a hit in

Fraser's in 1837 and 8 but you'd struggle to laugh at a volume now. (*The Fitzboodle Papers*, 1842-3, reads much the same.) Thackeray was satirising a common enough type of the time, the above-himself footman, but the words are dusty now; only the drawings are lively. His *Paris Sketch Book* (1839), *The Book of Snobs* (1848) and *The Roundabout Papers* (1860-3) are perhaps the best of these works. And the other great illustrated work, far shorter than *Vanity Fair* but fit to stand somewhere near, was the children's story, *The Rose and the Ring*, published as late as 1855. Among his serious works, *The Four Georges* (1857, about the four kings) and *The English Humourists* (1851, essays in criticism) remain sound if worthy stuff.

He should have lived comfortable well-off, but he lost his money early through gambling and speculation. He should have been happily married, but his wife suffered a mental collapse and spent much of her life in an institution. He should have found a new love, but his wife, who he never abandoned, long outlived him. He wasted a decade in a hopeless quasi romance with a friend's wife, Jane Brookfield (who led him on as wickedly as might any of his fictional characters). He had three daughters upon whom he doted, but one died young. (His third daughter became the first wife of Virginia Woolf's father; his first became a writer herself – Anne Thackeray **Ritchie**.) Thackeray was never a healthy man, and was seldom financially secure. Nevertheless, his death on Christmas Eve 1863, was unexpected.

W Brandon **THOMAS** (1856–1914)

Largely, perhaps only, remembered for his timeless farce *Charley's Aunt*, Walter Brandon Thomas first trod the boards in 1879, earning money on the side by writing sketches, plays and songs (often, dare we say it, 'coon songs', then very popular) until hitting the big time with his eighth play, *Charley's Aunt*, a genuinely funny piece, even today. It was first staged in 1892 in Bury St Edmunds, and when it came to London's Royalty Theatre it ran for four happy years.

The play had had a long gestation. The original script had numerous love scenes, all of which were excised: 'Farce,' admitted Brandon, 'is not written on a table but at rehearsal.' Much of the cutting was at the (correct) insistence of actor-producer W S Penley, who played the aunt originally. Penley claimed that at its first night a man came down from the gallery, saying he was lonely, and could he join the other two of the audience in the pit. Penley, too, was a comedian.

Francis THOMPSON (1859-1907)

Author of ornate, often religious verse (*Health and Holiness*, *The Hound of Heaven*, etc) who, having failed to become a doctor, had to be rescued from opium addiction and destitution in the 1880s by author Alice **Meynell** and her husband (editor, ironically, of *Merry England*). They did what they could for him, finding lodgings and placing his poetry, but his health never fully recovered and he died of tuberculosis. His overheated verse appeals particularly to some fervent Roman Catholics.

James THOMSON (1834-82)

> *I paced the silent and deserted streets*
> *In cold dark shade and chillier moonlight grey ;*
> *Pondering a dolorous series of defeats*
> *And black disasters from life's opening day.*
>
> from his *The City of Dreadful Night*

A poet not to be confused with James Thomson, 1700-48, author of *The Castle of Indolence*. The later Thomson was a gloomy Scot (early work: *The Doom of a City*, 1857) who failed to hold positions as a teacher or solicitor's clerk, and emigrated briefly to America in 1872. By then he had written for various magazines, was a friend of the elder Rossetti, and was drinking far too much. After a spell as Spanish Correspondent for *The New York World* he returned to London, and among pieces submitted to magazines was one that made him famous: *The City of Dreadful Night* (1874 in the *National Reformer* magazine, 1880 in book form) – a long poem of extraordinary pessimism, dark and original enough to touch the nerve of a public overdosed on saccharine. He was now able to place a good deal of work, much of which still seems fine, but his growing alcoholism sped him to his grave.

Anthony **TROLLOPE** (1815-82)

Trollope's most controversial work was his own *Autobiography*, published in 1883, the year after he died, in which he set down with admirable frankness how he worked: three hours every morning before setting off for the day job (a senior post in the Post Office) and measuring his output by the clock. 250 words in 15 minutes meant 3,000 words a session meant 15,000 words a week. 'A week passed with an insufficient number of pages has been a blister to my eye, and a month so disgraced would have been a sorrow to my heart.' He has been much pilloried for this confession – often by people who have not read the *Autobiography* – how could a real writer be so mechanical? Yet, in the very paragraph quoted against him, Trollope said that his average varied greatly, according to circumstances, and that although he might average 40 pages (making 10,000 words a week, not 15,000) he could drop to half that or rise to almost three times as much when under the cosh. In other words, like many writers, he wrote regularly but responded strenuously to deadlines.

Trollope freely admits that one or two of his books (he mentions *The Bertrams* and *Castle Richmond*) were tackled at a rush – suffering from poor plotting, not from over-hasty writing: often, in fact, 'I believe that the work which has been done quickest has been done the best.' Like any other writer, he lived with his characters, 'crying at their grief, laughing at their absurdities, and thoroughly enjoying their joy.' Trollope, ever professional, horrified his critics (who presumably did not earn their living from writing books) by admitting that as soon as a book was finished he went straight on to the next. 'A shoemaker when he has finished one pair of shoes does not sit down and contemplate his work in idle satisfaction.' But this alarming admission was followed by Trollope saying, 'An author may of course want time to study a new subject' – although: 'I could be really happy only when I was at work.' To me, there is little in these confessions that hasn't been said since by many an author. Trollope was a professional.

His mother, Frances, was a successful novelist before him (see below) and, rather than encourage her son to follow her, found him his position in the Post Office. (It is a myth that he invented the pillar box. It was invented years before he joined.) Only when he was in his thirties did he begin to write, and his first novel, the little-read *The MacDermotts of Ballycloran* came out in 1844. His fourth novel made his name: *The Warden* (1855), began the wryly comic, well observed Barchester series (or the *Barsetshire Novels*), a series never since out of print and seldom out of favour. His second series, of political rather than clerical characters, was the Palliser Novels, beginning with *Can You Forgive Her?* (1864-5) and becoming more political – or more parliamentary – as the series progressed. *The Eustace Diamonds* (1871-3) may be the best of this fine series, though fans will want to read them all. ('Plantagenet Palliser' appears in all six.)

The two series are only part of his huge output, practically all of which remains easily readable today. *The Way We Live Now* (1874-5) with its plot of financial swindles, dupes and sharks is the most apposite to our present troubled times, and should remain the greatest of his non-series novels, though *Orley Farm* (1861-2), *The Claverings* (1866-7), and *He Knew He Was Right* (1868-9) will always have their fans. For many of those fans, Trollope's novels are addictive.

On 3rd November 1882, wrote Trollope's son, his father 'was seized with paralysis on the right side, accompanied by loss of speech.' He drifted on through November until: 'He died on the evening of the 6th of December following nearly five weeks from the night of his attack.'

Frances (Fanny) TROLLOPE (1780-1863)

A mother wants the best for her son, but how does she feel if he overleaps her in a profession where she excelled? She was a best-selling travel-writer and novelist, having become a travel-writer almost by chance when her husband, following the failure of his business, sent her to Cincinnati to establish a fancy goods emporium. It inevitably failed, but on her return she recorded her experiences (non too flatteringly) in *Domestic Manners of the Americans* (1832). Had she praised America the book might not have sold so well. Frances, to her surprise, found herself a best-selling author at the age of 52 – best-selling but still in debt. Despite recurrent illness – and would it be unkind to say, despite her age? – the indefatigable woman (a family trait: see Anthony above) went on to write an astounding 40 more books in the next 25 years. Mainly she wrote novels, though she did produce more travel books (*Paris and the Parisians* in 1835, *Vienna and the Austrians* in 1838, *A Visit to Italy* in 1842). Notable among her novels were *Michael Armstrong, the Factory Boy* (first issued in parts, 1839-40), one of the first 'industrial' novels, and *Vicar of Wrexhill* (1837) which, bravely for its time, attacked organised religion. When she died she had restored the family's finances and had seen two of her sons begin writing novels; Anthony (above) and Thomas Adolphus, the now ignored author of some 60 assorted books, and a useful *Diary*.

Martin Farquhar **TUPPER** (1810-99)
Famously bad poet who was read by millions. At the time they took him seriously (he took himself seriously) but he has subsequently become a figure of fun. After the pious *Sacra Poesis* (1832) he issued a warning to students about vice: *A Voice From the Cloister* (1835). But his major work – half a lifetime's work, running as it did from 1838 to 76 and coming out in four solemn volumes and some 50 editions – was *Proverbial Philosophy, a Book of Thoughts and Arguments, Originally Treated*, full of maxims and commonplaces and a great deal of padding (much like a modern 'How to Succeed' manual, come to think of it) in which he hails his readers: 'Come again, and greet me as a friend, fellow pilgrim upon life's highway; Leave awhile the hot and dusty road, to loiter in the greenwood of Reflection.' At the same time he predicted the book's formal reception:

> *That book is doomed to be condemned; the critic must not read it;*
> *Some awkward beauties in the thing might tamper with his verdict.*

'WALTER'

Pseudonymous author of the century's most famous work of pornography, *My Secret Life*, a vast tome running to over a million words and published in stages between 1888 and 1894. His identity is not known for certain, although Henry Spencer **Ashbee** is the name most often cited.

Mrs Humphry **WARD** (1851-1920)

In the respectable late Victorian home Mrs Ward's writings were well-known. She was a moralistic novelist and journalist, of the kind who wrote high-minded pieces in middlebrow magazines. She was niece to Matthew **Arnold** (whose views on religion she supported), aunt to Aldous Huxley (whose views she would have abhorred) and was married to an Oxford don (who became art critic to the *Times*). She became secretary to Somerville College in 1879, and in the 1880s was active in social missionary work in London. At this time she met and became a close friend of the American writer Henry James. With some encouragement from him, Mrs Ward wrote an ill-advised first novel, *Miss Bretherton* (1884), transparently based on the career of the real-life American actress Mary Anderson, and fatally flawed by being written in a quasi-Jamesian florid style. It flopped, but she continued writing. Her 1888 novel *Robert Elsmere* displayed her (and Matthew Arnold's) interpretation of Christian duty, and all her subsequent novels stood on this firmer ground of practical religion, social service and human politics. She argued for higher education for women but, in common with a number of intelligent women of the time, was unable to agree with the cause of female suffrage. In 1908 she would become president of the Women's Anti-Suffrage League. She has not endeared herself to women readers since.

Theodore **WATTS-DUNTON** (1832-1914)

His gypsy novel *Aylwin* (1898) was a hit in its day but would be utterly forgotten now were it not that it contains a barely disguised portrait of the fading D G **Rossetti** (there named 'Haroun-al-Raschid the Painter'). Watts-Dunton knew Rossetti and other Pre-Raphaelites personally, though from 1879 his more famous, and no doubt more demanding, relationship was with the increasingly unpredictable Swinburne, with whom he lived and who he looked after at the Watts-Dunton villa – 2, The Pines, Putney – for 30 years. He produced a volume of poems, *The Coming of Love*, in 1897, and edited *Borrow's Lavengro* and *The Romany Rye*.

Beatrice and Sidney **WEBB** (1858-1943 & 1859-1947)
A famous and long-lived socialist couple. She was a daughter to the wealthy and well-connected Potter family, while he was the son of a London shopkeeper. They helped found the Fabian Society in 1884, married in 1892, helped found the LSE in 1895 and the *New Statesman* in 1913. Among their sturdy socialist writings were *The History of Trade Unionism* (1894) and *Industrial Democracy* (1897), before others on similar topics which fall outside our period.

Julia **WEDGWOOD** (1833-1914)
A Victorian bluestocking from the seemingly inexhaustible Wedgwood/Darwin clan, the great granddaughter of Josiah Wedgwood and the niece by marriage of Charles **Darwin**. Though deaf, she taught herself Latin, Greek, French, and German, and became research assistant to Mrs **Gaskell** on her *Life of Charlotte Brontë*. No one should have been surprised when she wrote a couple of novels, the first of which, *Framleigh Hall* by 'Florence Dawson' (1858), was advanced and, by the standards of the day, shocking in its coverage of sexuality and confused gender – too advanced for her father, who insisted on proof-reading and censoring her second, the much tamer *An Old Debt* (1859). This latter, under her own name, was the last novel she would write. (She started a third but gave up.)

She later wrote a critical biography of John Wesley (1870) and, shortly after, helped Darwin translate *Linnaeus*. She contributed to serious magazines and eventually published *The Moral Ideal: a Historic Study* (1888, dedicated to **Browning**), and six years later a book-length critique, *The Message of Israel*. The book was poorly received and she turned to a simpler – though, in her hands, never completed – project: a biography of her great-grandfather Josiah Wedgwood. She was, by now, becoming blind as well as deaf and had a perhaps non-fatal cancer. When she died she left most of her money to the anti-vivisection movement.

H G **WELLS** (1866 – 1946)
Famous as he is, Wells only just slips into this book as his first was published in Victoria's last decade. *The Time Machine*, although written in 1888 for *The Science Schools Journal*, came out as a book in 1895; it looked forward first to the year 802,701 and then to the end of the world, 30

million years ahead. In Victorian times, Wells kept to science fiction, a field in which he was pre-eminent, with *The Wonderful Visit* (1895), *The Island of Dr Moreau* (1896), *The Invisible Man* (1897), *The War of the Worlds* (1898) and *When the Sleeper Wakes* in 1899. 1900 saw his first more conventional fiction: *Love and Mr Lewisham*. Thereafter his output included works of both conventional and science fiction – as well as science fact and, later, some political pieces.

Wells had no fear of controversy. He had risen from the lower middle classes (his father an unsuccessful tradesman), had acquired a first class honours degree in zoology, had taught, written science textbooks, had survived a mistaken marriage to his cousin, and had eventually married the student with whom he'd eloped. His 'advanced' views on sex would hit back at him at intervals throughout his life. None of his science fiction predicted a joyous future: humankind would degenerate through its own foolishness in *The Time Machine*; eugenics and science would betray us in *Dr Moreau*; the gift of invisibility would be abused in *The Invisible Man*; *The War of the Worlds* would be disastrous; *When the Sleeper Wakes* it would not be to a cheerful cup of tea. (Decades later his final novel would be the deeply pessimistic *Mind at the End of its Tether* in 1945.) Yet despite his themes, Wells is a cheerful and entertaining writer (some of his 20th century novels were altogether lighter) and, if his predictions did not all come true, they remain arresting and inspired.

Oscar **WILDE** (1854–1900)

Life imitates art, Oscar insisted, but Wilde's life was nothing like his art. His plays teased convention and were the funniest of the 19th century, his poetry and prose exalted beauty, but the society he mocked rose up in ugly rancour to tear him down. He had asked for it, of course, and he knew that he'd done so – but in the liberal-thinking fin de siècle he thought he could sail above convention and disarm it with bon mots. That he and Lord Arthur **Douglas** were lovers was an open secret (though it appears they spent much of their time trawling together for rough trade) and when Douglas's infuriated father – the Marquess of Queensberry, renowned for his bellicose intolerance – left his misspelt card at Oscar's club Wilde should have known better than to respond. Would any of his languid heroes have done anything more than raise an eyebrow? To have returned the card with a spelling dictionary might have been more sensible. But Wilde, disastrously, sued for libel. It was unnecessary, futile, and he couldn't win. He couldn't be allowed to win – as he, of all people, should have known.

The court case (1895) was a media frenzy; Wilde lost, was sent to jail, and was disgraced. No theatre dared stage his plays. No person dared buy his works. His name became unutterable. He died alone.

Oscar Fingal O'Flahertie Wills Wilde, the son of an Irish surgeon, attended Trinity College, Dublin, then Magdalen College, Oxford, where he made himself deliberately prominent in the 'art for art's sake' movement. He was outrageous, and the public loved it. His *Poems* (1881) were enough to earn him a lecture tour in the States. ('Have you anything to declare, sir?' 'Only my genius.') His play there, *Vera*, was a flop and is never revived. Despite his flamboyant image, he married (in 1884) and had two sons. He produced a surprisingly good book of fairy stories, *The Happy Prince and Other Tales* (1888), then more stories: *The Picture of Dorian Gray* (1890), *Lord Arthur Savile's Crime*, and *Other Stories* (1891), and more fairy stories, *A House of Pomegranates* (also 1891). Brilliant as these pieces were, there was little sign of his becoming a genius of the theatre; his second play, *The Duchess of Padua* (1891 again) was dull, but the next four saw Wilde home in with devastating precision upon his target. The plays which made him king (queen would be too cheap) of the London stage came dancing from his pen: *Lady Windermere's Fan* (1892), *A Woman of No Importance* (1893), *An Ideal Husband* (1895), *The Importance of Being Earnest* (1895). The very different verse drama, *Salome* (1894), written in French (to emphasise its fashionably perfumed decadence) had been translated back into English by Lord Arthur Douglas (graced with fashionably perfumed illustrations by Aubrey Beardsley), but could only be performed in Paris (in 1896).

The *Importance of Being Earnest* was Wilde's best play; he was at the apex of his career, the outrageous darling of society and the stage – and, as if he were reliving an old Greek tragedy, at the height of success came Nemesis, in the form of the Marquess of Queensberry's card. Wilde's later works were *The Ballad of Reading Gaol* (written there, and published after his release, in 1898) and *De Profundis*, published in various, argued-over versions from 1905.

> *Never speak disrespectfully of Society, Algernon. Only people who can't get into it do that.*
>
> from *The Importance of Being Earnest*

Mrs Henry **WOOD** (1814–87)

It is only actresses of very advanced age today who cry, 'Gone – and never called me Mother!' in the expectation of a wry smile. The line is from the melodrama made from Mrs Wood's most famous novel – once very famous, but who reads it now? – *East Lynne*, a one-time stalwart of weekly rep. The novel, published in 1861, was her first, after she had written magazine short stories, and although she followed it with many others (good, workmanlike mysteries and domestic dramas, though somewhat worthy) and although they sold hugely in their time, she is no longer read.

W B YEATS (1865-1939)

One of the greatest, perhaps the greatest Irish nationalist poet and dramatist, although in the public mind – certainly the English public mind – he is remembered for his romantic image and for remarkably few of his many poems. Even to his contemporaries, he became more tiresome as he aged: vain and faded, over-reliant on his early reputation. But that was in the 20th century; his rocket soared in the 19th. Educated in Dublin, he began as a literary editor (helping found the Irish Literary Society and the Irish national theatre). His play *The Countess Cathleen* was staged in Dublin in 1892, and he remained immersed in the romantic Irish tradition of myth and revolution – *Fairy and Folk Tales of the Irish Peasantry* (1888), *The Celtic Twilight* (1893) et cetera – together with his poetical works, *The Wanderings of Oisin and Other Poems* (1899), *The Wind among the Reeds* (1899), *The Countess Kathleen and Other Legends and Lyrics* (1892), *The Land of Heart's Desire* (1894), *The Shadowy Waters* (1900). In the 20th century the romantic tone of his poetry would shift towards less accessible mysticism and political grouse, and ultimately he would receive the Nobel Prize for Literature (1923) and become an Irish Free State senator (1922-28). He died in the South of France.

YELLOW BOOK authors

For a literary magazine that ran only between 1894 and 97 the *Yellow Book* has an extraordinary reputation. Its eye-catching yellow and black covers reflected its intentionally shocking content – content which would shock nobody today: the magazine was often too 'aesthetic' to be enjoyable, the poems fey and the articles wilfully obscure. Illustrations, by Beardsley and the like, could be superb, and not all of the literary content was poor: how could it be, when there were contributions from Max Beerbohm, Henry James, Edmund Gosse, Arnold Bennett, H G Wells, W B Yeats, Earnest Dowson and Richard Le Galliennne? The magazine was published and, to an extent, reined in, by John Lane, and was edited by Henry Harland with assistance, of a kind, from Aubrey Beardsley.

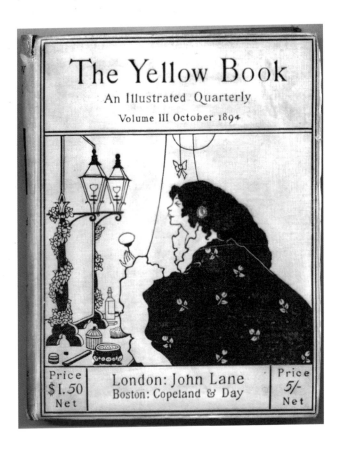

Charlotte **YONGE** (1823-1901)

The Victorian high priestess of sound moralistic writing. There was a great deal of moralistic writing in that century but most, unlike Miss Yonge's, was stodgy and indigestible. Charlotte Yonge could write, even if her subjects and teachings are not to our taste today. The Victorian nursery was not complete without a sprinkling of her books – she did, after all, write at least 120 of them. A hint of what was to come lies in her first published title, *Abbeychurch: or Self-Control and Self-Conceit* (1844). *The Heir of Redclyffe* (1853) was her first success, and was swiftly followed by a succession of worthy works, not all of which were for children: she wrote historical romances, biographies and tales of family life. *The Daisy Chain* (1856) began a popular series of books about a large family which included the widowed Dr May and his appealingly-drawn ugly duckling of a daughter, Ethel.

Despite her fame Charlotte Yonge lived all her life in a Hampshire village, Otterbourne from where, for 40 years, she also edited a girls' magazine, *The Monthly Packet*. She is still read, partly for the quality of the books themselves, and partly for the insights those densely packed stories give on everyday life in the 19th century.

Israel **ZANGWILL** (1864-1926)

Writer, political activist and translator, whose novel *Children of the Ghetto* (1892) remains the classic account of immigrants (in this case, London's impoverished and often stateless Jews) trying to settle in an alien city. The book exposed their struggles and vicissitudes and the open prejudice against them, and was followed by *Ghetto Tragedies* (1899) and *Ghetto Comedies* (1907). Alongside these ran his non-fiction history, *Dreamers of the Ghetto* (1898) and a collection of lighter tales in *The King of Schnorrers* (1894). Zangwill also edited the humorous magazine, *Ariel*, and wrote one notable detective novel, *The Big Bow Mystery* (1892), listed by the great American mystery writer Edward D Hoch as one of the ten greatest locked room mysteries of all time.

Sleep!

INDEX

Find the book you're looking for here. (Authors are listed in the A to Z above.)

A Blighted Life, 55
A Boy's Adventures in the Wilds of Australia, 103
A Chaplet of Verses, 148
A Child of the Jago, 139
A Child's Garden of Verses, 173
A Christmas Child, 137
A Daughter of Heth, 39
A Day's Ride, 123
A Dream of John Ball, 138
A Flat Iron for a Farthing, 83
A Girl in the Karpathians, 76
A Good Time Coming, 66
A Hard Woman, 105
A House of Pomegranates, 194
A Journey Due North, 161
A Life for a Life, 68
A London Plane-Tree, 124
A Modern Lover, 137
A Modern Minister, 79
A Mummer's Wife, 137
A New Spirit of the Age, 102
A Pair of Blue Eyes, 96
A Romance of Two Worlds, 66
A Shropshire Lad, 102
A Song of Italy, 177
A Study in Scarlet, 77
A Summer in Skye, 167
A Voice From The Waters, 36
A Woman of No Importance, 194
A Woman with a History, 94
A World of Girls, 132
Abbeychurch: or Self-Control and Self-Conceit, 197
Adam Bede, 81
Adèle, 111
After London, 108
Agnes Grey, 44

Ainsworth's Magazine, 25
Alice Lorraine, 40
Alice's Adventures under Ground, 59
All The Year Round magazine, 123, 126, 149
Allan Quatermain, 95
Almayer's Folly, 64
Alton Locke, 113
Amenophis, 144
Amours de Voyage, 62
An African Millionaire, 26
An Epic of Women, 142
An Ideal Husband, 194
An Inland Voyage, 173
An Irish Cousin, 167
An Old Debt, 191
Arabian Nights, 55, 119
Armadale, 63
Arms and the Man, 164
At The Back of the North Wind, 128
Atalanta in Calydon, 176
Athenaeum, 3, 39, 52, 75, 79
Athens: its Rise and Fall, 54
Atherton, and Other Tales, 136
Atlantic Monthly, 62
Aunt Judy's Magazine, 83, 89, 90
Aurora Floyd, 44
Aylwin, 190
Azeth the Egyptian, 126

Bad Child's Book of Beasts, 37
Balder the Beautiful, 52
Ballads of Scotland, 30
Barabbas, 66
Barsetshire novels, 188
Basil: A Story of Modern Life, 63
Beauchamp's Career, 133
Beeton's Christmas Annual, 77

Belford Regis, 136
Belgravia, 25, 44
Bentley's Magazine, 49
Bentley's Miscellany, 25, 33, 143
Bevis, The Story of a Boy, 108
Black Beauty, 162
Blackwood's Magazine, 30, 79, 81, 89, 142
Bleak House, 72, 99, 105
Born in Exile, 91
Boy's Own Paper, 150
Boys' Own Magazine, 100
Brother Fabian's Manuscript, 82

Can You Forgive Her?, 188
Candida, 164
Carrots, 137
Casa Guidi Windows, 51
Catriona, 173
Cautionary Tales, 37
Celebrities I Have Known, 123
Chambers' Journal, 61, 76, 132
Charles O'Malley, 123
Charley's Aunt, 185
Chartism, 58, 113
Cheveley, 55, 79
Children of the Ghetto, 197
Christie Johnstone, 149
Christmas-Eve and Easter Day, 51
Clara Vaughan, 40
Clayhanger, 38
Cock House at Fellsgarth, 150
Colonel Blood, 42
Cometh Up As A Flower, 49
Comic History, 24
Con Cregan, 123
Confessions of a Young Man, 137
Confessions of Harry Lorrequer, 123
Coningsby, 75
Contemporary Review, 52
Conversations with Lord Byron, 41
Cornhill magazine, 25, 82, 99, 158, 172, 183
Crabbet Club, 41
Cradock Nowell, 40
Cranford, 88, 89
Cripps the Carrier, 40
Cruikshank's Magazine, 166

Culture and Anarchy, 14, 29
Cunning Murrell, 139
Currer, Ellis and Acton Bell, 45

Daily News, 102, 118
Daily Telegraph, 105, 161
Daniel Deronda, 82
David Elginbrod, 128
Days and Nights, 179
De Profundis, 75, 152, 194
Dead Man's Rock, 148
Dealings With the Fairies, 129
Dear Faustina, 49
Death's Jest-Book, 36
Deerbrook, 131
Demos, 91
Departmental Ditties, 116
Desperate Remedies, 95
Diabolus Amans, 70
Diana of the Crossways, 133, 142
Diary of a Nobody, 94
Dictionary of National Biography, 172
Dombey and Son, 72
Domestic Manners of the Americans, 189
Dover Beach, 14, 27
Dr Jekyll and Mr Hyde, 173
Dracula, 122, 174, 175
Dream Days, 94
Dreamers of the Ghetto, 197
Dreamthorpe, 167
Dublin University Magazine, 121, 123
Dulcamara, 90
Duty and Inclination, 118

East Lynne, 194
education, 13, 16, 21, 104, 113, 117, 127, 145, 156, 166, 179, 190
Edwin of Deira, 166
Eminent Victorians, 12
England Arise, 59
England's Forgotten Worthies, 87
Eothen, 113
Erewhon, 56
Eric Brighteyes, 95
Eric, or Little by Little, 84
Esmond, 183

Essays in Criticism (Arnold), 28
Esther Waters, 137
Ethel Churchill, 118
Eugene Aram, 53
Evan Harrington, 133
Evening News, 98
Evolution and Ethics, 106
Evolution, Old and New, 56

Fabian Society, 82, 164, 191
Falkland, 53
Familiar Studies of Men and Books, 173
Far From The Madding Crowd, 95, 96
farthing poet, 102
Father and Son, 92
Father Damien, 174
Fatherless Fanny, 147
Felix Holt, the Radical, 82
Festus, 32
fin de siècle, 26, 36, 67, 77, 122, 165, 193
Firmilian, 30
Fleet Street Eclogues, 70
Folle-Farine, 143
Footprints of Former Men in Far Cornwall, 98
Fors Clavigera, 158
Fortnightly Review, 98, 124, 133
Foul Play, 149
Framleigh Hall, 191
Framley Parsonage, 183
Frank Farleigh, 166
Frank Mildmay, 130
Frankenstein, 165
Fraser's Magazine, 26, 57, 113, 183, 184
Frederick the Great of Prussia, 58
Fun magazine, 90, 100

Gallia, 76
Gaston de Latour, 144
Geoffrey Hamlyn, 114
Ghetto Tragedies, 197
Goblin Market, 153
God Debate, 8, 20, 28, 61, 108
Godolphin, 53
Golden Treasury, 143, 144
Government by Journalism, 171
Grass of Parnassus, 119

Great Expectations, 55, 123
Great St Benedict's, 132
Griffith Gaunt, 149
Gutta Percha Willie, 129

Handley Cross, 175
Hang in Haste, Repent at Leisure, 149
Hard Cash, 149
Hard Times, 71, 72
Harry Coverdale's Courtship, 166
He Knew He Was Right, 188
Heart of Darkness, 64
Held in Bondage, 143
Hereward the Wake, 114
Hide and Seek, 63
High History of the Holy Graal, 83
Hilda Strafford, 97
Hilda Wade, 26
Hillingdon Hall, 175
History of Civilisation in England, 52
History of the French Revolution, 57
HMS *Beagle*, 68
Homogenic Love, 59
homosexuality, 40, 59, 73, 75, 82, 114, 152, 193
Horae Subsecivae, 49
Hours in a Library, 172
Household Management, 36
Household Words, 63, 89, 102, 148, 161
How I Found Livingstone, 169

Idle Days in Patagonia, 104
Idle Thoughts of an Idle Fellow, 108
Idylls and Songs, 144
Idylls of the King, 181
Illustrations of Political Economy, 131
Imaginary Conversations of Greeks and Romans, 119
In a Glass Darkly, 122
In Darkest Africa, 170
In His Own Image, 67
In Memoriam, 180
In the Year of Jubilee, 91
In Vinculis, 41
Index Librorum Prohibitorum, 29
Ingoldsby Legends, 13, 33
Isaac Casaubon, 145

Island Night's Entertainments, 173, 174
It Is Never To Late To Mend, 149

Jack of all Trades, 149
Jackanapes, 83
James Merle, an Autobiography, 39
Jan Vedder's Wife, 35
Jane Eyre, 45, 46, 47
John Halifax, Gentleman, 67
John Inglesant, 165
John Marchmont's Legacy, 44
Jorrocks's Jaunts and Jollities, 175
Journal of a Residence on a Georgian Plantation, 112
Journal of the Discovery of the Source of the Nile, 167
Jude the Obscure, 97
Just So Stories, 115

Kailyard school, 35, 39, 128
Kama Sutra, 55
Kelmscott Chaucer, 138
Kidnapped, 173
Kim, 117
King of the Golden River, 157
King Poppy, 127
King Solomon's Mines, 95

Lady Audley, 13, 43, 44
Lady Windermere's Fan, 194
Lavengro, 42, 190
Lays of a Wild Harp, 65
Lays of Ancient Rome, 127
Lays of the Scottish Cavaliers, 30
Leila, or, The Siege of Granada, 54
Leopold Leuniger, 124
lesbianism, 82, 124
Lewis Arundel, 166
Liberty, 135
Librorum Absconditorum, 29
Life and Labour of the People, 42
Life of Charlotte Brontë, 191
Lilith, 128
Literary Studies (Bagehot), 31
Little Black Sambo, 32
Little Dorrit, 16, 72

Lloyd's Penny Weekly, 161
Lloyd's People's Periodical, 147
Lloyd's Weekly Newspaper, 109
Lob-Lie-by-the-Fire, 83
Locksley Hall, 22
Lombard Street, 31
London Assurance, 43
London Children, 132
London Labour and the London Poor, 131
London Miscellany, 161
London Nights, 179
London Poems, 52
Lord Arthur Savile's Crime, 194
Lord Jim, 64
Lorna Doone, 40
Lost and Saved, 141
Lothair, 75
Love and his Mask, 76
Love and Mr Lewisham, 192
Love Me Little, Love Me Long, 149
Love's Meinie, 158
Lovel the Widower, 183
Luck or Cunning, 56

Macmillan's Magazine, 153
Madeleine, 111
Mademoiselle Mathilde, 115
Man and Woman, 82
Margaret Ogilvy, 35
Marian Withers, 110
Marino Faliero, 178
Marius the Epicurean, 144
Marriage in Free Society, 59
Martin Chuzzlewit, 72
Martin Hewitt, 139
Mary Barton, 88, 89
Masterman Ready, 130
Maud, 181
Maurice Tiernay, 123
Mehalah, 34
Memoirs of Casanova, 129
Micah Clarke, 77
Michael and the Lost Angel, 110
Michael Armstrong, the Factory Boy, 189
Middlemarch, 82, 145
Miss Bretherton, 121, 190

Miss Brown, 121
Miss Marjoribanks, 142
Miss Meredith, 124
Modern Money-Lending, 59
Modern Painters, 157, 158, 159
Mogreb-el-Acksa, 93
Montezuma's Daughter, 95
Moonfleet, 83
Mr Facey Romford's Hounds, 175
Mr Midshipman Easy, 130
Mr Sponge's Sporting Tour, 175
Mrs Armytage: or, Female Domination, 92
Mrs Bligh, 49
Mrs Caudle's Candlelight Lectures, 109
Mrs Margaret Maitland, 142
Mrs Warren's Profession, 164
Mudie's Library, 133, 137
Munera Pulveris, 158
Music and Moonlight, 142
My Life and Loves, 98
My Secret Life, 189
Myth, Ritual and Religion, 119

Naboth's Vineyard, 167
Nathalie, 111
National Review, 29, 31
Natural Selection, 69
New Arabian Nights, 173
New Grub Street, 91
New Monthly Magazine, 33, 100
New Poems (Arnold), 28
New Woman, 76, 80
Newgate Novels, 24
Newgate School, 53
News From Nowhere, 138
Nicholas Nickleby, 71
Norman Sinclair, 30
Not Wisely, But Too Well, 49

Obiter Dicta, 39
Old Sir Douglas, 142
Old St Paul's, 24
Oliver Twist, 72
On Heroes, 58
On Races, Species and their Origin, 106
Once A Week magazine, 38

Origin of Species, 68, 69
Orion, 102
Orley Farm, 188
Our Mutual Friend, 16, 72
Our Village, 136
Outcast of the Islands, 64
Over The Cliffs, 61
Oxford Dictionary, 140
Oxford English Dictionary, 87, 176
Oxford Movement, 14, 101, 140, 141, 145, 165

Pall Mall Gazette, 108, 134, 170, 171, 172
Palliser novels, 188
Parables from Nature, 90
Paracelsus, 51
Paris Sketch Book, 184
Past and Present, 58
Patricia Kenball, 126
Paul Clifford, 53
Paul Ferroll, 62
Peg Woffington, 148
Pelham, 53
Pendennis, 182
Penny Dreadfuls, 13, 146, 160, 161
People's Palace, 39, 139
Peter Ibbetson, 79
Peter Pan, 35
Phantastes, 128
Pharais, 163
Philista, 25
Phoebe the Peasant's Daughter, 147
Physics or Politics, 31
Physiological Aesthetics, 25
Pierrot!, 169
Pisanus Fraxi, 29
Plain Tales From The Hills, 117
Plato and Platonism, 144
Plays Pleasant and Unpleasant, 164
Poems before Congress, 51
Poems in the Dorset Dialect, 34
Political Economy of Art, 158
Praeterita, 159
Pre-Raphaelites, 26, 63, 105, 110, 138, 145, 153, 154, 156, 162, 176, 180, 190
Prince Zaleski, 165
Principles of Geology, 69

Principles of Political Economy, 135
prisons, 20, 41, 72, 91, 104, 132, 149
prostitution, 24, 133, 170
public works, 21
Punch, 24, 48, 49, 79, 92, 94, 109, 122, 132, 148, 179, 183
Put Yourself In His Place, 149
Pygmalion and Galatea, 90

Quality Street, 35

Rab and his Friends, 49
Rambles in Germany and Italy, 165
Ranald Bannerman's Boyhood, 129
Ranthorpe, 125
Ready-Money Mortiboy, 38
Rebel of the Family, 126
Redskin and Cowboy, 100
Remember the Alamo, 35
Reuben Sachs, 124
Review of Reviews, 171
Reynolds' Miscellany, 161
Richard Feverel, 132, 133
Richard Savage, 35
Richelieu, 54
Rienzi, Last of the Tribunes, 54
Robert Elsmere, 190
Robert Falconer, 128
Robin Hood and Little John, 80
Rockwood, 24
Rodney Stone, 78
Romance of a Shop, 124
Romola, 82
Rosa Amorosa, 80
Rosamund, 176
Rose, Blanche and Violet, 125
Rupert of Hentzau, 101
Ruth, 88

Saints and Sinners, 110
Salome, 75, 194
Sartor Resartus, 57
Savage Africa, 150
Savoy magazine, 36, 90, 94, 179
Scenes of Clerical Life, 81
science fiction, 17, 26, 132, 165, 192

Self-Help, 166
sensation novel, 43, 62
Sentimental Tommy, 35
Sesame and Lilies, 156, 158, 159
Sex-Love, and its Place in a Free Society, 59
Sexual Inversion, 82
Shapes in the Fire, 165
Sherlock Holmes, 77, 78, 139
Ships That Pass In The Night, 97
Shirley, 46
Sigurd the Volsung, 138
Silas Marner, 81
Sing-Song, 154
Sir Jasper's Tenant, 44
slavery, 20, 114, 131
Social Diseases and Worse Remedies, 106
Soldiers Three, 117
Some Experiences of an Irish R.M., 167
Some Whims of Fate, 77
Songs Before Sunrise, 177
Sonnets and Songs by Proteus, 41
Sonnets from the Portuguese, 50
Sordello, 51
Spasmodic School of Poetry, 31, 166
Springhaven, 40
Stalky & Co, 116
state of the nation' novels, 21
Stories Toto Told Me, 67
Strand magazine, 26, 78, 107, 132, 170
Strangers Yet, 136
Stuart of Dunleath, 141
Studies in the History of the Renaissance, 144
Studies in the Psychology of Sex, 82
suffragism, 97, 190
Sunrise, 39
Sybil, 75
Sylvie and Bruno, 60
System of Logic, 135

Table Talk, 105
Tails with a Twist, 76
Tales of Mean Streets, 139
Tales of the Toys, 100
Tancred, 75
Tell Me A Story, 137
Temple Bar magazine, 44

Tess of the D'Urbervilles, 95, 97
The Academy magazine, 76
The Admirable Crichton, 35
The Adventures of Harry Richmond, 133
The Affairs of the Heart, 105
The Amateur Cracksman, 102
The Amateur Emigrant, 173
The Amateur Poacher, 108
The Angel in the House, 144
The Angel World, 32
The Athelings, 142
The Authoress of the Odyssey, 56
The Autobiography of a Thief, 149
The Bab Ballads, 90
The Ballad of Reading Gaol, 194
The Battle of Marathon, 50
The Beach of Falesá, 174
The Bible in Spain, 42
The Big Bow Mystery, 197
The Black Arrow, 173
The Black Monk, 161
The Blue Fairy Book, 119
The Bon Gaultier Ballads, 30
The Book of Beauty, 41
The Book of Nonsense, 120
The Book of Snobs, 184
The Boy Hunters, 151
The Boy's Country-book, 103
The British Barbarians, 25
The Brownies and Other Tales, 83
The Calendar of Horrors, 147
The Case of Rebellious Susan, 110
The Castle of Indolence, 186
The Celtic Twilight, 195
The Charge of the Light Brigade, 181
The Children of Tomorrow, 163
The Christian Year, 111
The City of Dreadful Night, 186
The City of the Soul, 76
The Claverings, 188
The Cliff-Climbers, 151
The Cloister and the Hearth, 149
The Colleen Bawn, 43
The Colour of Life, 134
The Colour Sense, 25
The Coral Island, 32

The Corsican Brothers, 43
The Countess Cathleen, 195
The Criminal Prisons of London, 132
The Crook of the Bough, 76
The Crown of Wild Olives, 158
The Cry of the Children, 50
The Crystal Age, 104
The Cuckoo Clock, 137
The Daisy Chain, 197
The Dancing Girl, 110
The Dead Secret, 63
The Defence of Guenevere, 138
The Descent of Man, 69
The Desert Home, 151
The Devil's Disciple, 164
The Dialect of the Southern Counties of Scotland, 140
The Doctor's Wife, 44
The Dolly Dialogues, 101
The Doom of a City, 186
The Drawing Room Scrap-Book, 118
The Dream of Gerontius, 141
The Dublin Mail, 174
The Duchess of Padua, 194
The Eagle's Nest, 158
The Early Kings of Norway, 58
The Earthly Paradise, 138
The Economist, 31
The Edinburgh Review, 125, 127
The Egoist, 133
The English Constitution, 31
The English Humourists, 184
The Englishwoman's Domestic Magazine, 36
The Ethics of the Dust, 158
The Eustace Diamonds, 188
The Evidence of the Miracle of Resurrection, 106
The Exploits of Brigadier Gerard, 78
The Expression of the Emotions, 69
The Fair Haven, 56
The Fairies, 27
The Fairy Godmothers, 90
The Field magazine, 122
The Fifth Form at St Dominic's, 150
The Fitzboodle Papers, 184
The Fleshly School of Poetry, 52
The Flying Dutchman, 84

The Footprints of the Creator, 136
The Forsaken Merman, 27
The Four Georges, 184
The Fowler, 97
The Gamekeeper at Home, 108
The Garden That I Love, 29
The Germ magazine, 145, 153, 155, 156, 162
The Girl of the Period, 126
The Golden Age, 94
The Golden Bough, 86, 120
The Golden Butterfly, 38
The Gordian Knot, 49
The Gorilla Hunters, 32
The Great God Pan, 129
The Greek View of Life, 74
The Growth of Love, 44
The Half Sisters, 110
The Happy Prince, 194
The Headless Horseman, 151
The Heir of Redclyffe, 197
The Heroes, 114
The Heroes of Asgard, 111
The Hillyars and the Burtons, 115
The Hole in the Wall, 139
The House by the Churchyard, 121
The House of Life, 155
The Human Interest, 105
The Hunting of the Snark, 60
The Idler in France, 41
The Idler in Italy, 41
The Idler magazine, 108
The Importance of Being Earnest, 194
The Intended, 169
The Invisible Man, 192
The Island of Dr Moreau, 192
The Jungle Book, 115
The Keepsake, 41
The King of Schnorrers, 197
The Lancashire Witches, 24
The Land of Heart's Desire, 195
The Last Days of Pompeii, 54
The Life of Charlotte Brontë, 89
The Life of Christ, 84
The Light That Failed, 116
The Little Lame Prince, 68
The Little Minister, 35

The Lives of the Saints, 34
The Lord of the Sea, 165
The Lost Stradivarius, 83
The MacDermotts of Ballycloran, 188
The Magistrate, 146
The Maiden's Progress, 105
The Man From The North, 37
The Man of Destiny, 164
The Maniac Father, 147
The Manliness of Christ, 104
The Martian, 79
The Master of Ballantrae, 173
The Matyrdom of Man, 150
The Mayor of Casterbridge, 96
The Meaning of Good, 74
The Mighty Atom, 66
The Mill on the Floss, 81
The Monthly Packet magazine, 83, 197
The Moonstone, 63
The Morning Chronicle, 126, 132
The Music Master, 26
The Mystic, 32
The Negro of Wapping, 84
The New Spirit, 82
The Newcombes, 183
The Nigger of the Narcissus, 64
The North Wall, 70
The Novel on Blue Paper, 138
The Octoroon, 43, 151
The Odd Women, 91
The Ogilvies, 67
The Old Arm Chair, 65
The Old Curiosity Shop, 1, 72
The Old Red Sandstone, 135
The Old Wives' Tale, 38
The Oxford Book of English Verse, 148
The Palace of Truth, 90
The Passionate Pilgrim, 144
The Penny Press, 174
The Perfumed Garden, 55
The Philanderer, 164
The Picture of Dorian Gray, 194
The Pilgrims of the Rhine, 54
The Poor Man and the Lady, 95
The Prince's Progress, 154
The Princess and Curdie, 129

The Princess and the Goblin, 128
The Prisoner of Zenda, 101
The Private Papers of Henry Ryecroft, 92
The Professor, 45, 47
The Purple Cloud, 165
The Purple Land, 104
The Quadroon, 151
The Queen-Mother, 176
The Quest of the Sangraal, 98
The Real Charlotte, 167
The Return of the Native, 96
The Rhythm of Life, 134
The Rifle Rangers, 150
The Ring and the Book, 51
The Romany Rye, 42, 190
The Rose and the Ring, 184
The Roundabout Papers, 184
The Rubáiyát of Omar Khayyám, 85
The Saturday Review, 98, 126
The Scalp Hunters, 150
The Scholar Gipsy, 27
The Scouring of the White Horse, 104
The Second Mrs Tanqueray, 146
The Seraphim and Other Poems, 50
The Seven Lamps of Architecture, 157
The Shadowy Waters, 195
The Shaughraun, 43
The Shaving of Shagpat, 132
The Ship of Stars, 148
The Sign of Four, 77
The Silver Fox, 167
The Silver King, 110
The Silverado Squatters, 173
The Simpleton, 149
The Sorceress of the Strand, 132
The Sorrows of Rosalie, 141
The Sorrows of Satan, 66
The Soul of Lilith, 66
The Spirit of Place, 134
The Splendid Spur, 148
The Sport of Chance, 163
The Stones of Venice, 157
The Story of a Short Life, 83
The Story of Elizabeth, 151
The Story of my Heart, 108
The Story of Venus and Tannhauser, 36

The String of Pearls, 147
The Subjection of Women, 135
The Sundering Flood, 139
The Tenant of Wildfell Hall, 44
The Thousand and One Nights, 119
The Time Machine, 191, 192
The Tower of London, 24
The True History of Joshua Davidson, 126
The Trumpet-Major, 96
The Twilight of the Gods, 87
The Two Paths, 157, 158
The Universal Hymn, 32
The Vampire, 43
The Virginians, 183
The Wages of Sin, 130
The Wanderings of Oisin, 195
The War of the Worlds, 192
The Warden, 70, 188
The Water Babies, 113, 114
The Way of All Flesh, 56
The Way of Marriage, 105
The Way We Live Now, 16, 188
The Well at the World's End, 139
The Wheel of God, 80
The White Company, 78
The White Slave and Amy, 161
The Wife and Woman's Reward, 141
The Wind among the Reeds, 195
The Wind in the Willows, 93, 94
The Woman in White, 63, 68
The Woman Who Did, 25
The Wonderful Visit, 192
The Woodlanders, 97
The Wreck and the Reef, 84
The Yellow Danger, 165
The Yellowplush Papers, 183
The Young Fur Traders, 32
The Zincali, 42
Thespis, 90
Things I Have Seen, 162
Things Will Take A Turn, 97
Thirty-Five Years of a Dramatic Author's Life, 84
Three Men in a Boat, 108
Three Plays for Puritans, 164
Through Fire and Flame, 34

Through the Dark Continent, 170
Through the Looking-Glass, 60
Ticket of Leave Man, 179
Time Flies: A Reading Diary, 154
Tiny Tadpole and Other Tales, 100
Tit-Bits, 37, 170
Tom Brown's Schooldays, 27, 104
Tommy and Grizel, 35
Towards Democracy, 59
Tractarianism, 110, 111, 153
Tracts for the Times, 112, 140
Travels in West Africa, 115
Travels With a Donkey, 173
Treasure Island, 173
Trelawny of the 'Wells', 146, 152
Trial By Jury, 90
Trilby, 79
Tristam of Lyonesse, 178
Troy Town, 148
Truth (newspaper), 118
Twice Around the Clock, 162
Two Little Waifs, 137
Two Little Wooden Shoes, 143

Uncle Bernac, 78
Uncle Silas, 122
Unconscious Memory, 56
Under Drake's Flag, 100
Under The Greenwood Tree, 96
Under The Hill, 36
Under Two Flags, 143
Undertones, 52
Union Jack magazine, 100
Unkist, Unkind, 105
Unto This Last, 158

Vanity Fair, 16, 98, 123, 182, 183, 184
Varney the Vampire, 13, 161
Vera, 194

Vestiges of Creation, 61, 69, 136
Vicar of Wrexhill, 189
Villette, 47
Virginibus Peurisque, 173
Vivian Grey, 74
Vulgar Verses, 140

Weir of Hermiston, 174
Wessex Poems and Other Verses, 97
Westminster Gazette, 101
Westminster Review, 81
Westward Ho!, 114
When the Sleeper Wakes, 192
White Rose and Red, 52
Widowers' Houses, 164
Wild Life in a Southern County, 108
Wild Wales, 42
With Clive in India, 100
Wives and Daughters, 88
*Woman in France During the Eighteenth
  Century*, 111
Woman magazine, 38
Woman, and her Place in a Free Society, 59
Women Adventurers, 76
Wonderful Stories for Children, 103
Wood Magic, 108
Workers in the Dawn, 91
Wuthering Heights, 47
Wylder's Hand, 122

Xantippe, 124

Yeast, 113
Yellow Book, 36, 37, 67, 70, 76, 77, 80, 94, 122,
  169, 196
Yellowplush Correspondence, 53
You Never Can Tell, 164

Zöe, 109